I0797534

Tidying the Abyss

A Practical Guide to
Cleaning and Organizing While
Exhausted and Overwhelmed

Tidying the Abyss

AMANDA STUCKEY DODSON, LCSW

New York Boston

Cover design by Terri Sirma
Cover illustration by Giselle Dekel

Balance
Hachette Book Group
1290 Avenue of the Americas
New York, NY 10104
GCP-Balance.com
@GCPBalance

First Edition: November 2025

Balance is an imprint of Grand Central Publishing. The Balance name and logo are registered trademarks of Hachette Book Group, Inc.

Print book interior design by Amy Quinn.

Library of Congress Cataloging-in-Publication Data

Names: Dodson, Amanda Stuckey author
Title: Tidying the abyss : a practical guide to cleaning and organizing while exhausted and overwhelmed / Amanda Stuckey Dodson, LCSW.
Description: First edition. | New York ; Boston : Balance, 2025. | Includes bibliographical references and index.
Identifiers: LCCN 2025024132 | ISBN 9781538770467 hardcover | ISBN 9781538770481 ebook
Subjects: LCSH: Housekeeping | House cleaning | Orderliness
Classification: LCC TX324.5 .D637 2025
LC record available at https://lccn.loc.gov/2025024132

ISBNs: 9781538770467 (paper over board), 9781538770481 (ebook)

Printed in the United States of America

LSC-C

Printing 1, 2025

For Kathleen,
who would've bought a hundred copies.
And for Copper,
who sat with me while I wrote every word.

Contents

Me, My House & the Pit of Despair

THE YEAR I TURNED THIRTY, CHAOS, PESTILENCE, AND PLAGUE STRUCK MY household like some kind of biblical punishment. To say I was caught off guard would be an understatement.

I was a diligent disciple of order. I believed in tidiness the way one believes in prayer—that if I did it often enough, with a virtuous heart, I would be admitted to some sort of squeaky-clean heaven on earth, a realm of austere, serene predictability (which, in my mind, resembled the IKEA showroom).

I. THE CHIANTI INCIDENT

The first ill omen came on a Friday evening, after a preweekend cleaning rampage. I was sweaty from vigorously vacuuming rugs and nose blind from accidental bleach inhalation. I lit a scented candle—the symbol of domestic nirvana—and settled in for an evening of blissful relaxation.

Then, my husband tripped and sent our two glasses of red wine catapulting through the living room in a trajectory I can only describe as "blood spatter."

As our dinner went cold, we grabbed dish towels and mopped wine from the floors, furniture, and (amazingly) ceiling. The surface area covered was, from a physics standpoint, impressive.

I cleaned meticulously, wedging my arm around furniture to reach errant drips. He, to my frustration, cleaned haphazardly, dripping wine everywhere he walked.

"Let's eat. I can't see any more spills," he said in the good-natured way he says everything.

"But it's everywhere!" I screeched, pointing at a small puddle right by his foot.

And he *shrugged.*

As I gaped at his beloved face, trying not to scream, I felt a yawning pit of futility open in my cozy domestic sphere.

If you have peered into the chaotic flames at the bottom of that domestic abyss, you know what I was feeling at that moment, unzipping my so-recently-clean couch covers while my husband peered around the room looking lost: a tightly restrained despair.

II. AMANDA TRIES TO AVOID THE PIT OF DESPAIR (WITH MIXED RESULTS)

You may be acquainted with this abyss. It opens in your home, like a portal to a demon realm, when order unravels into disorder. You spend your precious free hours on dirty laundry, grubby floors, and cleaning your ungrateful kitchen, only to have your labor promptly undone by unforeseen messes, your own forgetfulness, or the reliable passage of time. Worse, the agent of chaos is frequently someone you've promised to love forever, such as a child, a pet, or in my case, a man.

It wasn't just the wine. It was *all of it.* I felt like, every time I got our home under control, something immediately got broken or ruined.

"I'm like a bull in a china closet," Tom apologized, a few weeks before the wine incident, after accidentally breaking our last drinking glass while trying to wash it.

"It's supposed to be 'china shop,'" I laughed. But really, the image of a bull trying to navigate a closet was a little more accurate. He just couldn't stop making messes. *Really big* messes—dropping things, breaking things, spilling things, tripping and sending stuff scattering. And by and large, it fell to me to clean them up. He just didn't seem to notice.

Taking care of my home, myself, and my loved ones was once so sweet, a way to comfort myself in an unpredictable world. But in the abyss, these compulsory labors of adulthood had developed a bitter aftertaste.

But I didn't want to be bitter—I wanted to be happy! So, I cast my desperation questions into the dark ocean of the internet, hoping to hook some answers.

I asked: *What to do if husband nice but won't stop spilling stuff and not cleaning it up?* The results were unsatisfying.

Divorce him (no, I liked him!), compromise my home standards (no, I liked my standards!), work on accepting imperfection (lifelong struggle with minimal progress!). Queasy, I read countless stories of failed relationships, tanked by inattentive, neglectful husbands and exacting, unforgiving wives.

Luckily, or unluckily, that isn't where my story was headed. In the midst of our domestic squabbling, my husband and I couldn't see that our destiny had already drastically changed. Because we weren't headed to divorce. We were headed, instead, to a hospital room.

III. A PLOT TWIST AT URGENT CARE

Tom's degenerative neurological illness had gone undiagnosed for years, only identified by a clever urgent care doctor who noticed his wobbly balance while walking. I had also noticed his worsening balance, which is why he went to the doctor.

"Go to urgent care and see if they can look at your ears. Maybe you have, like, vertigo, or something," I had suggested. An hour later, he called me from the doctor's office.

"Don't immediately Google this and freak out, okay? But they think I might have MS."

I, of course, immediately Googled it. And freaked out.

MS is a disease of interrupted neurological messages. My husband's brain could still send signals to his body. (*Don't spill that wine in your hand!*) But his limbs didn't always receive the message in time. (*Too late, I already did it!*)

When Tom told me he couldn't see the mess he had made, he wasn't being willfully difficult. In a twist so dark it was almost funny, the doctors confirmed that Tom really could not see the red wine he had spilled because his vision was too damaged to easily differentiate similar colors. Crumbs on a white counter, red wine on a dark wood floor had become functionally invisible.

The reality that my bright, beautiful husband was suddenly diagnosed with multiple sclerosis seemed, in my feeble judgment, unfair.

"Couldn't it have just been one single sclerosi?!" he joked in the car after his first doctor's appointment while we laughed-cried or cried-laughed—I'm not sure which.

His illness just didn't make any sense. Had I not devised elaborately organized systems to hold us in health and longevity? But the sensible meals, the supplements, the faithfully attended annual medical exams had been no protection at all against disability.

Tom's illness unceremoniously launched me (much like the aforementioned glass of Chianti) to a new and unmanageable level of domestic responsibility. I drove him to appointments, negotiated with doctors, and set up systems in our home to accommodate his reduced coordination.

I kept the floors clear of tripping hazards. I took over all tasks requiring acute vision or dexterity. Filled with love, fear, and the prickly determination of a rigidly organized person, I kept our small world as peaceful as possible, so Tom could focus on maintaining his ability to walk, drive, and work.

But no matter how hard I tried, I could not hold it together. Every time I got myself organized as a caregiver, some fresh hell was revealed.

IV. PLAGUE OF BOILS & LOCUSTS

We started waking up in the morning with red, painful welts. Bedbugs: our own personal little plague of locusts. Shuddering at their unseen but certain presence, we threw our clothes, sheets, and curtains into apocalyptically hot washers and dryers. Drowning doesn't kill the little devils. You have to burn them into nonexistence.

We stored our decontaminated clothes and linens in tightly sealed black plastic bags, awaiting the exterminator. We couldn't unpack the bags until our apartment was coated in pesticides to kill the bugs.

Broke from graduate school and medical bills, we had no money for a hotel. So, we sat in our bare apartment, surrounded by piles of trash bags. It was not dissimilar to living in a miniature landfill.

V. PLAGUE OF PESTILENCE

Next, a pandemic sparked and raged around the world. This was singularly difficult for our newly immunocompromised household. We were two therapists, squeezed together in our revolting apartment, desperately trying to separately conduct confidential sessions.

Tom showed himself to be an admirable compartmentalizer—relaxed, flexible, with a good attitude. I did not.

I have been called capable and productive but have never once been accused of being flexible. In the absence of my carefully ordered systems of work-life balance and home care, I was totally off kilter. It took everything I had to be emotionally available for other people. I felt the threads that wove my orderly life together straining, snapping, one by one.

VI. ANOTHER PLOT TWIST AT URGENT CARE

I got tired (to be expected), then exhausted (troubling but understandable). Then, undeniably sick. I rested but did not recover. Sleep did not restore me. Every day, everything hurt. And I developed a very troubling habit of passing out cold at inconvenient moments.

The urgent care doctor suggested I was depressed, which honestly baffled me. I *was* depressed, obviously—what reasonable person wouldn't be depressed? But I knew depression, personally and professionally. And I knew it couldn't make me feel *that sick*.

Nevertheless, I dutifully took the Cymbalta prescribed to me, though it only made me feel more exhausted and nauseated. In lieu of any better explanation, I diagnosed myself with a hysterical psychosomatic illness.

Maybe I just wasn't selfless enough to be a good caregiver. Maybe I was just selfish enough to unconsciously concoct a way to steal my husband's disability thunder?

When I told my new therapist my theory, she told me, gently, "That's not how psychosomatic illnesses work. Those illnesses thrive on emotional repression. You aren't repressed, you're just exhausted."

It got worse. My head swam, my blood pressure plummeted. My body felt like a little neutron star—disproportionately heavy, dense, impossible to move. I collected a small batch of tentative medical diagnoses, amounting to "something's definitely wrong but we're not quite sure what."

The lack of a definitive answer was the most maddening part—a definite illness was theoretically treatable. A collection of vague but debilitating medical complaints just had to be endured.

VII. INTO THE DOMESTIC ABYSS

All through my life, I had nimbly tiptoed around the domestic abyss when it showed up in my life, a malevolently widening aperture. I covered it with plastic organizing bins, spreadsheets, and a can-do attitude bordering on hubris.

But one evening, sitting on my kitchen floor in a snowdrift of dog hair, too dizzy to stand lest I lose consciousness, coffee stains dripping down the cabinets around me, I realized that, without my notice, the abyss had already swallowed me up.

I was sitting at the bottom, peering at the distant light, waiting for my old self to come rescue me. But my old self was gone—she had slipped away without notice or apology. I was too tired to maintain the elaborate systems she devised in her energetic days.

Everything in my life was a maelstrom of disorder: my unruly internal organs, my barely passable work, my uncharacteristically and (for me) intolerably messy house.

VIII. AMANDA PRACTICES NONACCEPTANCE (WITH MIXED RESULTS, AGAIN)

But like a bird repeatedly flying into a window, I kept expecting my old ways not to harm my new body. Grasping for a sense of control over my life, I reorganized closets and scrubbed bathrooms, only to end up all but passed out on the floor—or, as my Texan father called it, DFO'd (translation: done fell out).

I got up and did it all over again. I was riddled with nonacceptance. I was convinced that there was some sort of secret cheat code of actions I could execute to make my life feel manageable. I just wasn't clever enough to figure it out.

But the more I resisted, whined, and refused to accept that my brain and body no longer worked, the more exhausted and miserable I felt. I had no path forward but acceptance.

IX: AMANDA, NEWLY HUMBLED, PRACTICES ACCEPTANCE

Ruminating on the unfairness of a situation does not make it fair. Endlessly interrogating the cause of my fatigue did not make me energetic. Working hard to put my life in order did not prevent disorder. I needed to improve my situation, not by working harder, but by making it easier to bear.

My old self, that little overachiever, used hard work to solve problems. I couldn't work hard anymore, so I devised clever ways to make my work easier. I used assistive tech, such as a watch my husband bought me to alert me when my heart rate was skyrocketing (which it did at odd moments), so I knew to stop working and rapidly assume a supine position. I hired helpers and relied on the generous support of family and friends.

I felt both physically and emotionally feeble, which I hated, but couldn't change. Life had forcefully humbled me. And the humility, it turned out, was good for me.

As my life stabilized, Tom and I got used to living in needy bodies. My home was slowly put back in order—nowhere near my old standards but much closer to tolerable. I, too, started, slowly, to feel better. Then, unbelievably, I started to feel happy.

I liked my simplified life—the very life I had been dragged into kicking and screaming. In my worst moments, I found a passion for creating simplified, streamlined systems, so easy to maintain that they required almost no energy.

On the way into the abyss, my chores, those burdens of adulthood, had been transfigured from compulsory to burdensome. On my climb out, they were transformed again, from burdensome to interesting to *fun.*

X: AMANDA ACCIDENTALLY BECOMES A HOME ORGANIZER FOR FELLOW STRUGGLERS

On a medically necessary break from my job as a therapist, I started looking for something fun to occupy my time. I started a low-pressure small business, cleaning and organizing for people with similar challenges. I wanted to share the practical comfort.

My company, Nesting Your Life, took off online. I was frequently enlisted, through virtual coaching, to help people all over the world solve their organizational quirks. They were fellow strugglers. I loved working with people with complicated relationships with home care, whether because of disability, grief, or dire circumstances. They were my people.

XI: MY ORGANIZING PHILOSOPHY

I'm not a minimalist or a maximalist. I'm a whatever-works-ist.

If you're disorganized, it's natural to want your life fixed as quickly as possible. It would be so nice if there were some revolutionary advice that could turn your home from chaos to order in one attempt.

But as you begin this book, I encourage you to turn your mind away from quick fixes.

Nothing we put in order can stay in order for perpetuity. Every good system (time management, chores, dishes, meal planning) will eventually fall apart when we encounter some insurmountable obstacle.

When my life fell apart, I felt like a failure. That's because, for so long, I saw disorder as the failure of order. It isn't.

Disorganization is organization's twin, its natural successor. Anyone can get organized. But you already know that the real problem is *staying organized*. To be truly organized, you must be comfortable, flexible, and persistent in the face of inevitable chaos.

Our homes fall apart. Our plans fall apart. We, too, are always falling apart. We put everything back in order, and we fall apart again. This isn't failure. This is the nature of the world—like the winter and summer, like sickness and health, like life and death, chaos and organization belong to one cycle.

And wherever you are, no matter how scattered or how rigid, whatever the state of your home and life, you are part of that cycle too.

HOW TO READ THIS BOOK: A NONTRADITIONAL HOME CARE MANUAL

This book contains what I've learned in my career as a therapist turned home organizer.

This is not a book of traditional, aesthetically pleasing organizing solutions. This is a book of weird organizing solutions for struggling people.

Struggling people have short attention spans. I know, I'm one of you!

That makes reading a book (like this one!) kind of challenging. So, feel free to jump around and find the advice most relevant to you. Here's a preview of what's coming up so you can go where you need to go first.

PART I: INTO THE ABYSS

An Exploration of All the Theoretical Factors That Make Homemaking So Hard for Some

1. **Facing Chaos:** Gaining the emotional skills you need to start addressing your mess
2. **Uncovering Barriers:** Identifying why homemaking can be so challenging
3. **Breaking the Rules:** Defining new standards for your home
4. **Dishes Are the Marriage-Killer:** Navigating differences in home standards
5. **Family Baggage:** Figuring out how your family passed their cleaning quirks to you
6. **The Abyss Widens:** Digging deep into unhelpful attitudes about home care

PART II: OUT OF THE ABYSS

This "practical" part of the book walks you through putting your home, and life, in order. It starts with the areas most crucial to your functioning and builds upward from there.

First: Getting Yourself Ready

1. **Self-Care Before Home Care:** Getting you fed, rested, and cognitively prepared to organize
2. **Managing Motivation & Overwhelm:** Dealing with tricky emotions that get in the way of progress

Next: Addressing Your Basic Needs

1. **Trash & Recycling:** Figuring out what's trash, what's recycling, what's donation, and how to get rid of it
2. **Kitchen & Dishes:** Systems for kitchen organization, kitchen cleaning, and dealing with dirty dishes

3. **Laundry & Clothing:** Getting your laundry running smoothly, even if you have a terrifying amount

Then: Creating Order in Your Most-Used Spaces

1. **Decluttering & Organizing:** Resolving Doom Piles and making homes for your stuff
2. **The Bedroom:** Creating a space to retreat from the chaos (and figuring out where to put all those clothes)
3. **Bathrooms & Personal Hygiene:** Making a clean space where it feels good to get clean

Finally: Dealing with the Most Difficult Organizational Tasks

1. **Rooms to Live In:** Living rooms, dining rooms, offices, and creative spaces
2. **Paper, Admin & Life Skills:** Addressing your paper piles and undone to-do lists
3. **Routines That Work:** Finding systems that work for your brain

PART III: BEWARE THE BACKSLIDE

These final three chapters are for troubleshooting the complications of life. They address the factors most likely to upset (and enrich) your hard-won domestic harmony.

1. **Expanding the Nest:** Dealing with chaotic pet situations, one issue at a time
2. **In Sickness & in Health:** Managing housework as an ill person, caregiver, and together
3. **Training the Next Generation:** Engaging children in housework

PART I

Into the Abyss

What Makes Homemaking So Hard

1 Facing Chaos

Abandoning the Fantasy of a Perfect Home

MY PROFESSIONAL NICHE, AS A THERAPIST TURNED HOME ORGANIZER, IS the subjective realm of domestic chaos.

Mess does not necessarily equal chaos. Chaos happens when your mess exceeds your ability to live inside it.

You can be cozy in your mess, like a cute little field mouse in its warm nest. Or your mess can gather force, like an avalanche, and bury you in a chasm, leaving you to pray for a highly trained Saint Bernard to dig you out with its giant paws and revive you with a nip of brandy.

Domestic chaos can be visible: unmanageable clutter, overflowing sinks, moldy showers. It can also be invisible: unpaid bills, undone paperwork, or difficulty caring consistently for your own body.

In the abyss, facing chaos feels dangerous. Out of the corner of your eye, its shadowy form starts to look like a monster—the kind that could paralyze you with direct eye contact. The closet of too-small clothes feels like a judgment of your body. The pile of unopened mail seems to confirm that you, at your core, are an irresponsible baby.

But here's the trick: When you muster the support and courage to face your mess, you will find that it is not a monster. It's only a simple pile of mundane objects and boring administrative tasks.

Resolving chaos requires nothing more than patience—patience to learn how, and patience with yourself as you get the job done in slow, faltering steps. There's only one way to put a life in order: one piece at a time.

I have worked with so many people who believed their messy lives were beyond help. None of them was beyond help. With compassion, persistence, and a sense of humor, any mess can be cleaned up. Yours can too.

Tidying Tidbit

The more you avoid looking at your disorganized house, the scarier it seems to clean it up. Facing your problem makes it less intimidating.

ABANDONING THE FANTASY OF PERFECTION

In your most desperate domestic moments, you are vulnerable to the siren song of the traditional home organization—the kind you see in magazines or targeted ads online. This kind of organizing involves putting your stuff into tiny, beautiful boxes in an open, airy home that costs several grand more than you have in your bank account.

Seduced by the ethereal atmosphere of the Container Store, you plan projects you're too tired to do, buy products you're too broke to afford, and worship at the altar of that indifferent god, the plastic storage bin.

When you try to organize your home in this way, you buy into the fantasy that with enough effort and money, you could have a stress-free home and, by extension, a stress-free life. And that you could be a stress-free person, imbued with calm, orderly competence by your peaceful environment.

I can tell you from personal experience: This is not the case. Occasionally, a clever storage solution (a revamped closet, an ingeniously shaped container, an aesthetically pleasing shelf of jars) is the answer to a complex problem. But more often, the problem doesn't lie with your storage—it's you, baby. It's not your containers, or even lack thereof. It's your humanity.

A tidy house is lovely, but it is also fickle. It can be undone as fast as you can say "My pharmacy is out of Lexapro."

Illness, injury, grief: There are so many things that can push you beyond where the bright light of traditional homemaking advice can reach you. If you struggle with the general keeping-it-together of life, your goals need to be different. You don't just need organizing tips and products that make your home look nice. You need a home that is resilient to disruption.

Organizing your life this way isn't something you buy but something you do—not just once, but over and over again. It is not a product, it's a process. It is not a goal, it is a practice.

In bad times, you need an arsenal of skills that help you manage the practical work of living when everything about living hurts. Not only the technical knowledge of how to clean out a pantry, arrange a wardrobe, or keep track of incomplete tasks. But also, the ability to carry out these tasks while being assailed by sadness and frustration.

Without these skills, you feel like a child in too-big clothing, impersonating an adult. Each new crisis threatens your shaky performance. You anxiously sweep the floor, do the taxes, and wait to be either caught or rescued.

With the right skills, you feel like the adult who does the rescuing.

SKILL 1: SELF-ACCEPTANCE

Accepting What You Can't Easily Change; Changing What You Can Slowly

If you want to have a more functional home, you will have to change. That's tricky because people are involuntarily, magnetically drawn to maintaining the status quo—even if the status quo is a distressing state of complete chaos.

When you try to change yourself too much, too fast, you experience what therapists call internal backlash. This is a kind of revolt staged by your inner self because it doesn't want to be different and you're being so mean!

Case in point: I often work with clients on their household routines. Many of them don't get out of bed until the very last minute, leaving no time for breakfast, self-care, or sometimes even hygiene before work.

They come to me to help them execute their shock-and-awe plans for change. Usually it's something like "I'd like to wake up at six in the morning, exercise, meal prep for the week, reset the house, and do a deep-cleaning task every day."

"Okay," I say, already sensing what's coming. "And what time do you usually get out of bed?"

They look at me with an evasive expression somewhere between a smile and a grimace. "On a good day . . . ?"

"No, not a good day." I say, "What time did you wake up *today*?"

"Like . . . eleven . . . ish?"

Then, they cave, because even though I'm not a therapist anymore, I still have resting therapist face.

They admit that every attempt at a morning routine has resulted in catastrophic failure. Even though they set multiple alarms, dragged themselves out of bed, and struggled through their desired routine with grim determination, they could only keep it up for a few days, max, even though they were animated by ecstatic hope that they were changing for the better.

But then their boss was mean to them, or they caught a cold, or they forgot to set their fifth alarm. And they ended up back at square one, feeling the shame of thwarted effort.

"Based on past data," I ask, "is it possible that you are just not a morning person?"

"But I want to be!" they insist. But unfortunately, wanting to be different doesn't automatically make you different. You can't base a plan to get your life together on who you wish you were. You must build it on how you actually are, today. That's how we create sustainable change—by not expecting ourselves to change too much.

To my clients, I suggest an alternative. "How about you just try to get up by ten, eat a granola bar, and clean one thing before work? Then, you can work backward from there."

"Fine," they sigh morosely, and then succeed at reclaiming an hour of their day.

To arrive at self-acceptance, nonjudgmentally assess your weaknesses. Reflect on your disorganization with curiosity. Your forgetfulness, your disabilities, your hatred for repetitive tasks—accept these things as they are. Do not expect some new, higher self to wake up in your place tomorrow. If you wait for change to come to you, you'll be left waiting in chaos.

Tidying Tidbit

Try to be realistic when setting your goals for self and home improvement. Getting too ambitious can lead to burnout and eventual failure.

BABY STEPS TOWARD SELF-ACCEPTANCE

Remember that you are who you are for a reason. Whether you're fastidious or messy, controlled or scattered, it probably isn't your fault that you're that way. Your past, your culture, your biology, your current situation: These forces have molded you without your awareness or permission. This isn't good or bad. It just is.

Find understanding for the people who made you this way. It's easy to turn self-hatred outward, directed toward the people who made you so dysfunctional—whether it was your parents, past teachers, or ex-partners. Anger is natural. But just as you are who you are for a reason, the person who hurt you was that way for a reason too. Understanding isn't the same thing as forgiveness. It just puts things in perspective. Instead of seeing the world as a collection of people who screwed you up, you see the world as a collection of people who suffer too. This can help diffuse your anger so you can work toward your goals in a productive (not vengeful) way.

Harness the limited capacity for change. Self-acceptance doesn't mean you stop changing. It means quieting the storm of self-hatred and defensiveness just enough that you can see yourself clearly, then assess what needs to change, calmly and thoughtfully. You can, and should, change as you age and grow. But we're not very good at changing. It works best if we do it a little at a time. So, try to focus your efforts on first changing your most destructive habits (those that inconvenience you and others most).

SKILL 2: STREAMLINING

Solving Problems with Simplicity & Creativity Rather Than Effort

After you accept yourself as you are, it's time to set up your life to accommodate your imperfections. Sustainable organization comes from accepting that chaos will come (sometimes with you as its maker). Then, creatively planning for its arrival.

I once had an organizing client who worked overnight shifts at a hospital. In the small hours of the morning after work, all she wanted to do was strip off her scrubs and shower the night away.

She criticized herself for her habit of leaving her dirty clothes strewn all over the bathroom floor, where they got soaked with bathwater and seasoned with cat hair. This drove her housemates crazy, because the shared bathroom was small, and not improved by the presence of sopping wet, hairy hospital scrubs.

"Why can't I just put the clothes in the hamper in my bedroom? It's right there! It's so easy!"

"If it's so easy," I asked, "then why don't you do it?"

"Because I'm a lazy wretch?!" she laughed. I smiled.

"Okay, but seriously, without judgment, why are you lazy about this thing specifically?"

The forbidden question: Why are you lazy about that chore? This is the most important question, the one we don't feel allowed to ask ourselves. We just assume that if we're slacking, it's because we're wretched worms.

But hear me out. **If something is easy, it requires no effort. If it requires effort, it isn't easy—and there's a reason that it isn't.**

Uncovering that reason is often the secret to streamlining. Streamlining is making something easy that we once found challenging.

My client considered my question for a moment before answering.

"I'm just exhausted after work. I feel like I have hospital germs all over me. I don't like to take my clothes off and walk naked to my shower from my bedroom, because it's cold. I don't like to pick up a pile of dirty clothes on my way out of the shower, either, because it feels like I'm making myself dirty with hospital germs after I just went through the trouble to get clean. But that seems silly."

It may or may not have been silly. But it also made sense.

I suggested: "Why don't you just add an extra laundry hamper to your bathroom? You could put the dirty clothes in there. It will be a little bit in the way. But it won't be more in the way than a floor full of wet scrubs. Or you could get a bathrobe."

"That's so obvious," she laughed. "Why didn't I think of that?"

That's so obvious, why didn't I think of that describes about 80 percent of my work. I'm not an innovator of organizational schemes. I'm an observer of human nature. And our tender egos often get in the way of doing what makes sense. We are so convinced that the path to order lies in being more disciplined. But overreliance on discipline clouds your ability to find creative (and sometimes obvious) solutions to your problems.

Tidying Tidbit

If you want your life to be easier, don't make yourself stronger. Make it simpler and faster to do the things you need to do.

Streamlining your life requires giving up your pride and getting out of your own way. Give yourself permission to make things easy. There is no annoyance too small or too silly. If it is in your way, it requires fixing.

SKILL 3: SUPPORT

Reducing Your Burden by Surrounding Yourself with Helpers

Sometimes, feeling overwhelmed is perfectly valid. It is the correct emotional response to a problem too big to solve alone. Sometimes, the chaos is too big for one person—or one household—to clean up. In that case, getting outside help is necessary.

There are so many reasons not to seek help: You don't have the money, you don't want to be a bother, you will spontaneously combust if a single person sees how you are living.

After all, what if you work up the courage to ask for help, but they say no? Worse, what if they say yes but are judgy about it? There are some really compelling reasons to keep a problem to yourself.

I still think you should ask for help. Even if the help is subpar. In a totally unmanageable situation, even condescending help is better than isolated desperation.

In all the homes I have worked in, the only people I have seen fail were those who refused to enlist support—even when it was available. They kept vowing every night to clean up their lives, on their own, ignoring the fact that every morning, they failed to enact that plan.

If you keep fumbling your attempt to get organized, it's a good sign that you might need more support. But support can be hard to find these days. Often, you hold out hope that a Perfect Helper will come along—a best friend, always available, who is excellent at cleaning, and whose home care opinions exactly align with your own. You could ask the Perfect Helper for assistance without any risk of judgment, burden, or conflict.

But for most people, that Perfect Helper does not exist.

More often, the people available to help are just as imperfect as you are. They're busy. They're distracted. They talk too much (or too little). They're not a best friend. They're just a neighbor, or a coworker, or a sibling with whom you have a complicated relationship. Asking them for help involves a bit of interpersonal risk.

That doesn't mean that they can't help. Imperfect helpers are all we have. Imperfect helpers can change lives, if we let them.

Identify the safe people in your life, however imperfect they may be, who might be willing to help. Open up about your struggles. Ask what they are good at. People are usually delighted to assist with a task that they do well. You can offer a trade, or just let them feel rewarded by helping you.

Then—and this is the hard part—let them help. Don't ask yourself whether they are helping out of pity. Trust me, a little pity won't hurt you too badly. Choose (or at least try to choose) not to interpret their every word, glance, and breath as a judgment.

Keep it in perspective. Remember how little you care about the state of your friends' homes.

Remember, no one ever perished because their friend saw their messy house.

Remember that we weren't meant to live in little cubicles of isolated responsibility. We were meant to keep our lives together in community, held by the flawed hands of others.

Tidying Tidbit

If your situation is out of control, it's worth it to ask for help. Even if your available helpers are subpar organizers.

SUPPORT OPTIONS

Assistive Technology

- Devices that help you physically complete chores (*e.g., mobility aids or accessible cleaning tools*)
- Technology that helps with the cognitive aspect of home care (*e.g., timers or alarms to help with time management and memory*)

Medical Support

- Mental health treatment to address underlying emotional issues
- Occupational therapy to help solve functional barriers
- Physical therapy to address pain and mobility associated with home care
- Medication to alleviate relevant medical/mental health conditions

Hired Support

- Cleaning service to help keep your home feeling manageable
- Personal assistant to help keep up with administrative tasks
- Personal organizer to assist with decluttering
- Junk haulers to assist with a big declutter

Community Support

- Family, friends, or neighbors to help with the basics of cooking, cleaning, and home maintenance
- A designated friend to keep you company while you do administrative tasks and errands

2 Uncovering Barriers

Cognitive, Emotional & Physical Challenges

My first job out of graduate school was with a child welfare agency as an in-home therapist. If that sounds way too advanced for a freshly graduated social worker, it was. But it was a job entirely populated by brand-new social workers. Experienced social workers are much too wise to accept a job with so much responsibility and so little pay.

I provided court-mandated therapy to parents whose children had been temporarily removed from their care—many because of the deplorable physical condition of their home.

Structural damage, pest infestation, and florid mold growth were common, often not the fault of the parent, but of their neglectful landlords. But sometimes, the homes were piled up with more concerning signs of suffering, such as rotting trash or animal waste. Other times, hoarding rendered kitchens or sleeping areas inaccessible.

My job was straightforward: Get the house under control, so the kids could reunite with their parents. Looking back, it seems inconceivable that my superiors sent me—a basically clueless twenty-three-year-old neat freak—to discern the underlying cause of these chaotic homes and support their rapid transformation. But the kids were often desperate to go home, and their parents were desperate to have them back, and I was desperate to help. We were all united in one objective. That was a good place to start.

Still, I was completely off the grid, training-wise. I had no silent office, and no psychotherapist's armchair, in which to conduct my therapy sessions. Instead, I sometimes spent sessions on my hands and knees next to my clients, scrubbing walls and filling trash bags while music blasted and children and cats ran in and out of the house.

Among the overflowing litterboxes, the unwashed dishes, the piles of unanswered mail, we cleaned. And we talked. And I learned how they ended up in their personal abyss. For me, it was an invaluable education.

HOW COULD YOU LET IT GET SO BAD?

The Understandable Descent into Chaos

How could you let it get so bad? People tsk-tsk at out-of-control homes. But, honestly, it's easy! And it can happen to anyone.

When we see people in desperate situations, we are quick to sympathize but also quick to explain to ourselves why that couldn't be us. We could never live in squalor—we're just too responsible!

But the truth is, responsibility does not save us from desperation and chaos, always waiting in the wings, a few unlucky events away.

Home chaos takes hold gradually when barriers get in the way of living. Barriers are problems that take precedence over cleaning. The death of a caregiver, the loss of a job, the unexpected plummet into mental illness—there are an infinite number of very good reasons that a home descends into chaos.

Once you're living in chaos, you learn to adjust, because you must. Equipped with highly adaptive powers of avoidance and compartmentalization, you learn not to see the mess because it's too distressing to see.

As one of my clients described it, "A home this crazy is like unmanageable credit card debt. You just make the minimum payment and pray you'll die before the full bill comes due."

When life is upended, your dishes, your laundry, and your bills mercilessly persist, piling around you, an oppressive burden. There is always a barrier—colicky baby, broken ankle, incontinent cat—that caused the home to fall apart. And once you understand that barrier, compassion is the natural consequence, and also hope, because if you can understand a problem, you have a shot at fixing it.

Tidying Tidbit

It's no good judging people who end up living in unmanageable situations. We're all a bad event or two away from being them.

BARRIERS VS EXCUSES

How Can You Tell the Difference?

Barriers and excuses aren't the same thing. But they are occasionally coworkers.

Barriers are real-life circumstances, internal or external, beyond your control, that prevent you from keeping your life together.

Excuses are fibs you tell about your barriers—to other people and to yourself. Obviously, flat-out lies about ability are excuses. *I have a rare and definitely-not-made-up skin condition that makes me unable to touch sponges!*

But it works the other way too. Insisting that you don't have barriers, when you actually do, is also an excuse. Refusing to accept that I was too weak to mop my floors, that I needed to find ways to manage my energy, didn't result in cleaner floors just because I was trying so hard and being so good. It resulted in my husband finding me, semiconscious, at the junction of the mopped and unmopped sections of my kitchen floor.

"I'm fine!" I said bravely, lying on the flat of my back. "Just resting!" (This excuse was arguably more unpleasant for everyone than a dirty floor would have been.)

No matter whether your home is immaculate, mildly cluttered, or hazard level—if something is making functioning hard for you, it's a real barrier. It doesn't matter *why* you find a home task difficult. You only have to contend with the fact that you *do* find it difficult.

Whether your reasons feel valid or silly, your struggle is a fact. Trying to escape the facts, or convince yourself that housework shouldn't be difficult, will not make you any better at it. It will only make you more ashamed, less capable, and greatly at risk of driving your loved ones crazy.

Tidying Tidbit

Barriers are valid reasons why you can't keep your life organized. Barriers can be both internal and external.

COGNITIVE BARRIERS

Stuff Your Brain Is Bad At

Cleaning and organizing seem simple on the surface but actually involve a complex network of interconnected brain skills called executive functioning. There are a wide range of biopsychological factors that can interrupt these capacities, temporarily or permanently, in childhood or adulthood.

Those interrupted capacities are called executive dysfunction. In other words, when these capacities are offline, your brain just ain't working.

Here is a tale of how executive dysfunction can get in the way of home care.

Trouble with Planning Ahead: Imagine this. You're lounging on the couch. All of a sudden, you remember—people are coming over tonight. *What rascal invited them? You?! God!* Time to clean your house, with the spicy addition of cognitive barriers! Should you have planned ahead and cleaned your house yesterday? Possibly, but it's too late for all that now.

Difficulty with Starting & Transitioning Tasks: Suddenly, your body feels as if it weighs a million pounds and no force on earth could get you from sitting to standing. Getting yourself from one state of being (not doing a thing) to a different state of being (actively working) has always been difficult for you.

Time Management Challenges: So, you delay. How long does it take to clean a house, really? Two minutes, two hours, two years? You've never been good at estimating how long a task will take. Last time you had company, you finished party preparation a whole four hours early, and had to sit there twiddling your thumbs until people arrived.

Problems with Prioritizing: With two hours left, the pressure to clean pushes you over the edge into action. But where to start? You look around. Absolutely everything is dirty. Should you clean the bathroom first? The floors? Clear the couch of laundry? You spend five minutes gazing around, running the calculations. You finally give up and *eeny-meeny-miny-moe* to pick the kitchen.

Confusion on Sequencing: You wander into the kitchen with the intention of doing the dishes. But the sink is too full of dirty dishes to run the faucet. How to do the dishes if you can't access the sink? Jesus, it's like a logic puzzle. You try to move the dirty dishes to the counter to access the sink.

A Hard Time Focusing: But there's no space on the counter because you forgot to finish your project from last week, decanting your spices into adorable identical jars. Organized people have organized spices, and you want to be organized. Maybe spices are the answer to serenity. You spend fifteen minutes alphabetizing your spices until your friend calls you to ask about the party tonight, and you suddenly snap out of your distraction detour. *Yikes!*

Slipping Memory: Okay, you urgently need to do the dishes. Wait, you're out of soap. Where is the new bottle of dish soap? It's lost in the jumble of shopping from last week. You know you're prone to losing things, so you try to leave Important Stuff, such as dish soap, out on the dining table, where you can easily see it. But your Important Stuff Pile has gotten so big that you can't find anything in it. You have bought nine dish soaps in the last month.

Category Confusion: The dishes are done (you found three unopened bottles of dish soap under the sink). It's time to tidy the living room. The coffee table is absolutely brimming with mysterious objects that need to go somewhere else. But they don't seem to *belong with* anything else. Do your batteries belong with electronics, tools, or your junk drawer? What about the tiny rubber duck you got at your nephew's birthday party?

Agonized Decision-Making: The unanswerable questions just keep coming. Do you need to keep that user's manual for your dishwasher? Or that very nice but apparently useless box your phone came in? How many pens is one person supposed to own? How in God's name did all these things find their way to your coffee table?

Tricky Spatial Reasoning: You need to contain all this *stuff.* In your Important Stuff Pile, you have a chic organizer bin that could contain all these objects. But fitting those objects into the existing space requires thinking in three dimensions, which you can't easily do. You can barely navigate to the grocery store. You dump everything onto a bookshelf—a two-dimensional solution, and a problem for Future You!

Inflexible Thinking: With a few minutes left, you notice the floors are visibly dirty. You know that the optimal cleaning method is to sweep, then vacuum, then mop. But your vacuum is broken. If you can't clean the floors the best way possible, what's even the point of cleaning them at all?! Your best friend arrives early and reminds you that sweeping alone would still make the floors cleaner than no action at all. (Sounds fake.)

A NONEXHAUSTIVE LIST OF CONDITIONS THAT INTERFERE WITH EXECUTIVE FUNCTIONING

Developmental Disorders

- ADHD
- Autism spectrum disorder

Acute Mental Illness

- Major depressive disorder
- Postpartum depression
- Bipolar disorder
- Obsessive-compulsive disorder

Neurological

- Brain injury
- Multiple sclerosis
- Parkinson's disease

Environmental Factors

- Grief
- Sleep deprivation
- Malnutrition
- Chronic stress and trauma

EMOTIONAL BARRIERS

Managing Life with Unmanageable Feelings

Emotional disturbance often doesn't do the polite thing and stay put inside your little brain. It creeps out into your body, overflowing into your physical environment, like a visible scavenger hunt of invisible anguish.

Sadness shows itself in the loss of connection to everyday life—the grim bedroom nest of tangled sheets, unwashed dishes, and overflowing trash.

Anxiety about home care, visible in obsessively cleaned spaces, comes to the sufferer in piercing mental flashes of "What if?"

What if you get salmonella? What if there's an unpaid bill in the mail pile? What if your mean aunt comes to visit unexpectedly and chastises you for doing everything wrong?!

Boredom, our old enemy from childhood, rears its head when it's time to do tedious tasks, which is *all the time*. Adults try not to acknowledge they're bored (to set a good example for the children!). But it's a shoddy performance at best. We get sucked into preferred tasks (e.g., scrolling) over nonpreferred tasks (e.g., folding the laundry) all the time—proving that difficulty tolerating boredom is rarely left in childhood.

Shame, the conviction that something is inherently wrong with you or your life, causes you to hide your home chaos, from a fear of being humiliated or rejected by others. Housekeeping shame thrives on the belief that people *just know* how to be adults. And because you don't *just know*, you must just be an immature slob at your core.

This isolation, unfortunately, prevents the flow of any information that would disprove your self-loathing theory. That's where connection comes in. If you find yourself unable to manage your feelings related to housework, it is probably time to seek additional support.

Emotions are a part of life, but they shouldn't prevent you from functioning—at least not for very long. When they do, it's time to consider therapy. A therapist can help you diagnose the cause of your distress and support you in understanding how your emotions affect your behavior and, by extension, your home.

DYSFUNCTIONAL RELATIONSHIPS WITH POSSESSIONS

Barriers in How We Think About Our Stuff

We aren't always cold and logical when it comes to the stuff we own. We're sentimental. We're impulsive. We imbue objects with more meaning than what they really have.

We equate what we own with who we are. I once organized for a person who spent weeks crying about donating her old flight attendant uniform, one she hadn't worn for years, since being forced to quit her job due to illness. The uniform had grown to represent everything she left behind in her old career.

We make possessions proxies for people. Personally, I have kept a set of my grandma's stationery (that even she didn't want) since she died twenty years ago. I can't use it, and I can't get rid of it. To me, that creamy stationery with the lilac trim *is* Grandma.

We assign our possessions personalities. Have you ever tried to get rid of a beloved toy from your childhood? It's excruciating. You know that your teddy bear isn't sentient. But you also know that you're hurting its feelings by even thinking about giving it to Goodwill.

Emotional relationships with possessions are deeply understandable. Buying and saving things that don't make sense is relatively harmless. And often, it's well intentioned. But when compulsive saving or buying fills your home with a cascade of items you can't use, it becomes a barrier.

THE COMPULSIVE SAVERS

Three types of people who save more than they can use.

1. **Environmental:** This saver fears destroying the planet by contributing to landfills. They are driven by a very real anxiety about climate change. Often, they don't have the time or resources to recycle and reuse everything they save.
    - *Quirky Saves: packaging from purchases, so many jam jars*
2. **Financial:** This saver *hates* wasting money. They are driven by genuine fears of financial insecurity. They save anything that could be fixed or reused because the money may not be there to repurchase it in the future. And even if they have the money, repurchasing is a waste they can't tolerate.
    - *Quirky Saves: gift bags and tissue paper, mystery nails and screws*
3. **Creative:** This saver has creative and innovative ideas for reusing an impressive stash of hobby supplies. They are driven by creativity and passion. They have difficulty mourning the reality that they can't execute every creative idea into real-life results.
    - *Quirky Saves: old paper for collage, fabric scraps, junk with potential*

What they have in common: Compulsive savers are full of admirable intentions. But they lack the self-awareness and foresight to see that they may not have the time, energy, or functioning to make use of what they have saved.

THE COMPULSIVE BUYERS

Two types of people who buy more than they can use.

1. **The Self-Soother:** This buyer feels overwhelmed by stress. To feel better, they chase the good feelings that come with a shiny new purchase. Often, they feel guilty after shopping. They miss return-date windows due to avoidance of the guilt associated with buying.
    - *Quirky Purchases: clothing, makeup, gaming equipment*
2. **The Fixer:** This buyer feels in chaos and is sure their new purchase will fix their personal problems. They feverishly purchase cleaning, organizing, or self-care supplies. But by the time they get the purchase home, the magic is already starting to wear off, and they rarely end up using everything they buy.
    - *Quirky Purchases: workout equipment, fancy cleaning supplies, organizing bins*

What they have in common: Compulsive buyers often feel a lack of enjoyment, or even shame, about purchases. They fail to remember that each purchase carries the responsibility of unpacking and assigning each item a designated home.

Self-compassion is a helpful tool in managing emotional relationships with objects. It is normal to feel sentimental. We all make mistakes about what we buy and save. But at the end of the day, objects are just objects. And we only have so much time, money, and thought to give the things we own.

Try to be honest with yourself about why you buy and save. Look at past evidence to determine your chances of using your stuff. If you can, try to do this with a spirit of curiosity, not judgment.

SENSORY BARRIERS

Stuff You Find Icky

The squish of the burned rice soaking in a pot in a sink. The nose-stinging smell of disinfectant. The rumble of the dryer. For people with sensory issues, the smells, sensations, and sounds of cleaning can cause distress bordering on pain. They have a heightened awareness of texture, sound, temperature, light, and smell.

Unmanageable sensory issues are most commonly seen in people with developmental disorders such as autism. But most adults have at least one sensory quirk—a sensation that they can't stand, either because it's associated with a bad experience or just because it's yucky. And fear of feeling that sensation can cause chore avoidance.

SENSE	IRRITANT	DIFFICULT CHORE
Touch	Squishy, slimy, rough, prickly, or tickly textures	Cooking and dishes Bathing, hygiene, and dressing Cleaning up spills
Smell	Rotting smells, chemical smells, or body smells	Cooking and dishes Litterbox and bathroom cleaning Laundry General cleaning
Sound	Loud, clanging, roaring, clicking, or repetitive noises	Sweeping and vacuuming Unloading dishwasher Drying laundry
Temperature	Too hot or too cold, or the transition from one to the other	Bathing Taking out the trash

PHYSICAL BARRIERS

Stuff Your Body Is Bad At

Physical disability simply means "I can't do that because my body won't let me."

Home care can be very physically demanding—even something as simple as cleaning up a spill. You have to be able to see the spill, locomote your body to it, then contort your limbs to clean it up. An able-bodied person can do that without any interruptions or protests from their body.

But what if you can't see very well? Or you can't stand for long? What if your back spasms every time you bend down, or your hands don't have the dexterity to hold a rag? For people with physical disabilities, cleaning tasks can be (on the mild side) a great frustration and (on the severe side) an agony.

I wish I could go back in time and share this wisdom with my newly sick household. Use every single accommodation, hack, and as-sold-on-TV device you can get your hands on. There are scores of clever people who develop technology that makes cleaning, if not easy, then slightly less difficult for people with disabilities. I wish I had known that I didn't have to suffer through housework, in pain, short of breath, struggling, and stymied by useless pride—at least not all the time!

PHYSICAL CAPACITIES NEEDED FOR CLEANING

Physical Challenge	Affected Chores	Possible Accommodation
Standing/Stamina: the ability to keep upright for an extended period of time	Cooking, washing the dishes, cleaning the floors, changing the bedsheets	Stools, chairs, and walkers that allow sitting while working; doing only a bit at a time
Mobility: the ability to move over distances without falling	Sweeping, mopping, laundry, taking out the trash	Mobility devices such as walkers, canes, carts, and chairs

PHYSICAL CAPACITIES NEEDED FOR CLEANING (continued)

PHYSICAL CHALLENGE	AFFECTED CHORES	POSSIBLE ACCOMMODATION
Flexibility: the ability to bend and reach without pain	Cleaning the bathroom, organizing, putting away dishes, groceries, or laundry	Long-handled extendable cleaning brushes; reacher-grabber tool; using only easily accessible cabinets
Lifting: the ability to move heavy items without strain	Laundry, taking out trash, organizing	Wheeled carts to help move items without lifting
Vision: the ability to perceive dirt, dust, and messes	Cleaning the kitchen, floors, bathroom, and surfaces	Bright lighting, thin cloths that allow you to feel whether a surface is clean
Chemical Tolerance: the ability to interact with cleaning supplies without allergic reaction	Cleaning the bathroom, doing the dishes, laundry	Hypoallergenic cleaning supplies; protective gloves, masks, and aprons

Note: In the second half of this book, you will find practical chapters on how to clean and organize each room of your home. In each chapter, you will find tips for managing physical and sensory difficulties with that task. Chapter 19 is devoted to dividing up chores and caregiving tasks in homes with disability.

3 Breaking the Rules

Standards Beyond Moralism & Self-Criticism

I TEACH ART TO SIX-YEAR-OLDS ONCE A WEEK. MY CLASSROOM RULE IS THAT everyone cleans up after class. Without this rule, the classroom quickly devolves into complete chaos.

I teach the kids to put away supplies, wash paintbrushes, and wipe down the tables at the end of class. They don't do it perfectly. But they do it well enough for kindergarteners, so I pick up their slack.

Now, let's imagine that I drop the hammer on these kids. I announce: "No more messes! I'm sick of this sloppy behavior! We're tightening up the rules around here!"

So, on top of what they're already cleaning, they also have to wash the windows, mop the floors, and do mechanical maintenance on our terrifying kiln, the technologically advanced fire robot we use to cook pottery. I provide no instruction. I only expect results. It's never too early for these kids to learn some good habits!

How do you think that would go? They would gape at me with their bright little kindergartener faces. Then, mayhem. Tears. Screams. And revolt. Not a paintbrush would get cleaned. And nary a window washed.

And why? It is not because my kindergarteners are incompetent rule breakers. (They are actually lovely.)

The only person to blame, of course, would be me. I made a bad rule, out of proportion to their capabilities. It would be insane to expect them to live up to that standard.

You are just a grown-up kindergartener. You also struggle to follow rules beyond your capacity. We don't resolve chaos in the long term by imposing harsher rules but rather by making rules that fit circumstances.

And yet, when someone we love falls into the homemaking abyss, we shout *our* rules down at them as if the rules were highly motivating universal truths, flimsy little ropes they could use to shimmy out of the pit—if they just gave it a little effort!

Clean as you goooo!

One item in, one item ouuuut!

Don't put it down, put it awaaaaay!

But those rules aren't helpful. If they were able to follow those rules, they never would've ended up in the pit of despair.

A rule that you can't follow is just another barrier.

There are a few hard-and-fast rules we can all agree on: Don't rub raw chicken all over your walls. Use the toilet per its manufacturer's instructions. Beyond that, most things are really a matter of individual function and preference. If you're safe and healthy and your household is working, there's no right or wrong way to do it.

Tidying Tidbit

Such rules as "Clean as You Go" are only helpful if you can follow them. A rule beyond your capabilities is just another barrier.

THE TYRANNY OF THE INNER CRITIC

When I was younger and healthier, I spent every Saturday cleaning my house. I dusted high to low, scrubbed baseboards, and carried out a very specific (some would say a little insane) vacuuming routine.

My cleaning habits were like a ballet: carefully choreographed, obsessively practiced. Designed to look beautiful and effortless while requiring incredible stamina.

At the time, I felt that this was the Correct Standard for cleaning. I was following the rules! (The rules that I made up.) But I did have some help.

You see, in my brain, there lived a tiny homemaking critic. For brevity, let's call her *Demanda* (a demanding version of Amanda; an unflattering but unfortunately hilarious nickname coined by one of my high school boyfriends).

Demanda was my internal judge—self-appointed and unelected, I might add—of all matters cooking, cleaning, organizing, and administrative. And if anyone did a homemaking task incorrectly within a 10-mile radius, she filled my head with a hair-raising screech. Demanda believes she should be writing this book, not me.

Like many critics, Demanda had forceful opinions on her subject of interest but very little real-world experience. She insisted I run the dishwasher every night, but also that I *never ever* run the dishwasher half full. (What was the correct action on a day with few dishes? Demanda had no suggestions.)

Demanda wanted my laundry done ASAP. She also insisted that I hand wash my delicates, which was counterproductive to the goal of having laundry done ASAP. Informed by theory rather than practice, she was weirdly worried that the dryer would wear out the elastic on my sports bras. She was not receptive to feedback that sports bras can easily be replaced.

I just couldn't live up to my inner critic's demands for home care. Perhaps you have an inner critic too—a single director of the board insisting on the correct way to be an adult. They wield their rules with an iron fist and sound vaguely like your grandma, but way meaner.

When I got too tired to be so zealous about cleaning, I had to put Demanda into retirement and drastically reconsider my standards.

Standards—your collection of rules about how to keep house *the best way*—are not facts. They are opinions. They are desires.

I desire to load my dishwasher with sacred geometric perfection, to allow the maximum amount of water to reach the maximum amount of dishes. It is not true that this is the only one, single, correct way to load a dishwasher. It is not true that I can't do it differently if I'm rushed, tired, sad, or assailed by any other of life's unpleasant surprises. It is not true that I am superior to my family members because of my incredible dishwasher-loading skills. It is only true that I have very strong (*strangely strong?!*) opinions about the dishwasher.

KNOWING YOUR VALUES

Core Motivations That Animate Your Rules

So, you've thrown out the rule book on housekeeping. Good for you! Also, urgently, now what?

Now it's time to make your own rules. Rules are guided by values. That's because, if you don't truly care about a house rule, you won't follow it. Your heart won't be in it. That's why your first step to developing new standards is determining your values. Let's find yours.

Aesthetics: You want your home to look beautiful, cozy, or interesting. Your main goal for cleaning and organizing is pleasing your eye.

Efficiency: You are most interested in your home being functional, streamlined, and easy to maintain. Your home serves you, not the other way around.

Familiarity: You want your home to feel *like home*, with everything in the same place. And, ideally, no disruptions or surprises.

Freedom: You don't like to be tied down by the obligations of housekeeping. You value time spent relaxing or doing enjoyable activities rather than cleaning.

Health: You want to avoid potential risks to safety. You dust to prevent allergies, or sanitize to prevent germs, or keep floors clear to prevent tripping.

Hospitality: You want your home to feel comfortable for guests. You feel motivated to clean before they arrive. You prefer not to show any of the behind-the-scenes work involved in preparing for their visits.

Relationships: You care less about the state of your home, and more about being in harmony with the people you live with. You align yourself with the preferences of the people who live with you.

Responsibility: Your home and your possessions are a privilege. You are obligated to take care of them, so they can last as long as possible, in as good a condition as possible.

Exercise: From the preceding list, choose three values that matter most to you. Consider how you could honor these values in the care of your home. Do you have any habits that are in conflict with those values?

KNOWING YOUR CLEANING STYLE

How Clean Is Clean Enough for You?

Functional (and dysfunctional) houses can be tidy or cluttered, sanitized or natural, and everything in between. Everyone has their own cleaning preferences—somewhere at the intersection of those four factors. That's your cleaning style.

I have a theory that by the time you reach adulthood, your cleaning style is pretty much established. You will proceed to keep house in that style, unless something comes along to disrupt your life (e.g., getting married, or welcoming a baby, or having an existential crisis).

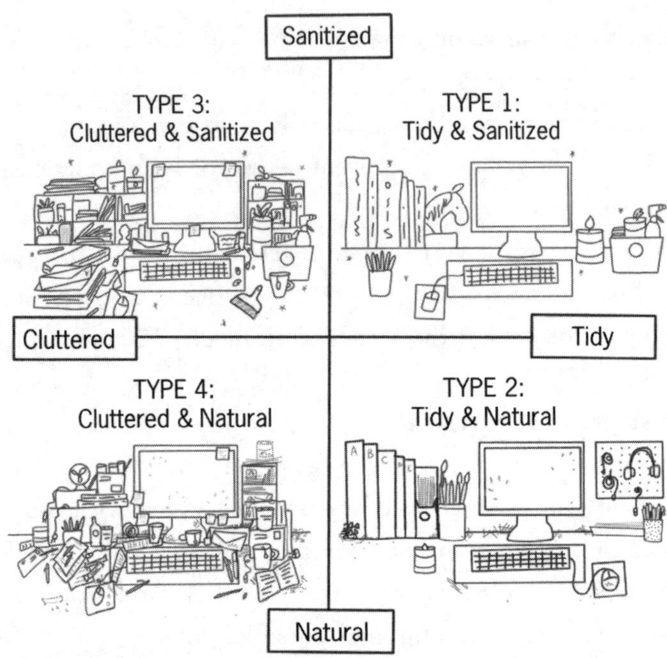

Understanding that your cleaning style is a preference, not an objective truth about the world, can save you lots of suffering. It helps put your homemaking quirks in perspective. I hope you can find yourself (or your baffling loved ones) in these four types of homemakers.

TYPE 1: TIDY & SANITIZED CLEANERS

| Squeaky Clean with Everything in Its Place |

Core Values: health & aesthetics

These housekeeping superstars are talented—and slightly unsettling! They genuinely enjoy tidying and organizing. They also might snatch your coffee cup away and wash it the second you set it on the coffee table. They feel the presence of a mess with almost physical pain.

How do they manage to keep things so clean? It's not just that they don't procrastinate. They *can't* procrastinate, even when they want to, because they can't relax until their environment is reset.

Their home looks uninhabited, magazine-like, pure. Their strength is in their attention to detail, focus, and capacity for hard labor. Their weakness is in their inability to tolerate chaos.

TYPE 2: TIDY & NATURAL CLEANERS

| Everything's in Its Place, but It's Not Squeaky Clean |

Core Values: efficiency & aesthetics

This highly organized but down-to-earth housekeeper values tidiness above all else. They don't stress about scrubbing or sanitizing—just organizational schemes. Their home is meticulously clutter-free but lived in: jam on the counters, dog hair on the floors. All objects are carefully tidied away into cubbies, and the cubbies are dusty.

They are usually excellent at color-coding, decision-making, and spatial reasoning. Their weakness lies in their avoidance of unseen but urgent cleaning tasks, such as the colony of mold hiding behind the beautifully organized shower caddy. They are sometimes former Type 1s, forcefully reformed by the presence of a child or rowdy pet.

TYPE 3: CLUTTERED & SANITIZED CLEANERS

| Squeaky Clean & Things All Over the Place |

Core Values: health & responsibility

A scattered housekeeper with a stubborn streak of discipline—and perhaps a small chip on their shoulder! Laundry and papers might be strewn about, but there's not a germ in sight (metaphorically, of course, as you can't see germs). They make piles of clutter, then they vacuum around the piles. They might readily admit that they struggle with organization. But they can muster vigorous stores of intensity when it comes to scrubbing a kitchen sink.

Their homes can be identified by their sparkling, chemically scoured bathrooms and disastrously messy bedrooms. They can get a ton of functional cleaning done in a cluttered environment, which not everyone can do. Their battle cry is "Sure, I'm messy, but I'm not dirty!"

TYPE 4: CLUTTERED & NATURAL CLEANERS

| Things Are All Over the Place & They're Not Squeaky Clean |

Core Values: freedom & efficiency

This is who Type 3s are trying not to be. These misunderstood souls have an admirable ability to thrive in conditions that others might find intolerable. Their homes are cluttered and grubby, though not necessarily unpleasant. They can go through life, adaptable, happy, focused on pursuits beyond the practical, with the blessed and cursed ability to ignore a house that's gotten out of hand.

Unfortunately, the practical sometimes comes back to bite them in the ass—usually in the form of a new housemate, romantic partner, or a bitter dose of public shaming. Healthy Type 4s demand mutual respect while putting reasonable restrictions on their highest value—freedom. This prevents future problems, practical and relational, from getting out of control.

Tidying Tidbit

Knowing your cleaning type can help you understand why you make the rules you do (and why other people seem to have such trouble following your rules).

BAD RULES I SUGGEST YOU FOLLOW

| Alternative Standards for a Functional Home |

Once you know your cleaning values, and your cleaning style, you are ready to replace your outdated cleaning rules with new ones. To help you with that process, I would like to humbly suggest a few controversial cleaning rules for your consideration.

HALF-ASS YOUR CHORES

Stop delaying a task because it can't be done perfectly. I see you! I know what you're doing—waiting to pick up that chip you dropped on the floor two days ago until you can sweep the entire room, because it's more efficient. Just pick it up. Leaving a chip on the floor for two days isn't efficient.

Stop waiting, and waiting, and waiting for the energy to clean your entire dirty bathroom before you clean anything at all. Just wipe that toothpaste out of the sink. It's been there for seven weeks, and you aren't getting any more energetic.

Perfection is scrumptious when it's attainable, and useless when it isn't. **When efficiency isn't attainable, be pragmatic. Doing your chores badly is better than not doing them at all. Doing your chores partially, even 1 percent, is an improvement on 0 percent.**

BECOME A "CORRECT CLEANING FREQUENCY" AGNOSTIC

If you want to destroy your friends group, ask them the correct frequency for cleaning a bathtub. Everyone, from the once-a-day to the once-a-year cleaners, believes they are correct. But as with all cleaning tasks, there is no correct answer because it depends on a complex range of factors.

How many people use that bathtub? How often? How much of your body is in direct contact with the tub—just the bottom of your feet? Or are you submerging your entire body in bath soup? Is the bathtub frequently inhabited by children who haven't quite mastered potty training? Do you live in a climate that promotes mold growth? Is your water mineral rich? How psychologically distressed are you by the unseen presence of germs?

Unfortunately, there is no one correct answer or guideline to follow. Only you can know how often to clean your home. In Part 2, you'll find guidance for defining your own cleaning frequency.

GIVE UP ON PERFECT PRODUCTS

Stop delaying cleaning because you need to find the perfect product to spray, scrub, or disinfect the mess. Obviously, glass cleaner works wonders on windows when compared to furniture polish. A well-designed cleaning or organizing product can certainly help a job go well. But let's not forget that most of our ancestors cleaned with little more than vinegar, hot water, and homemade soap (and probably the power of fervent prayer).

Personally, I'm a big fan of modern specialty cleaners and disinfectants. But needing the best product for a task, when a good-enough product would suffice, is just a barrier. Expensive and precious items deserve to be cleaned carefully. Most everything else can still benefit from a swipe with a soapy rag.

BE LAZY

Have you ever seen that "As Seen on TV" aisle at the supermarket? It's full of devices to help complete simple household tasks. I used to scoff at that aisle as a waste of money, an indulgence of laziness. Why would I need a sponge with a long handle when I can just bend down?

Wow, did adulthood knock me down a peg with herniated disks, blood pressure drops, and a loss of zeal for doing hard things! Now I relish those lazy shortcuts. Life is hard. What can be made easy should be made easy.

DIVORCE CLEANLINESS FROM GOODNESS

Take it from me, a very clean but not especially virtuous person. Clean and happy aren't the same thing. Clean and healthy aren't the same thing. Mess does not equal chaos. Mess does not equal wickedness. Mess is just a life that is put in order less frequently.

A clean and organized life can *feel* good, but it does not *make* you good. It can bring you pleasure but not happiness. Know that difference and keep it in perspective.

Exercise: Minimum Household Standard

CIRCLE YOUR TOP THREE MOST IMPORTANT HOUSEHOLD VALUES.

Aesthetics   Efficiency   Familiarity   Freedom

Health   Hospitality   Relationships   Responsibility

CIRCLE YOUR HOME CARE STYLE.

Tidy & Sanitized   Tidy & Natural

Cluttered & Sanitized   Cluttered & Natural

WHAT CHORES NEED TO BE DONE FOR YOUR HOUSE TO FEEL IN LINE WITH THOSE VALUES?

(e.g., dishes done, laundry done, meals planned, house tidy)

____

____

PROVIDE RATIONALE: WRITE WHY EACH CHORE MATTERS TO YOUR FUNCTIONING.

(e.g., I need the dishes done so I have something to cook and eat on.)

____

____

MAKE IT CONCRETE: DEFINE HOW FREQUENTLY, AND HOW WELL, EACH CHORE NEEDS TO BE DONE TO ENABLE YOU TO FUNCTION.

(e.g., I need the sink clear and the dishwasher run by the end of each day.)

____

____

MAKE A BAD DAY PLAN: IF YOU CAN'T DO EVERYTHING ON YOUR LIST, WHAT'S THE LOWEST STANDARD YOU COULD STAND AND STILL GET BY?

(e.g., switch to disposable dishes and frozen meals)

____

____

4 Dishes Are the Marriage-Killer

Homemaking & Relationships

In training to be a therapist, I learned all sorts of techniques to help couples understand each other and get along. But in practice, instead of delving deep into past traumas and relationship dynamics, I instead found myself refereeing bitter debates about laundry, cooking, and taking out the trash.

My training left me woefully unprepared to confront the practical. I was taught that an argument about "who loads the dishwasher" was petty and insignificant—a distracting proxy for the core wounds within the relationship. If someone couldn't stop talking about vacuuming during a therapy session, they were probably deflecting from the Real Conversation. When it came to chores, I was instructed to guide couples to basically get over it and get on with it.

This did not work. I can't even describe how much this did not work.

If you have ever lived with someone with vastly different housekeeping values and standards of living, you know how maddening and polarizing it can become. That's because long-term love isn't just a romantic endeavor—it's also a partnership of practicality. It became clear to me early on: Love does not protect you from the annoyance of cohabitation. Dishes are the marriage-killer.

Tidying Tidbit

"Who does the chores?" isn't a trivial relationship question. It is one of the central tasks of building a life together.

YOU ARE DIFFICULT

Seeing Yourself as You Are

One of the trickiest parts of cohabitation is the incorrect assumption that you are, at all times, a very reasonable person who is pretty much easy to live with.

So, when someone challenges your homemaking habits, you (quietly or loudly) infer that they are the crazy one.

Imagine that what I'm about to tell you is wrapped in a warm, affectionate hug. This belief is semidelusional. It cannot be correct that everyone else is difficult, and you're so easy-breezy. You are not easy to live with either. You too are difficult.

You have quirks and foibles. You're what my family calls "particular," which really means "strange." You are probably also lovely but, still, difficult.

"I'm not weird," you say; "my standards are totally reasonable!"

"I just like things a certain way."

"I just don't like to waste time on—" Stop it right there, buster. There you go again, being difficult!

It's okay that you're kind of difficult to live with. To be difficult is to be human. Difficult does not equal unlikable. At home, you are unmasked. You can't hide how strange you really are. Why can't you just put your socks in the hamper? Why leave them balled up under the coffee table?

Why do you insist on hand washing all those tiny vintage glasses? What do you have against the dishwasher?

I'm sure you have a good reason. That reason may also be—you guessed it—*difficult*.

I'm not suggesting that you resign yourself to living with someone you find intolerable, just because you're difficult too. I certainly believe that some couples just aren't destined to cohabitate, and that some divides are too wide to bridge.

What I am telling you is this: Have an inch of humility for every yard of self-righteousness. Remember that when you're at your wit's end with your Difficult Partner, they may also be at their wit's end with you. And miraculously, they still love you. Strive to be as mutually generous in your assessment of them.

THE UNION OF MESSY & NEAT

Seeing How the Other Half Lives

It's a tale as old as time. A messy person and a neat person fall in love. Messy admires Neat's competent, organized nature. Neat is seduced by Messy's relaxed attitude. They are aware that their homemaking proclivities aren't aligned—but do opposites not attract?

In a burst of optimism, they find a home, move in together, and hope the rest will work itself out. (Poor babies—they have no idea what's coming.)

Messy notices that Neat is mystifyingly particular about home care. Neat de-stresses after a long day by cleaning, of all things. This makes Messy uneasy. The home is so disturbingly perfect, like no one even lives there. It's almost as if Messy isn't allowed to live there! Trying to get comfortable, Messy forges a path of chaos through Neat's orderly life.

For Neat, untidiness and grime feel like a personal attack. They ask Messy to get it together. Messy wants to make Neat happy, but unfortunately they have different visions of what "getting it together" looks like. Marooned in clutter not of their creation, Neat looks at Messy, silently fuming. The unappreciative little rascal!

Messy feels increasingly criticized, controlled, and restricted. Jesus Christ, they just want to be able to relax at home! This causes Messy to develop a quiet rebellious streak. Determined to be able to be at peace at home, they passively resist Neat's demands by continuing to make messes. Which makes Neat apoplectic. Messy starts to suspect Neat might be a little bit mentally ill.

Neat is increasingly dysregulated by Messy's mutinous attitude. They try to adjust, and ignore Messy's chaos, letting Messy take care of it. But Messy never does. Or at least, not in any time frame Neat can tolerate waiting. How can they live in such disarray? Neat starts to suspect that Messy might be a little bit unhinged.

The mistrust grows like a bitter plant. Messy doesn't understand why Neat is constantly cleaning. Why can't they just relax and do it later? Neat doesn't understand how Messy can just relax in the presence of a mess, which will inevitably need to be cleaned up at some vague future date.

This creates a pattern of control and rebellion, a parent-child dynamic that is deeply unsexy for both parties. And conventional advice frequently fails to solve the problem.

Tidying Tidbit

Messy and neat people living together can struggle greatly to understand each other and find a common standard of living.

DON'T TRY THIS AT HOME

Conventional Relationship Advice That Might Not Get You What You Want

It's not that the conventional advice on cohabitation is bad. It's that it's far from universal. Relationship dynamics are as complex and varied as the people who live within them. That makes it maddeningly difficult to find advice that fits your situation. I can only advise that I've seen these popular bits of wisdom go sideways a time or two.

LOVE IT OR LEAVE IT

The Advice: Make uneasy peace with your partner's maddening home care habits. You've made your bed, and now you have to, you know, share your home with someone who's a nightmare.

The Problem: Although there is a grain of truth in this technique (it really is difficult for people to change, and you did choose to move in with this person), good relationships welcome adjustment, compromise, and growth. It is okay—healthy, even—to expect your partner to meet you halfway.

LOWER YOUR STANDARDS

The Advice: This is the most common advice for fastidious people living with their tornadic lovers. Just learn to live in a house that's way dirtier than you can tolerate!

The Problem: While it's true that standards should be adjusted, changing your standards (whether higher or lower) to precisely meet your partner's is rarely a recipe for happiness. Defining standards should be a collaborative process, a give-and-take on both sides that causes minimal disruption to both and preserves what each partner values most.

IF YOU WANT IT THAT WAY, DO IT YOURSELF

The Advice: There's no use upsetting your beloved by asking them to do chores your way! Avoid conflict by taking responsibility for everything on which you have a strong opinion.

The Problem: It's good in theory to delegate chores to the person with the most interest. But this tends to place the workload unequally on neat people, which makes them feel unappreciated and as if their partner doesn't care about what they value. Instead, collaboratively discuss standards and workloads so housework can be divided up fairly.

PRACTICAL WISDOM FOR COHABITATING

Loving Your Partner Even When They're Accidentally Messing Up Your House

It is easy to think someone is lovely and charming on dates. It is harder to see them as delightful when you have a front-row seat to their incomprehensible housekeeping habits.

Staying with someone when they won't stop putting empty containers back in the fridge? Adoring someone who can't physically sleep if the floor isn't vacuumed? Man hath no greater love than this.

We erroneously think that if we love someone, then living together should be effortless. I have found this to be mostly true for the emotional parts of the marriage but not at all true for the coworking partnership of creating a livable home. (Unless you've luckily fallen in love with someone exactly aligned in your habits. Most of us aren't so wise.)

After trying everything above and getting nowhere, personally and professionally, I was left with only trial and error. Luckily for you, by making lots of mistakes, I gained a bit of practical wisdom on the subject. Here's what I've seen work best for couples with vastly different cleaning styles and standards.

Keep Judgment Out of It: Even when you're certain of the rightness of your opinion, entering a discussion about housework (or anything, really) full of self-righteous fury is a good way to start a terrible argument. We are too naturally defensive to be receptive to self-righteous people. A healthy discussion is a conversation where you're open to seeing both sides. Avoid mocking your partner's habits, even when you think they're being indisputably weird.

Be on the Same Team: Housework isn't competitive, it's collaborative. It isn't you against your partner. It is you two against the problem of housework. You are on a team. Focus on problem-solving rather than keeping score. If you do need to get data on who is doing more housework, approach it with a sense of curiosity and fun rather than competition.

Explicitly Delegate Each Chore: Housekeeping isn't just dishes, laundry, and scrubbing the toilet. It's also dealing with the mail, arranging home maintenance, and monitoring the household supply of toilet paper. Don't assume that you will both pitch in equitably without any discussion. Sit down together to explicitly decide who is responsible for what.

Be Receptive to Changing: If you want to be able to make requests, you must be willing to fulfill requests too. When your partner asks you to do something differently, remember what it is like to be on the asking end. Use it as an opportunity to gain perspective.

Know Your Limits: Determine how much adjustment you can reasonably tolerate without going crazy. Adjustment makes cohabitation work, but not everyone is suited to living with other people. If your housemate's habits are beyond your ability to accommodate, know when it is time to start thinking about going solo. But before giving up, try talking things through.

NAVIGATING DIFFERENCES

Discussing Standards with Respect & Compassion

I have seen too many couples tiptoe around each other, hinting, building a case for a request about something as trivial and life-changing as laundry, worried that a direct conversation about housework will destroy the relationship. But a relationship that can't tolerate a practical conversation might deserve to be destroyed. Fighting for the ability to tolerate living with someone *is* fighting for the relationship.

Armed with compassion and patience, it's time to find common ground with your beloved—especially on those chores that cause you conflict and frustration. There's only one way to get started: Talk about it! If you struggle with these kinds of conversations, here's a protocol for opening the discussion.

1. **Set the Tone:** Even if you are very frustrated, try to start with an attitude of curiosity and compassion toward your partner.

Communicate your open attitude with a neutral, warm tone of voice and relaxed posture. Bring up the conversation at a time that is as calm and unhurried as possible (e.g., "*Can we problem solve about dishes?*").

2. **Ask for What You Want:** Make your request directly and neutrally. Don't hint that you want the dishes done. Don't tell them they're gross for letting dishes sit overnight. Just ask for what you want as neutrally as possible (e.g., "*Could you please put your dirty dishes straight into the dishwasher rather than the sink? I'll do it too.*").
3. **Bring Receipts:** Give a justification of why your request matters to you. If you don't have a good justification, admit that you are being a little bit weird. Being weird counts as a justification if you're willing to name it (e.g., "*When dirty dishes fill up the sink, it makes it harder to access the faucet, which makes it harder to cook and clean. Also, I know this is odd, but touching wet food makes me want to die.*").
4. **Negotiate a Concrete Standard:** Be willing to negotiate until you find middle ground. Then, define your standard explicitly. Do not, I repeat, do not assume that you both mean the same thing by "do the dishes." Agree on the standard for the task, and the interval at which it should be done (e.g., "*I can commit to unloading the dishwasher every morning so it's always accessible. If a few dishes pile up, that's okay with me. I just don't want them to go over the level of the sink because that blocks the faucet. Does that work?*").
5. **Plan for Mistakes:** Understand that even with the best intentions, change is hard. Discuss what you both should do if your agreed-on standard isn't maintained (e.g., "*Do you want me to remind you about the new plan for a few days, or should we put up a sticky note? Let's talk again next week to see if the new system is working. Which of us should bring it up?*").

A DISCLAIMER

People sometimes *hate* this communication protocol, on the grounds that it is (a) exhaustingly tedious, (b) cringe-inducingly nice, and (c) about as erotic as a work meeting that could have been an email. *If this is what it takes to live with someone*, they say, *I would prefer to be alone forever.*

I can only say: Yes! And that's okay!

Yes, the work of living with a partner can be incredibly mundane. You are your partner's coworker in life. Dishes, bills, and hair in the bathtub are part of the package deal. This is difficult to hold in tension with your romantic spark. Loving and respecting someone, while witnessing the most annoying parts of their personality, requires nauseating reserves of sweetness. And these direct conversations, boring as they may be, require frightening amounts of trust. But it would be a shame to let a good relationship die because you're too worried it can't withstand a few unsexy chats.

If you attempt a few of these boring but brave conversations, and things keep going badly, it might be time to start scanning your relationship for red flags.

COHABITATION RED FLAGS

Signs That Things Are Taking a Turn for the Worse

Let's talk bad relationship behaviors. To be fair, anyone could pull one of these not-so-good relationship moves on a bad day. It's not that each one is a relational death sentence on its own. What is more concerning is a repeated behavior pattern over time with no willingness to change.

A salvageable partnership is based on mutual respect, willingness to adjust, and aligned values. Those relationships can usually recover with a frank conversation about boundaries and values or, if necessary, couples therapy. If you observe these behaviors in your partner, it's important to recognize it, name it out loud, and determine if they are willing or able to change. If they aren't, it's time to get honest with yourself about whether the relationship can, or should, be saved.

SHOOTING YOU DOWN: REFUSING TO DISCUSS HOUSEHOLD STANDARDS

If you come into a conversation in a reasonable way, your partner (perhaps after an understandable few moments of defensiveness) shouldn't refuse to discuss your request. Rescheduling the discussion to a more convenient time is reasonable. But shooting down any attempt to discuss shared labor is not.

Tip: Firmly express that you need to have a conversation about the house and ask them to choose a convenient time. If they can choose a time and follow through, that's a good sign—they aren't unwilling, they're just overwhelmed.

RIDICULING YOUR REQUESTS: MAKING FUN OF YOUR REQUESTS AS BEING SILLY OR DRAMATIC

When you love someone, you want them to be happy, which means investing in what is important to them. You fold their laundry in the way they like, even if you think it's stupid, because it matters to them. A reasonable request deserves a reasonable response, not ridicule. It's one thing to tease affectionately, but outright contempt isn't helpful.

Tip: Out of an abundance of caution, poll two or three of your friends or coworkers to determine whether your request is as reasonable as you think. Either way, tell your partner that you do not want a relationship with ridicule or name-calling. (Hold up your end of the deal by not engaging in ridicule, either, and quickly ending any conversations that turn nasty.)

AGGRESSIVELY DEFLECTING REMINDERS: GETTING ANGRY WHEN YOU TRY TO REVISIT CONVERSATIONS

If you have agreed on a household standard and your partner fails to live up to it, it is reasonable to ask to revisit the conversation. A receptive partner will be open to this. They can admit when they've made a mistake or express the need for an adjustment to your agreement without exploding.

Tip: Refuse to continue conversations with yelling. Ask your partner how they would like you to bring up these kinds of conversations, and see whether they have a reasonable answer. ("Just don't bring it up" or "Stop making such a big deal out of nothing" isn't a reasonable answer.)

VASTLY UNEVEN WORKLOADS: AN UNFAIR DIVISION OF HOUSEHOLD LABOR

The division of labor in your household doesn't have to be exactly 50/50. Many factors can affect who carries more responsibility at home. That isn't a problem as long as both people agree the arrangement is fair. But if you are vastly outworking your partner on the domestic front, and they refuse to correct the imbalance, or even to recognize the value of your time and effort, it can be a sign that your labor is being taken advantage of.

Tip: Point out the problem and express your desire for an equitable workload. I highly suggest reading Eve Rodsky's book *Fair Play* with your partner, to help find a concrete middle ground.

WILLFUL INCOMPETENCE: REFUSING TO PARTICIPATE COMPETENTLY IN HOUSEWORK

It's okay to not know how to cook or clean. Everyone must learn at some point. A major red flag is when your partner, even with all the available resources, refuses to learn home care tasks so they can share your burden. Even worse is when they intentionally bungle a task so that they won't be asked to do it again. This is a form of manipulation, and it isn't okay.

Tip: Recognize and name the problem out loud. Refuse to complete chores your partner does badly or to save them from intentional incompetence. Express that you are willing to teach them to do chores at any time if they want to learn.

DISABILITY NOTE

Some disabilities can interfere with a person's ability to discuss, determine, and enact new chore agreements quickly. In that case, these behaviors may not be red flags but, rather, an expression of their disability. It's important to note that all of these disabilities have a range of expressions, and there is no one-size-fits-all approach for navigating these challenges. But compassion, nonjudgment, and cooperation are great places to start.

Autism: Autistic adults can struggle with impromptu, unexpected conversations involving demands. Being flexible in their routines and habits can cost them incredible effort and upset.

Tip: Preview or schedule house meetings; give them time and space to process new demands and form an opinion; have logical, concrete explanations for your requests prepared.

ADHD: If your ADHD partner looks a little squirrelly in these discussions, it might be a matter of focus, not intentional evasiveness. After agreeing to a new house rule, they might struggle to remember and enact the steps necessary for change, due to executive dysfunction.

Tip: Don't be offended by changes of subject or memory lapses; ask if they want help starting chores and staying on track; remember that it may take longer for them to form new habits.

OCD: Folks with obsessive-compulsive disorder may experience intense fear that something bad will happen if they change their habits and rituals. OCD doesn't always affect cleaning, but if it does, remember that they may be wrestling with overwhelming anxiety while adjusting their routine.

Tip: Ask whether your request will put a strain on their anxiety; invite sharing about obsessions and compulsions without judgment; ask how they would like to be supported.

GENDER ROLES AT HOME

The Hidden Hand in Uneven Workloads

The traditional model for sharing housework was: man works, woman cleans. But there have always been homes beyond "man works, woman cleans." Single dads, working moms, same-gender couples, and families with aging or disabled adults carried on with chores outside those traditional gender roles.

Interestingly, same-gender couples today are far better at dividing up chores equitably than their different-gender counterparts. Without the "man cooks, woman cleans" story to restrict them, they are free to divide up chores based on factors beyond gender, such as relative hours worked, skill level, and personal interest. (That leaves only culture, class, skill level, and standards to complicate matters on the domestic front, so it's not like they're totally off the hook.)

Different-gender couples are free to divide up labor in that same way. But puzzlingly, they don't.

Statistically, women still do twice as much household labor as the men they live with. Even when they both work outside the home. I can only assume that the old stories about how men and women should behave at home keep pulling at their ankles, dragging them back into roles that are no longer a comfortable fit.

THE DIFFICULTY OF BREAKING FREE FROM THE OLD STORIES

Once upon a time, the roles of men and women at home were clearly defined, like an old play performed over and over with different actors. The tone of this little performance could range from perfectly lovely (reasonably equal) to extremely grim (terribly exploitative), and everything in between.

The man had one important job: to provide money for the support and protection of the family. Then, his wife, sister, mother, or grown daughter took that money, stretched it, preserved it, and created a livable home. The man was the recipient of home care, not the provider of it, unless the tasks were suitably masculine seeming, such as lawn care, structural repairs, and car maintenance.

All other chores—the near-constant daily tasks of cooking and cleaning—were in the realm of women (with, of course, some variation by culture, class, and situation).

In the era of gender equity—or at least what I hope is valiantly attempting to have gender equity—the role of man living with woman is murky.

Our man shows up to perform his role of provider and protector, only to find his wife providing and protecting quite well on her own. She can earn money, she can mow the lawn, and she can do home maintenance. Even more, she still does twice as much housework as him, and she is *very tired.*

Our man, hoping to be useful and helpful, scrambles for some task to perform.

"How can I help?" he asks, not sure where to enter her tour de force of household tasks.

"Here, try out my role!" she says, flinging him her props (broom, frying pan, notebook for grocery list, crying infant).

"Uh, where's the script?" he asks, panicked.

"There's no script," she says, affronted and confused. "You just take care of the home. You just do it! Like I always have."

But our man is unprepared to *just do it.* He doesn't know how. He has so little experience. In the journey to become a man, he faced incredible pressure to avoid anything with even a whiff of femininity. He didn't babysit, he wasn't fastidious about grooming, and he certainly didn't clean with Mommy. And as a result, he has few useful domestic skills.

What is he to do? Insist she give his role back? Offer to take on her role but perform it so badly that it pains her to watch, so she *has* to take it back?

He can try, but he'd better be ready to recast the role of "wife" pretty soon. Because a man who refuses to become a competent partner at home, out of some misguided desire to preserve his masculinity, is a man that is hard to live with. Because by trying to stay a man (in the traditional sense), avoiding the feminine pull of housework, he is transformed into a child, unable to be of use in his own home.

This puts straight men in an uncomfortable position. They can either admit near-total incompetence in their own homes—never a pleasing prospect for anybody with even a tiny bit of pride—or they can foist an outsize amount of responsibility onto their already exhausted working wife.

Or, as a third option, they can assume a semidisdainful, self-protective attitude of teasing toward their wife's relentless interest in sustaining the livable state of the home they share. (And wait for the relationship to implode.)

A modern man without home care skills is a man adrift. His role in the relationship is shaky. But a man who is an enthusiastic participant in life, who can go to work, come home, sort the mail, bake a birthday cake, and fold laundry without being asked? He will always be wanted and needed. And luckily, it is never ever too late to learn.

No matter who you are or how you identify, if you struggle with home care, it's worth looking at your internalized beliefs about home care and gender. These beliefs tend to start in childhood and stick with you, subtly guiding your beliefs and behavior throughout adulthood. In the next chapter, we'll take a look at families of origin and how they affect our relationships with home care.

Tidying Tidbit

Traditional gender roles hurt modern working couples when it comes to dividing home care fairly.

Reflection Exercise

1. When did you first notice that there were different expectations for boys and girls when it came to home care?
2. Growing up, what did you learn were suitable chores for men? For women? Were there any gender-neutral chores in your house, which anyone could do?
3. What training did you get on home care as a kid?
4. Did you notice that your different-gender siblings or peers got different training?
5. If you had shown a great interest in cleaning as a kid, how would your friends or family have reacted?
6. What beliefs about gender and chores do you want to let go of?

5 Family Baggage

Our Imperfect Domestic Role Models

If you live with an apathetic boyfriend who refuses to clean a toilet, or an exacting girlfriend who delivers a performance review each time you fold laundry, it won't be long before you go looking for someone to blame. You will quickly zero in on the prime suspect: *their family.*

Family life is the first teacher of domestic management. In a perfect world, all parents are competent homemakers from Perfect Families. Perfect Families teach you everything you need to know about organization, such as how to keep your backpack tidy, your room clean, and your butt washed. You graduate to adulthood, a competent grown-up, a joy to cohabitate with.

THE CORE ADULTHOOD COMPETENCIES PERFECT FAMILIES TEACH AT HOME

Food Management

- Meal planning and grocery shopping within a budget
- Cooking basic meals
- Taking care of the kitchen environment

Trash Management
- Taking out trash/recycling on time
- Knowing what to throw away

Laundry Management
- Changing bedsheets
- Cleaning clothes regularly
- Organizing clothes into a closet or dresser

Cyclical Cleaning
- The ability to monitor the need for deep cleaning of bathroom, floors, etc.
- Knowledge of cleaning products and techniques

Basic Organization Systems
- How to organize belongings so they can be easily found
- Tackling administrative tasks

Self-Management
- Regular bathing and dental care
- Medical appointments and health maintenance
- Keeping a sleep/wake routine

Relational Management
- If you're reading this list like "Fabulous! I can do all that!" remember that you also need to be able to do these skills without terrorizing the people around you.

Unfortunately, very few of us grow up in Perfect Families with perfect home training. (And if you did, why did you pick up this book?!) Everyone else was raised by well-meaning (but unfortunately human) adults. And they taught us imperfectly.

Family life happens in the context of home. Home can't exist without domestic work. Meaning that the experience of family is intertwined with the experience of chores. Our relationships with our parents can't be separated from the practical care (or lack thereof) they provided.

ORIGIN STORIES

How You Got So Weird About Cleaning

No family is safe from cleaning quirks. Even I, a person with a reasonably happy childhood, managed to grow up to be very weird about cleaning. I blame country life.

I grew up in rural Texas, the youngest of five children. We lived outside Houston in the vast, steaming Piney Woods. It was an idyllic setting for family life, except that the woods kept trying to reclaim our home.

Our house was situated uphill from a sandy creek. Hurricanes frequently swelled the creek far beyond its banks, transforming our home from creekside to lakefront. When the waters receded, our yard was a new landscape—littered with sandbars, golf balls from an upriver course, and snakes both poisonous and benign.

Enormous bugs in the house (everything's bigger in Texas!) were a fact of life. Tiny green lizards occasionally found their way inside as well. At one point we had at least ten feral cats living on our back porch. They weren't pets. They just slunk out of the woods and draped themselves over our rocking chairs, permanent fixtures. To show their appreciation, they left shocking little hunting trophies on our welcome mat.

In such a *rustic* environment, only a persistent attention to cleanliness kept us from total disorder. In my childhood memories of my dad at home, he's constantly addressing cleanliness at the ground level. Either outside, mowing acres of wilderness into submission, or inside, sweeping the persistently sandy floor.

Then, the grass grew. The sand crept back into the house, smuggled on our bare feet. And my dad had to start all over again. Sorry, Dad.

My parents managed, rather deftly, to foster a friendly, cooperative attitude about chores. My brothers and I all helped with home care and yard work, without too much trouble. This environment of cooperation was enforced by a clever form of social control that my mom and dad called "Poor Form."

Picture this: Christmas dinner at my aunt's house. I finish my slice of pie, push back my plate, and stand up from the table, satisfied. As I walk toward the couch, my mother catches my wrist and whispers urgently in my ear.

"Poor Form." With a chill running down my spine, I pick up my dirty plate and take it to the sink, where my aunt is washing dishes. I set my plate next to the sink and point myself toward the fireplace, where I run into my father.

"P.F.," he says under his breath, in code, to maintain state secrecy. I turn around and wash the saucer myself, almost as if possessed by a very polite demon.

Poor Form ruled our house. Poor Form was akin to "good manners," but it went beyond being polite. Poor Form encompassed your duty to your loved ones and society in general.

Leaving your shoes where people can trip over them? Poor Form.

Grumbling when your mom asks you to help fold laundry? Poor Form.

Hiding in the bathroom, pretending to poop so you don't have to help your brothers with the dinner dishes? Poor Form!

Besides, my brothers were wise to my tricks (since they'd invented them) and would pound on the bathroom door until I came out. I still had to help with dishes. There was no escape.

The honor code of Poor Form was self-enforcing among my siblings, requiring almost no criticism, cajoling, or rewards from my parents. When it came to helping with chores, we simply did it. It would have been unthinkable not to do it. No one wanted to be the bad sibling (the one with Poor Form).

And that, I tell my invisible therapist now, is why I can't go to sleep with dirty dishes in the sink!

I'm thankful for all the skills my parents taught me. But that is not to say I have turned out totally normal on the home front. Neither have my brothers. I love cooking for them, because they're just like me. The second they finish eating, they jump up and start scrubbing pots and pans. They hover, waiting to snatch plates away from people after their last bite.

The dishes are done before dinner is actually done. It's unsettling, but it is responsible! Good form!

Now, as an adult, it's my job to help people figure out how to tackle their unmanageable homes, routines, and practical lives. It is my job to find their family baggage, expose it to the light, and put it in order. I was surprised to find that this work didn't feel so different from my life as a social worker.

True, rather than cleaning metaphorical skeletons out of closets, I now clean out literal closets. But the people who own those closets struggle with their own vulnerabilities, clinical diagnoses, and emotional baggage around housekeeping inherited from imperfect families.

In this chapter, we'll take a look at a few different sorts of families, how they dealt with home care, and the adults they produced as a result. I hope you can see yourself, or your bewildering loved ones, in some of these stories.

Tidying Tidbit

Very few of us survive childhood without inheriting emotional baggage around homemaking—domestic quirks that lie in wait to wreak havoc on our adult relationships.

LIVING IN PRIVILEGE

Zoe's Origin Story

A client of mine, Zoe, grew up in a home with a live-in housekeeper. The housekeeper, a consummate professional, handled all the cooking, cleaning, organization, and shopping for the family. So, when Zoe moved into her first apartment, sans housekeeper, she was totally lost.

She had a PhD but couldn't boil an egg. She could code a website but had no idea how to remedy the growing colony of mold in her bathroom. She worried: Why all the mess? Was it her? Did the mold spawn from her gross, incompetent body?

Zoe enlisted me to help her learn to clean a home. Room by room, she learned about necessary cleaning tasks and corresponding cleaning products. She came to each session prepared with a list of questions.

How do I keep my food from sticking to the pot? (Use oil.)

What is this weird ring around my toilet? (Hard water deposits; use a pumice stone.)

What do I do with my pile of clothes? (Purchase a dresser, put them inside.)

With time and practice, Zoe gained a new perspective on housework. In her childhood, cooking and cleaning were regarded as menial work, the realm of people with little education or skill. But in creating her own home, Zoe saw how much skill housework really required.

Her well-funded childhood had given her plenty of opportunities, but it couldn't purchase competency at home. Competency can only come with patience and practice. With time, Zoe developed into an enthusiastic homemaker, attacking home care with the same dedication and curiosity that drove her career.

Tips for Those Who Can Relate

1. Reconsider your belief that cleaning is an unskilled profession. Once you give it a try, you might find that it requires a lot more time, effort, and expertise than you once thought.
2. Don't be embarrassed by what you don't know. Everyone has to learn at some point! Find a friend or professional willing to teach you the basics of cooking and cleaning.
3. Cleaning is hard work. If you become able to hire cleaning help, make sure to compensate your cleaners fairly.

GOOD (BUT ANXIOUS) PARENTS

| Alex's Origin Story |

Alex had a wonderful childhood. He described his mom as "amazing, but a little high-strung about cleaning." Which was a compassionate understatement.

Alex's mom liked things done a certain way. She tried to teach her son to fold clothes, but Alex was *so bad at it*. It was so much faster to just handle the housework herself, with Alex's big sister as a much more competent helper.

Alex's mom had her own baggage. She grew up in a quiet, cold home, feeling a little neglected. Doting on her only son made her feel like she could give him the wonderful childhood she never had. It was hard work, but it was so rewarding!

And besides, Alex's mom reasoned, isn't it a fact of life that teenage boys are just gross? It didn't occur to her that grossness is a pattern of behavior, not a state of being, and that she could teach him not to be gross. She figured, Alex had his whole life to learn how to do laundry! Why not let him enjoy being responsibility-free a bit longer?

And Alex did enjoy being responsibility-free. In fact, he hardly noticed the work it took to care for a home. It just seemed to happen. Alex grew into a delightful and charming man, the kind of person people loved taking care of. Until they eventually realized that he wouldn't—*couldn't*—reciprocate.

The unfortunate side effect of Alex's loving childhood is that he never learned how to care for himself, much less other people. This skill deficit caused quite a lot of friction with his partners in adulthood. Alex was a happy, healthy adult man with the home care skills of an eight-year-old child.

Seeing how much stress he added to his wife's life and not wanting to set a bad example for his own children, Alex enlisted me to learn the basics of home care and caregiving at the ripe age of forty, which I admired. It's never ever too late to learn. Over time, he learned what his own mother always knew: just how rewarding it is to care for your family by caring for your home.

Tips for Those Who Can Relate

1. Resist the impulse to blame others (your parent for not teaching you well, your partner for their higher standards) and simply accept the situation as it is.
2. Don't be embarrassed by what you don't know. Do recognize the impact your lack of skill has on those around you. As a child, incompetence wasn't your fault. As an adult, it is your responsibility.
3. Admitting what you don't know can make you feel painfully vulnerable, but most people who cook and clean well are enthusiastic teachers. Enlist one as your mentor. Imagine how great your future competence will feel.

PUNISHING HOMES

| Martha & the Admiral |

By the time I met Martha, she was in her seventies. Martha's father was a naval officer. Every Saturday when she was a girl, he played a military tune and performed "inspection" on his children's rooms, to make sure they met expectations. This was the admiral's idea of fun.

The admiral knew he was strict. He was strict because he loved his children, and he wanted them to succeed. His father had never shown him such care and attention: When the young admiral made a mistake, he just got smacked upside the head.

The admiral was determined never to lay a hand on his own children. So, when Martha misbehaved, he assigned her chores instead. It seemed so much kinder than the physical abuse of his childhood. Plus, it was good for Martha to learn the value of discipline and hard work!

Unfortunately, this had the effect of making Martha feel that all cleaning was a punishment. When she grew up and got married, she woke up early each day and dusted the house from top to bottom as if her father might come in and perform inspection again. Grim-faced, she scrubbed, polished, decluttered, always with the vague sense that she was in trouble.

She never allowed herself to wonder, "Do I like cleaning? Does this even matter to me? Do I even want to do this?"

Turns out, she really didn't. Over the years, she allowed herself, bit by bit, to stop cleaning so much. She learned to see cleaning as something she *wanted* to do, occasionally, rather than a penance assigned to her from the universe. She gave herself permission to hire a cleaner to come once a month. She performed risky experiments with letting standards slide.

"Now," she told me conspiratorially, "I never dust unless someone is coming over. God forbid someone sees a speck of dust! The admiral would roll over in his grave."

Tips for Those Who Can Relate

1. Acknowledge that your parent may have been acting with good intentions; even if their parenting philosophy didn't get good results.
2. Ask yourself this question repeatedly: What's the worst that would happen if someone saw my house messy, and can I survive that worst-case scenario?
3. Try to find the joy in home care again. What tasks bring you pleasure and satisfaction? What tasks do you actually hate? Could those hated tasks be delayed or outsourced?

RIGID STANDARDS

| Delia's Origin Story |

Delia's family was working-class. Like me, she grew up in a small town in the South. After helping her clean out her wardrobe following a big weight change, I suggested Delia go thrift shopping to replenish her closet. She shook her head frantically. *No, no, no.*

"Why not?" I asked. "It's a great way to find deals!"

"That's fine for you," she said. "But you're you!" She flapped a hand toward my face to encompass my obvious white middle class–ness. "You don't have to worry about what you wear because people aren't going to assume you're poor if your stuff is thrifted."

And to her point, that thought had never once occurred to me.

Delia's parents worked hard to ensure she had everything she needed to be successful. In their words, they couldn't control being broke, but they could control *looking* broke. And so, they took care of their modest home, and personal cleanliness, with zeal. The kids never left the house with a hair out of place. They were the most polished, polite children in the neighborhood.

Delia and her siblings were expected to pitch in with housework. Everyone worked together. There were no excuses. *See a need, fill a need* was the family motto.

Saturday mornings, Delia woke up to the sound of music blasting and the vacuum roaring. There was no chance of relaxing before the house was clean, so Delia learned to clean quickly, efficiently, and spectacularly.

As an adult, in her own immaculate home, Delia struggled to relax. It always seemed that there was something more to do. She couldn't stand watching others lounging around, being lazy, because she herself had never been allowed to be lazy. Laziness was the crack in the door that could have let judgment into her home.

She was snappy with her partner and kids, neurotic about cleaning. This made Delia sad because she didn't work so hard to be stressed-out. She worked hard so she could be happy.

And so, Delia and I worked together to come up with a (for her) relaxed home care schedule, one that all her family members could agree to. Delia worked slowly and steadily to divorce her personal respectability from the state of her house, to see it as a refuge, a safe and unobserved place where she didn't have to worry about looking respectable. In other words, a home.

Tips for Those Who Can Relate

1. Search for understanding (and if possible, compassion) for why your family felt such immense pressure to appear clean and respectable. Chances are, there was a good reason.
2. Try to have a frank, nonjudgmental conversation with your household about what you need to feel okay at home. Attempt to find a standard that works for everyone. This might involve you feeling a bit of anxiety.
3. Experiment with leaving some cleaning tasks undone. How did it feel? Did anything bad happen? Use that information to inform your standards.

NEGLECTED HOMES

Candace & Patrick's Origin Story

"My parents were hoarders. Well, not actual hoarders," Candace clarified. "But there was shit everywhere."

Candace and her brother, Patrick, grew up in chaos. There was so much paper and laundry on the couch, it no longer functioned as a couch. The kitchen was barely usable—every inch of the counter was crammed with food containers. Everything smelled powerfully of cigarette smoke and cats.

When we think of neglectful homes, we think of cold, indifferent parents. But Candace and Patrick's mom wasn't indifferent, she was just overwhelmed. She wasn't a neglectful parent, she was just a neglectful housekeeper. Depleted by her work and her poor health, she had just enough energy left to care for her kids, and nothing left for her house.

Candace and Patrick diverged in their responses to a chaotic environment. Candace developed an adaptive, incredibly high tolerance for mess. She could let dishes sit in the sink for weeks without feeling a bit of internal pressure to wash them. She could live with smells that others felt an immediate need to escape.

Patrick couldn't ignore the mess. He was determined to escape it. Even though he loved his family, he couldn't wait for the day he could live on his own. And when he did, his apartment was pristine, almost empty. Any accumulation of stuff that wasn't absolutely necessary gave him flashbacks to his crowded childhood home. He was preoccupied with the fear that he would smell bad, and bathed compulsively.

Candace's and Patrick's homes could not have looked more different. But on the inside, they both felt the same fear—the fear that their mess would bury them. Candace was terrified of admitting that her mess wasn't a personal choice but a problem. Because a problem required her effort, and she was sure her efforts would fail. Patrick was also sure that his efforts would fail, which is why he never gave messes a single chance to form.

They both benefited from building distress tolerance. Candace practiced taking ownership of her mess, to assert autonomy over her home. She chose an area of countertop or table, about four square feet, and said, "I made this mess, and I can fix it." Then, she cleaned it up without the pressure to clean up the whole house.

Patrick practiced distress tolerance by letting his messes accumulate for a day or two, to see that they wouldn't bury him in a tsunami of uncleanliness. He started letting nonessential but fun items into the home, such as blankets and art. In a brave moment, he even allowed in a knickknack. And so his house turned into a home rather than an enemy lying in wait.

Tips for Those Who Can Relate

1. Accept that your parent struggled to keep up with life, whether or not there was a good reason, such as overwork, mental illness, or lack of support.
2. Try to create one corner of your home that feels maximally comfortable and safe. Create more corners. Fill your house with safe zones to feel a healthy sense of control over your environment.
3. If needed, therapy can help you cope with overwhelming feelings of sadness, anxiety, or anger about the state of your home.

YOUR ORIGIN STORY

| Building Self-Awareness |

In your search to understand your homemaking needs, you must understand your homemaking roots. Reflect on the following questions. If you discover a quirk, don't put pressure on yourself to fix anything (yet). Just sit with the understanding that you are the way you are for a reason.

Family Baggage Reflection Exercise

CIRCLE THE VALUES THAT WERE MOST IMPORTANT TO YOUR FAMILY.

Aesthetics Efficiency Familiarity Freedom

Health Hospitality Relationships Responsibility

CIRCLE THE CLEANING STYLE THAT BEST DESCRIBES YOUR PARENTS.

Tidy & Sanitized Tidy & Natural

Cluttered & Sanitized Cluttered & Natural

HOW DOES THAT COMPARE TO YOUR OWN VALUES/STYLE?

____

____

WHAT ARE YOUR MEMORIES OF CLEANING AND ORGANIZING DURING YOUR CHILDHOOD?

____

____

DO YOU REMEMBER BEING TAUGHT HOW TO DO CHORES? IF SO, BY WHOM?

____

____

IF YOU (OR YOUR SIBLINGS) FAILED TO DO YOUR CHORES, WHAT WERE THE CONSEQUENCES?

WHAT WOULD HAVE BEEN THE REAL-WORLD CONSEQUENCES FOR YOUR FAMILY IF THEY LOOKED DISORGANIZED OR DIRTY IN FRONT OF OTHERS?

WHAT CLEANING HABITS DID YOUR FAMILY FIND OVER-THE-TOP? WHAT DID THEY FIND DISGUSTING?

WHAT ANNOYED YOU MOST ABOUT THE WAY YOUR FAMILY KEPT HOUSE?

WHAT HOME CARE SKILL DO YOU THINK YOUR CAREGIVER WAS BEST AT?

6 The Abyss Widens

Digging Deep on Domestic Despair

An uneasy relationship with home care rarely exists independent of any other problems. It is, more often, just one facet of your uneasy relationship with life.

Your home is your designated refuge from the chaos of life. It should be a source of joy and comfort—the place where you feel safer than anywhere else in the world. But too often, home can be a source of frustrating obligation, where instead of feeling gently held, you feel squeezed.

Home care presents you with some of the oldest struggles known to humanity: difficulty facing suffering, resistance to accepting the indignities that life requires, and running away from boredom and responsibility as if you're being pursued. This chapter is a look into the deeper currents running beneath your difficult relationship with home care.

1. DOMESTIC WORK IS REWARDING

The path to becoming a therapist cost me years, tears, and nauseating amounts of money. But it was worth it to me because I wanted to help people. Being fully committed to the entire career aesthetic, I also wanted to wear turtlenecks and lounge all day in an overstuffed armchair.

"What do you do for work?" people asked me.

"I'm a therapist," I told them.

"Oh!" they would say. "That's such important work." And I *loved* that shit.

So, when five years after reaching licensure, my illness conspired to eject me from my chosen career, I felt adrift. My exhaustion was beyond medical description—less like chronic fatigue and more like my body was smothered by a hot, damp, weighted blanket.

One can't run a good therapy session with a brain that feels overstuffed with scratchy wool. So, it was obvious that I needed a break.

But inconveniently, I also needed income. You know, to live.

With the same financial acumen that led me to select social work as my profession, I chose cleaning as my backup profession because it was the only activity I could think of that I liked as much as therapy. (Other than painting, poetry, or not working at all, which were even more financially unpromising.)

"Maybe I should have been an accountant instead," I joked to my dad after I explained the necessity of leaving my job to rehabilitate my energy level. "Not as rewarding, but you can't beat the money."

"There's no doubt about that," he deadpanned, completely correct.

But when I started my little home care business, I was delighted by how rewarding I found domestic work. Therapists are in the business of making people feel better, but that work can take weeks, sometimes months, and occasionally *years*. It was gratifying, as a cleaner, to make people feel better—less stressed, more organized—almost immediately.

And yet.

"What do you do for work?" people asked me.

I'm a therapist, I almost said each time, which was technically true but practically false. I was licensed but nonpracticing. And I was weirdly hesitant to talk about my new business because, even though I was having the most fun of my adult life, there was still a part of me that saw domestic work as a demotion.

"I'm—an organizer."

"Like, a political organizer?" they asked.

"No," I said. "Homes. Cleaning. Kitchens. Closets."

"Ah! Great." And they did not say: *That's important work.*

As a therapist, I often questioned the ethics and efficacy of my career. The crimes of the mental health treatment complex are well documented. There were moments where our entire system of diagnosis and treatment felt as nonsensical as balancing black bile and yellow bile. But on reflection, is there any occupation more important, more essential, than domestic work?

I have never once questioned the necessity of domestic care: scrambling eggs for my husband's lunch, folding my mother's laundry, loading the dishwasher for my grandfather while I brewed him a fresh pot of coffee.

The utility, and goodness, of these tasks is universally apparent. Because there is no functional life without domestic work. You need food to eat, clothes to wear, a place to sleep that isn't being slowly overtaken by rubbish.

To neglect these tasks is not an option. When you neglect these tasks, people start trying to intervene, move in with you, or put you in the hospital. So, why do we look at domestic work, one of our most necessary and caring occupations, whether it is done privately or professionally, with so little respect?

Why don't we say, "*That's important work*" too?

Tidying Tidbit

Chores are the necessary, important work of living. Creating spaces where people feel calm, comfortable, and safe can be incredibly rewarding.

II. DOMESTIC WORK IS SKILLED

Humans have done horrific things to get out of doing chores. From serfdom to slavery to human trafficking, the devaluation and exploitation of domestic workers is as old as humanity itself. Masters foisted the care of their estates onto servants. Men foisted it onto women. Women foisted it onto women of lesser status who, out of necessity, foisted it onto children.

We have consistently outsourced domestic work, which none of us can live comfortably without, to the most vulnerable members of our society. Historically, these tasks have traditionally fallen to those with less power: women, immigrants, people in poverty. At best, the work has been modestly paid. At worst, it has been forced.

Our cruel attitude about domestic work persists today. In the United States, professional domestic workers—cleaners and caregivers—remain largely unprotected by federal labor laws. Minimum wage, sick leave, workplace safety: These basic protections do not apply.

We tend to see cleaning as the bottom rung of the professional ladder. Menial labor, we call it, meaning boring, repetitive, and low-status work that anyone could do.

But is that really true—that anyone can clean and tidy? A team of professional cleaners runs with the vigor and efficiency of a NASCAR pit crew. The idea that housekeeping requires no skill is preposterous. Just ask imaginary frat boys, Chet and Chad, sharing their first apartment, unsure about which part of the toilet one cleans with the brush (*inside, outside, or both?!*).

Tidying Tidbit

Society has a long (and deplorable) history of devaluing domestic workers, or so-called menial laborers. But the idea that domestic work requires little skill is a myth—one we tell to get away with underpaying for it.

We are absolutely dependent on the people who cook and clean for us, and yet manage to get away with treating them abominably. When we do domestic labor for our own home, we don't even see it as "real work," because it doesn't make money. It occupies an odd liminal space—not a job, not a hobby, but a duty. One that goes underappreciated and undervalued, from the economic sphere to our own little homes.

III. DOMESTIC WORK IS LOVING

When I was a teenager, I had dance rehearsal every morning at sunrise. No matter how early I set my alarm, my mom was *always* up and dressed before me.

She sent me off to practice every morning with a thermos of hot chocolate, two pieces of cinnamon toast, and a packed lunch with chilled hibiscus tea. Without fail. In response to this really luxurious treatment, I was invariably sullen. When I think of how little appreciation I showed her at the time, I want to invent time travel, go back to the 2000s, and strangle my spoiled-rotten teenage self.

When people care for us well, as my mother did for me, their work becomes invisible. I didn't see how much effort my mom put into caring for me, because she was so good at it. I just thought that was what she was like. I just thought that's what *moms* were like.

I didn't see all the years she cultivated her patience and skills, such as the ability to get a semicomatose teenager dressed in a fresh leotard, fed and provisioned, and out the door before sunrise. It wasn't until I was an adult that I realized how deft, how precious, those domestic skills really were. I didn't realize how much of my status as an "organized person" was really the culmination of her support, and of all the women who supported her.

I was birthed into adulthood, well fed and full of domestic competence, by the invisible work of women. Their work was not menial. It was not unskilled. It was not boring or repetitive or undignified. It was clever, creative, and forcefully competent. It was Important Work.

Tidying Tidbit

It takes a lot of skill to care for a home and the people within it. Counterintuitively, the better you are at domestic work, the more invisible your work becomes.

IV. DOMESTIC WORK IS NECESSARY

It took me a long time to figure out the value of my own domestic work as an adult. Throughout my twenties, I really struggled. Not with how difficult adulthood was, but how *tedious* it was.

Adulthood presented me not with freedom or novelty or even ease, but with a showcase of Stunningly Boring but Practically Essential Activities. Cleaning large, forgotten bits of food from the dark underbelly of my stove. Getting my tires rotated while I drank acrid coffee in the mechanic's waiting room, where the TV played a golf tournament so loudly it was basically compulsory to watch it. And horror of all horrors, buying specialty equipment for plunging a clogged toilet, then finding industrial-grade cleaners to deal with the grisly aftermath.

The further I got into my twenties, the more I struggled against the reality that *this is it*. Everything about my domestic life—the endless sweeping, the nonstop laundry, the dispiriting act of getting rid of clothes I was too fat for dropped me deeper into the abyss, where everything was leached of meaning.

Even simple chores, such as checking the mail, could send me spinning out. The idea that I would have to keep opening my mail weekly, even the junky coupons, and that this hated task would never end unless I stopped receiving mail, a situation for which I would probably have to fake my death and assume an alias in some mountain hamlet, was unbearable.

At the root of my (honestly, a little dramatic) domestic despair, there was the unspoken, and kind of yucky, belief that I was just *a little bit* better than cleaning. When I had to spend my weekends lugging sweaty sheets to the laundromat and back, I felt that some sort of mistake had been made. Had I accidentally slipped into some shitty, alternate universe where a new vacuum cleaner was the pinnacle of my week?

The belief that we're destined for something *greater* than housework is a thorny one. Of course, people who have toiled, underpaid and underappreciated, in service rightly deserve a break, a chance to do something different. **But if we believe that we are destined for greater things than chores, do we not also believe that other people *aren't*?** That there are some people out there who are too silly, too undignified, for anything but cleaning? That there is a class of people only fit to make the beds and scrub the tubs?

If you're a lord of a fiefdom, that hierarchy probably makes sense to you. For modern progressive people, it's a line of thinking that goes sour pretty fast.

Imagine that this news comes with a warm hug. You are not too good for chores. You aren't too interesting or clever to spend your time tidying up. You weren't meant for something better, or you weren't *only* meant for something better.

Tidying Tidbit

The idea that you're too good (clever, interesting, creative) for cleaning implies that there are people out there who *aren't* too good for cleaning. Which is more than a little elitist.

Cleaning is a part of human life, like it or not. Like everyone's, your underwear needs laundering too. Your options are as follows:

- Clean.
- Pay someone to clean.
- Villainously trick someone into cleaning.

If you don't have the money to pay a cleaner fairly, or you're too good a person to exploit others (*please, please say you are*), you have only one viable path forward: finding a way to embrace home care.

V. DOMESTIC WORK IS INTERESTING

Once, I was driving with my grandpa through the Great Divide Basin of Wyoming, on the way to a camping site in the mountains. In my mind, it was indisputable that this was the absolute worst part of the drive.

The Great Divide Basin is a barren, sunken area of desert in the middle of the Rockies. Its claim to fame is its rainfall flows neither to the Atlantic nor to the Pacific, which as far as I can see is a nonissue, since it never seems to rain at all.

"I *hate* this part of the drive," I whined, accelerating to a hair above the speed limit, trying to make the drive pass faster. Longingly, I pictured the next truck stop, roughly 200 miles ahead.

"You hate *this* part of the drive?" my ninety-year-old grandpa repeated back, scrunching his overgrown old-man eyebrows. He seemed truly bewildered.

My grandpa was a geologist, a man of persistent curiosities. To me, the desert was something to be endured. To him, it was a fascinating anomaly, full of geological history. And there was plenty in the barren landscape to engage his interest.

"It's a desert where no desert belongs! A place where the water runs nowhere! Created by a geological uplift in the Late Cretaceous Age!"

Not being a geologist myself, I struggled to match his enthusiasm.

"Well . . . it's pretty boring. Visually, I mean." I gestured vaguely to the dust, which is about all there is to gesture at. More than anything, the landscape looked like a place that you shouldn't go riding a horse into unless you want that horse to die of dehydration, and you with it.

My grandpa was a kindly man, but this was more than he could take.

"If you think this is boring," he said as disapprovingly as I had ever heard him, "then you need to learn to be interested in different things."

Damn, Charlie, I thought, decelerating back to the speed limit.

When I find myself bored by my housework, I think of his firm but ultimately helpful lecture. *I need to learn to be interested in different things.*

Each task is an opportunity to humble myself before the world. It is a chance to look beyond the barren surface of drudgery, to find a secret spring of interest.

If this is boring, I think, folding my laundry, which is made of textiles grown all over the world, assembled by industrial sewing machines that are marvels of modern engineering, laundered only by the grace of the laundry robots living in my house, folded in sacred geometry to fit my oddly shaped shelves, *then I need to learn to be interested in different things.*

If this is boring, I think, reading my junk mail, which exists only because ancient China invented paper, because Gutenberg invented a printing press, because forests grow, because chemists make ink, because my parents taught me to read with Hooked on Phonics tapes, *then I need to be interested in different things.*

If this is boring, I think, scrubbing a toilet—but no, don't get me started on the wonders of modern sanitation. I'll never stop.

You, modern person, have every technologically advanced marvel of cleaning convenience at your disposal. This is not only a privilege but a wonder. A dishwasher, a washing machine, a disinfectant spray? What a time to be alive.

Housework is only boring if you allow it to be, if you refuse to become interested. This is the core of mindfulness: that anything can be interesting, even transcendent, if you only pay attention.

Tidying Tidbit

If you find housework boring, try looking at it in a little more depth. There is plenty to be interested in (historical, technological, and relational) if you look deeply enough.

VI. DOMESTIC WORK IS CYCLICAL

Most days, I sweep the floor of my home. For a brief, shining moment, it's pristine. Then, my old long-haired dog ambles in from the yard, smuggling grass and mulch on his silky belly. He stretches out on the cool floor, totally at peace, and deposits a blast radius of hair and organic material around him. I scratch his ears. He hums with contentment.

Then, I fetch my broom from the closet and start the pointless work of sweeping again.

My clients are often pained by the circular nature of housework. They feel like Sisyphus rolling the boulder up the hill, except the boulder is a chaotic amalgam of laundry, unopened mail, and power cords too important-looking to throw away. And every time they reach that bright pinnacle—the clean and organized home—the boulder rolls back downhill, and they start their arduous work again.

It can leave a reasonable person wondering, Why bother? What's the point?

Why clean your house when it will just get dirty again?

Why shower when you'll just get sweaty again?

Why get a new shelf for storage when you'll only fill it with more junk?

Why have kids when they'll just mess up your house and get mad at you for asking them to clean up?

Seeing your hard work immediately undone is a spiritually depleting experience. It leaves you feeling that there is no point in cleaning because things will never stay clean. In this is our belief that if something is done right, it must be permanent.

This is a very hopeful, but unfortunately false, fantasy that your house *could* be clean and organized forever if you just did it the right way.

So, when entropy, that inevitable breakdown of order, strikes, it feels like an affront to your accomplishment. After all, if you have to do it more than once, it must mean either (a) you did it wrong or (b) the entire enterprise is doomed, so give up.

We resist investing in things that end up ruined. But not cleaning because things will eventually get dirty is kind of like not living because you'll eventually die. Everything gets ruined, us included. That doesn't mean that temporary things aren't worth tender care and attention.

If you want to have a home, you must clean a home. A home, at its very essence, is a place that humans maintain. When you clean a home, you separate it from the wild world of nature outside. You expel dirt, mold, insects, even weather. If you stop cleaning your home and just wait, nature will simply take it back.

There is no reality in which you could have a home with no maintenance. Your maintenance is what makes it a home. That process of homemaking is frustratingly cyclical. But it is also finite. Surrender to the cycle of homemaking while you have the privilege to do so.

Tidying Tidbit

Chores produce temporary results that are quickly undone. But temporary things can still be meaningful. It's not the results that matter. It's engaging with the cyclical nature of life.

VII. DOMESTIC WORK HAS SPIRITUAL VALUE

I once visited Magnolia Grove, the Buddhist monastery in the Mississippi Delta, founded by Thich Nhat Hanh. I was having a bad month, triggered by one too many bleak Saturdays, performing my weekend ritual of scrubbing away the extremely robust colony of pink slime from my bathtub's caulking. I just couldn't do it anymore.

I thought a meditation retreat would be just the thing to lift me out of my domestic abyss. Surely the monks and nuns at the monastery, living a life of spiritual enlightenment, had found a path to escape the very specific despair that's caused by living a perfectly ordinary life.

I drove through the riotously green forest and found the monastery. The small collection of buildings sits in a grassy clearing, like an island of exquisite calm. The wind rustled the trees, carrying the smell of incense and cooking over the walkways. The place was perfectly clean and tidy in a way that made me feel instantly peaceful. It hummed with the sounds of chanting, birdsong, and bells.

And also, very familiar domestic clatter.

I found monastics at their serious spiritual work. They were doing exactly what I had come to escape: cooking and cleaning. They bustled around, chopping vegetables, scrubbing toilets, and mopping the floors—just like me. But unlike me, they were treating the tasks not only with joy but with serious spiritual attention, with specific meditations for each cleaning task.

They already knew what it took me so long to figure out: Menial work is not devoid of meaning. It doesn't separate you from your higher purpose. It is an opportunity to connect with your environment. It is a chance to be with yourself, to put a mark on the world, however impermanent.

We are so sure that there is some clever hack we can use to escape boredom or drudgery. But drudgery isn't something you escape to become fulfilled. It isn't a distraction from your one wild and precious life. It is life.

When you clean, you ask nature to make space for you. When you organize, you are in conversation with the chaotic nature of the universe. When you care for others, you honor those who have cared for you.

Finding meaning in home care—whatever that is for you—is the surest way out of the abyss. Each meaning is a ladder rung, a firm place to put your feet as you raise yourself, slowly, gently, toward domestic enlightenment, which is not escaping drudgery but embracing it with joy.

EIGHT LADDER RUNGS

The Hidden Meanings of Chores

1. Chores connect you to generations of ancestors who also had to do boring chores (often, without the benefit of your modern conveniences).
2. Chores connect you with mentors and teachers. By doing chores in the same way an elder taught you, you keep their legacy alive, even after their death.
3. Chores allow you to make peace with entropy, chaos, life, and death. They are a kind of meditation on radical acceptance.
4. Chores give you an opportunity to gain skill and mastery, and it feels good to assert control over the world around you sometimes.
5. Chores are an opportunity to practice humility and self-sacrifice by not inconveniencing others, paying attention to others, and considering their needs.
6. Chores give you a chance to connect mindfully to the world around you.
7. Chores make your dwelling into a home. You pay to live there, so you might as well enjoy it. Your labor is what makes a place yours.
8. Chores are an opportunity to care for yourself because you deserve a peaceful environment.

PART II

Out of the Abyss

A Practical Guide to Putting Your Life in Order

7 Self-Care Before Home Care

How to Get Your Life Together

IT'S DARK IN THE ABYSS. AND CLUTTERED. AND—NO JUDGMENT—IT'S ALSO a little bit smelly. It's time to climb out. You don't deserve to live down there. Come, climb toward the light! Let's get your life together.

We're starting—not with your home—but with you. Before we get your home organized, we need to get you fed, rested, and functioning. I know that's counterintuitive, but hear me out.

HOW NOT TO GET YOUR LIFE TOGETHER

You've tried to get your life together before, haven't you? You've tried to crawl toward organization, only to go backsliding down the slope to chaos. Did your previous attempts go something like this?

1. Wake up.
2. Panic because your life is a writhing mass of disorder.
3. Resolve to change your ways starting . . . now!
4. Chug a caffeinated beverage and pray it will help you decide which project to tackle first.
5. Sit quietly and wait for motivation to arrive. Keep waiting.

6. Despair.
7. Scroll through inspirational content on how you *could* get your life together.
8. Get so focused on the inspirational content that you pass the day without committing one single act of organization.
9. Cue the simultaneous existential crisis and caffeine crash. Wait, did you remember to eat anything today?
10. Late-night panic meal.
11. Try to salvage the wreckage of the day by staying up late.
12. Eventually surrender to fatigue and go to bed. Toss and turn while fighting off the demon of self-hatred. Repeat.

If this feels familiar, worry not. You're in good company. It's very much a normal part of the process, and kind of the entire premise of this book. **Here's the biggest mistake people make when trying to get organized: They try to work from the outside in. They focus so much on what they have to *do*, that they forget about how they want to *feel*.**

I know this is swerving dangerously into touchy-feely-therapist territory, but just humor me for a moment. Forget cleaning plans. Forget organizational products. Put down the IKEA catalog.

Instead, turn your attention within. How do you feel when you think about getting your life together? Do you feel okay? Do you feel organized? Do you feel like a confident adult?

Or do you feel like a sullen preteen, dressed up in adults' clothes, exhausting yourself every day without anyone to take care of you?

GIVING YOURSELF A FIGHTING CHANCE

If you're sleep deprived, malnourished, and crusty because you haven't had a sip of water in three days, your brain *will not work* as well as it can.

If you try to organize in a haze of self-neglect, you'll ask your brain: *Hey brain, what's the best way to declutter my desk drawer?*

And your brain, after a long moment of radio silence, will be like: *Great question, but why are you trying to do this when you're so tired? Did you know that it's three p.m. and you forgot to eat both breakfast and lunch? Did you know that if you don't eat, you die? I'm worried but not about the desk drawer.*

Then, your tired brain will proceed to generate zero good ideas.

It's simple to build a life that looks organized on the outside. All it takes is a ton of time and money! But to be a person who *feels* organized, you have to get it together from the inside out.

There's no shame in going to bed late, eating at odd times, and keeping a scattered schedule. But living that way, you are always reacting to your body's needs when they're urgent rather than planning for their inevitable arrival. That sucks up all your brain's precious (and if you picked up this book, compromised) organizational resources.

That's why organization starts not with clutter but with what's going on in your brain, body, and belly.

Tidying Tidbit

You're going to be a lot better at organizing if you're fed and rested first. Nutrition and sleep enhance executive functioning. That's why we need to build a base of self-care before we take on home care.

EVERYBODY'S GOT A HUNGRY BRAIN

Fueling Your Brain with Food

If there's one thing I learned as an eating disorder therapist, it's that food has an almost magical ability to help you think more clearly.

Patients arrived at inpatient treatment with low executive functioning skills and by the time they left, they were like national merit scholars.

What changed? Weeks of intensive therapy and healing—but mostly, it was the three regular meals a day.

(I was okay at my job. But, honestly, the food did most of the work.)

Yet so many adults operate under the erroneous belief that they don't *really* need to eat, because they don't *look* malnourished. But if you combine calorie restriction with a vigorous activity like cleaning, you know what you get? Short-term cognitive impairment! And usually some emotional dysregulation thrown in, for dramatic tension. You might not die, but you won't be very creative or clever either.

Let me be direct with you. Just because you're carrying around some body fat doesn't mean you're exempted from the biological rules of life. **Everybody needs to eat. Your brain doesn't want to burn your fat for fuel. It wants a gosh darn turkey sandwich. And it's going to hold off getting organized until it gets one.**

EXECUTIVE DYSFUNCTION & FOOD

Hunger cues are your body's warning signs that you need to eat (e.g., "My stomach is growling, I feel vaguely lightheaded, and why can't I stop thinking about chicken potpie?").

It's easy to develop a scrambled relationship with food when your hunger cues are—medically speaking—all jacked up. These cues can act up for a variety of reasons—medication side effects, irregular schedules, health problems.

Mental illness, especially depression, is also well-known to interfere with hunger cues. And sensory problems can make hunger difficult to respond to because, despite hunger, all food sounds disgusting.

When your hunger cues are offline, it's easy to disregard food. So, instead of being able to greet your hunger at the door like an expected guest, it busts in through the windows like an enraged moose at odd hours, rampaging around the kitchen, making it *very difficult* to decide what to eat because of the general environment of panic and disaster. The moose can talk and it asks increasingly troubling questions, like little emotional bombs, invoking the frightening specters of appetite, body image, and money:

What could you eat?!

What could you eat that wouldn't make you fatter?

What could you eat that wouldn't make you poorer?

What could you eat that would improve your overall health and longevity and stave off the looming certainty of death?

There's so much riding on that snack! Every meal takes on an emergency-level intensity, draining the day's serenity and brainpower. This does not create a climate conducive to organizing.

Tidying Tidbit

A lack of caloric intake creates temporary deficits in your ability to think clearly, manage emotion, and make decisions. Colloquially, we call this "hangry."

Hangry people aren't very good organizers.

ORGANIZATIONAL TRICKS FOR EATING ENOUGH

Fortunately, my career has put me in a position to witness and help problem solve a myriad of logistical issues around food. Here are a few of my favorite hacks for getting nutrition.

MECHANICAL EATING

| Eating at Mealtimes Whether You're Hungry or Not |

"Eat when you're hungry" is sensible conventional advice. But if you struggle with appetite, you are sure to feel hungry only at times of great inconvenience. **Instead, try what dietitians call mechanical eating.**

Eat at set times of the day whether you feel hungry or not. Most dietitians agree that three meals per day is a good place to start. No pressure to cook a full, balanced, three-course meal (though bonus points if you do!). Oftentimes, the noble intention to eat the "right thing" is a barrier to eating anything at all. Just focus on getting calories in. Gradually, eating at regular times, even in the absence of hunger can, counterintuitively, help restore hunger-fullness cues.

KNOW YOUR MVP FOODS

| Which Foods Can You Eat with No Appetite? |

Keep a list of simple meals—your Most Valuable Players—that are easy to eat and prepare, even when you don't feel like cooking, even when you have no appetite. For example, I could eat a piece of warm buttered toast even on my deathbed. This is especially helpful for people with sensory or appetite issues. Rotate the list as items become unappetizing. Remember, your goal isn't to eat the most appetizing, nutritious meal possible. Save that for the days when you have a higher capacity for caring. Instead, just focus on getting calories in—especially carbs and protein.

Common MVP Foods

Noodles with jarred sauce
Scrambled eggs with toast
Instant rice with canned beans
Instant rice with frozen edamame
Frozen pizza with prepackaged salad

GET AHEAD OF HUNGER

| Decide What You Are Going to Eat Before You Feel Hungry |

Most scattered people know that the problem isn't eating; it's choosing what to eat. The hungrier you get, the less equipped you are to choose

what to eat. Get ahead of the problem by making a daily deadline for choosing meals. Set daily alarms, not for mealtimes, but for "decide on a meal" times. Ideally, the deadline happens before you get too hangry to make good decisions.

For example, by six o'clock every night, I have to decide what I'm making (or ordering) for dinner. Once six o'clock comes around, I *must* choose. Even if the only meal idea I have is too expensive, too time-consuming, or too bland, I must choose. Any idea is better than hemming and hawing for three hours only to end up eating an unsatisfying bowl of stale cereal.

FOOD STREAMLINING

| Put the Food Where You Will Eat It |

Instead of trying to get yourself to the food (often a doomed endeavor), put shelf-stable snacks and drinks where you will already be, such as your desk, car, or nightstand. You can use these as Thinking Snacks—little bits of food that stave off hunger while your brain works through what to cook or buy for the meal.

My bouts of catastrophic hunger tend to strike when I'm out and about, and because I have food allergies, it's not always simple to find a restaurant with accessible meals. Instead, I keep my car's glove compartment stocked with nuts, crackers, or jerky to stave off blood sugar crashes while I come up with a plan for my next meal.

SNACK MEAL

| Build a Meal from Nutritious Snacks |

The pressure to create a perfect meal—one that's maximally nutritious, tasty, thrifty, and environmentally responsible—is just another barrier when you don't have the capacity to cook to those specifications. **If you can't come up with a single idea of an appetizing meal, broaden your idea of what qualifies as a meal. Build a meal from snacks.**

I know, I know—snacks aren't "real" dinner. But you're an adult, and you get to decide what real dinner is. (*Really, you get to decide what every meal is. Who says you can't eat soup for breakfast?*) Fill a large fridge bin with your preferred snacks. Include a hook: one food you really love and can get excited about eating.

SNACK MEAL IDEAS

TRY TO INCLUDE ONE FOOD FROM EACH CATEGORY

Protein	Hummus, deli meat, nuts, peanut butter, jerky, cheese
Carb	Crackers, chips, pretzels, toast
Fiber	Apple slices, baby carrots, snap peas, mini peppers
Fun	Chocolate, cookies, or other preferred treats

RECHARGING YOUR COGNITIVE BATTERIES

| Fueling Your Brain with Sleep |

Organizationally speaking, a sleep-deprived brain is about as useful as a skull full of Jell-O. Fatigue obliterates focus. Deliberate sleep deprivation, I will remind you, is considered torture. You won't be organizing any cupboards with a tormented brain, babes.

Sleep deprivation is the great enemy in my life, and I have in fact been diagnosed with a rather rare and incurable sleep disorder. So, when my brother had his first baby, and he lived for months on barely any sleep, he called me, the reigning expert on sleep-related suffering, to complain.

"I'm so loopy," he told me. "I don't know how you function like this," he said.

"I don't!" I said. "That's why I don't have a real job anymore."

There are so many circumstances, medical and circumstantial, that interfere with sleep and sabotage internal organization. So many of those—family, illness, mood—are out of your control. And even with the best of intentions, lying in the dark mentally chanting "Go to sleep! Go to sleep, you fool!" has a perversely stimulating effect on the mind. Luckily, there are a few tried and true methods for summoning sleep.

SLEEP HYGIENE

Theoretically, all you need to do to sleep is lie down and close your eyes. If you can do that, you lucky soul, just skip this section and enjoy your life. Leave, I'm jealous.

For the rest of us, sleep doesn't come so easily. It must be summoned with a bedtime routine—not just for kids anymore! Experiment with a few sleep hygiene practices and calming activities.

SLEEP HYGIENE MENU

Choose one to three activities to wind down for bed.

Attempt a Schedule: Just as irregular eating scrambles your hunger/fullness cues, irregular sleeping scrambles your sleep/wake cues. Try setting a reasonable bedtime. No need to be aspirational about this. Be realistic about your impulse control, sleep needs, and past success with routine.

Put the Screens to Bed: Electronic screens are proven saboteurs of sleep, but few of us have the self-control not to pick up that bright screen and scroll. Don't rely on self-control.

- Put your phone to bed in another room or out of reach.
- Use a restriction app to close down all the fun apps for the night.
- Use an analog alarm clock.

Put the House to Bed: Knowing that you will wake up to a marginally more functional house is a favor for future you, and can send you to bed feeling calm and accomplished.

- Spend one to three minutes throwing away trash and putting items in their place.

- Wash a few dishes or start the dishwasher.
- Tend to pets and children.
- Close windows, turn off lights, and lock doors.

Ease the Transition to Bed: The walk from the couch to the bed sometimes feels so far! Trick your brain into thinking it's easier by smoothing the transition.

- Ease yourself into the dark with mood lighting. Turn off overhead lighting and light only necessary lamps.
- Take the mental stimulation of television with you. Listen to an audiobook on your way to bed.
- Take the couch with you. Put on a robe, slippers, or wearable blanket to ease the transition to bed.

Tend to Yourself: Spending a few minutes tending to your body in a loving way can be a great springboard to the calm of sleep.

- Take a warm shower (use a shower cap if you don't want to sleep with wet hair).
- Brush your teeth (use the kitchen sink, or a disposable toothbrush, if you struggle to transition to the bathroom).
- Wash your face. Using a headband, sweatbands, or even just face wipes can help reduce the splashiness of this task.
- Do skin care. Moisturizer isn't just for the bathroom! Keep a basket of products in your bedroom so you can wind down while you do your skin care.

Calming Stimulation: Time for bed, which means it's time to be alone with your own thoughts! If your thoughts are bad companions, have a few wholesome distractions at the ready.

- Watch a calming show or movie. I know we're battling the screens, but sometimes we have to make concessions.
- Read a book in bed.

- Listen to an audiobook on wireless headphones, so you don't have to pick up your phone.
- Keep a basket of puzzles or notebooks and pens next to the bed, to doodle or journal.

ENLISTING MORE SUPPORT

Good sleep and food habits aren't always completely within your control. If you try to manage your basic self-care and find yourself consistently failing, don't berate yourself. It's just a sign that you need more support. Enlist a helper on your organization team.

PROFESSIONAL	CAN HELP WITH
Registered dietitian	Meal planning and special dietary needs
Occupational therapist	Sensory issues and executive functioning challenges around food preparation and sleep hygiene
Mental health therapist	Anxiety and emotional issues interfering with eating and sleep
Medical doctor	Digestive problems and assessment for sleep disorders
Grocery/meal delivery	Decreasing the burden of food preparation by automating your grocery shopping

8 Managing Motivation & Overwhelm

Finding a Way to Get Started

IT WOULD BE SO CONVENIENT, WHEN YOU URGENTLY NEED TO GET YOUR LIFE together, to actually feel motivated to get your life together. Ideally, that motivation would exactly align with your free time. Then, you wouldn't need this book!

But, frustratingly, motivation isn't so obedient. It isn't like a loyal dog you can summon to your side at any moment, eager to be useful.

Motivation behaves more like my semiferal cat, Penny—unpredictable. Sometimes, she's sweetness itself. Other times, when I call her, she darts out a window and disappears.

Once, I spent hours running around my neighborhood in tears, calling for Penny. After dark, I found her sitting serenely under a shrub. Elated, I reached out my arms. She looked me dead in the eyes and ran away.

Two weeks later, after many Lost Cat posters, after many visits to the Humane Society to see whether she had been turned in, after I had given up in despair and mourned Penny's loss and probable death, I sat on my couch, feeling bereft.

Then, I heard the sound of meowing from the front porch.

I ran to the door, threw it open, and there she was—the return of the prodigal cat. Penny sauntered in, unfazed by my incredulous shock. She curled up on the couch as if nothing at all had happened and fell asleep purring like an engine.

Motivation is like that.

You can love it, but you can't trust it. You can't seize it on command. You can *try* to call it, but you can't predict the results. It's a welcome visitor but an unreliable ally. It's just a feeling like any other. And if you wait for it to come save you from the bottom of the abyss, you might be waiting for a very long time.

Tidying Tidbit

Don't wait around, hoping to feel motivated to change. You can't depend on motivation to come.

THE AVOIDANCE TRAP

A Sad Quirk of Human Nature

We all know the logical answer to resolving chaos: Clean it up! Sadly, it turns out, we are illogical creatures.

So, in the presence of an unmanageable mess with motivation lost somewhere in transit, you don't clean it up. You avoid it.

You avoid seeing, talking about, or doing anything at all to address the chaos. You slam the closet door, shove the junk drawer closed, and hide the important papers in another godforsaken bin.

You hope, with childlike faith, that someone, *anyone*, perhaps some future and completely changed version of you, will arrive to clean up the mess. And while you wait, the chaos grows.

As the chaos grows, so does your anxiety. As your anxiety grows,

so does your avoidance of it. Chaos, avoidance, and anxiety follow one another in an endless loop.

Meanwhile, your difficulty keeping your life in order—a problem suffered by so many throughout the vast span of time—feels like a shameful secret that you must hide at all costs. You draw inward, isolating yourself in your own personal abyss with your one companion—your loathed mess.

Eventually, some grave and time-sensitive issue (*Mom's visiting!*) forces you to act. The cleaning feels pressured and grim. Your brain forms a memory of housework as nauseating, stressful, and anxiety provoking. And your brain will remind you of that any time you are faced with cleaning in the future, making motivation even harder to find.

Tidying Tidbit

Avoiding a big mess (though understandable) only increases your shame and fear of cleaning it up.

ACTING WITHOUT MOTIVATION

Avoiding Avoidance

The paradoxical secret to finding motivation is this: Don't wait for motivation. Don't avoid the dreaded task. Avoid avoidance.

This is the most difficult part of resolving chaos: getting yourself to start cleaning when it feels really, really bad to start cleaning. But weirdly, the more you clean, the more you will want to clean.

The secret to getting started is finding a mini-task—the smallest first step you can take. A step so small that it barely feels like a step at all.

Create motivation to do the dishes by washing a single fork.

Create motivation to take out the trash by putting on your shoes.

Create motivation to sort your mail by simply putting your hands on the stack of unopened letters and waiting to feel brave, like some clerical self-guided exposure therapy.

Remember, motivation is like a feral cat. If you come right at it with grabby hands, poof, it's gone! It may be a long time before you see it again. But if you set out a little food, perhaps a water bowl, and a warm box full of blankets consistently over a few days, you might find motivation clawing at your door, waiting to be invited in.

Tidying Tidbit

Reverse psychology! If you clean when you don't feel motivated, you'll feel more motivated to clean in the future.

MOTIVATION TRICKS & TRAPS

Outsmarting Motivation Without Getting Outsmarted Back

Motivation, like all human emotions, is a delicate creature. It can be loved, even befriended. But it's also fickle and has the tendency to bite you if you try to outsmart it.

Here are three trusted tricks for building motivation. They work, but they're not without risk. Each comes with a corresponding pitfall, sure to send you tumbling back into the abyss. Tread carefully.

THE TRICK: CREATE NOVELTY IN BORING TASKS

Make a familiar task like cleaning more interesting with the addition of a new cleaning supply or gadget—one you'll be excited to use.

Beware the Trap: Your floor is dirty. You want to clean the floor, but your mop kind of sucks, so what's even the point? You suspect that, if you had the right tool for the job, you would *want* to mop. After all, what's the point of mopping if you can't mop in the most perfect, optimal way possible?

The prospect of novelty fills you with energy. You spend a frenzied evening obsessively researching mops. You are now a mop expert. You wait six weeks for your fancy mop to arrive from Scandinavia or wherever.

But here's the trap: By the time the mop arrives, the magic is gone. You leave the box unopened. The floor remains unmopped. Where's your optimization now, Buster? Lost! Should've just used your crappy mop six weeks ago.

Don't burn your precious resources obtaining supplies. Always account for the time and energy it takes to obtain, assemble, and learn to use new supplies. *And* to recycle the box. **If you can't create novelty fast, it's better to just half-ass the job with suboptimal supplies, just to get it done.**

THE TRICK: FOLLOW A CLEANING ROUTINE

Doing the same cleaning task on the same day each week, and tracking your results, can be really satisfying.

Beware the Trap: When overwhelmed, many of us turn to the internet for expert-endorsed cleaning routines. These routines are developed by professionals who *really love* cleaning. If you, a person barely holding it together, try to follow these sorts of routines, you might quickly end up feeling like a failure. As an alternative, it's easy to fall into the opposite trap: spending so long devising your personal cleaning routine that you run out of energy to actually clean.

But routines are only helpful *if* they *can be followed*. A routine that doesn't allow for bad days is a routine that is doomed to fail. Remember to only follow routines that you can feasibly do, and redo, over time.

THE TRICK: GET INSPIRED

Browse home organization inspiration online to get ideas for your own house and life.

Beware the Trap: You have a room absolutely filled to the brim with clutter. After browsing a few aspirational catalogs, you create a divine plan to get your life organized. The divine plan for new shelving, new furniture, and (an ideally) new you will cost thousands of dollars and require mechanical skills that you do not possess.

So, before even starting, you're stuck.

Be honest with yourself. Are you ready to pull the trigger on that inspired plan right now, or in the next three months? If the answer is no, your dream is too big for right now. Which means it isn't doing you a bit of good. **Keep your home inspiration helpful by keeping the ideas small and attainable.**

THE TRICK: WAIT FOR THE RIGHT MOMENT TO DO A PROJECT

Tackle organization and cleaning projects when you have plenty of time.

Beware the Trap: Having limitless time to complete a task can be almost as bad as having no time at all. We are creatures of urgency, and when there is no urgency, we are pretty much lazy. We need a compelling reason to start an unpleasant project. That gets us in trouble when procrastination creates terribly stressful periods of intense motivation right at the deadline.

Try using this sad quirk of human nature to your advantage. Create a *little* (not a lot of) pressure by engineering a timeline. Invite a visitor to stay with you next month, so you have to tidy the room they'll stay in. Come up with a totally fake deadline, then enlist a friend to hold you to it. **Find the just-right amount of pressure that makes you act without feeling overwhelmed.**

DEALING WITH TOTAL OVERWHELM

| You Can't Mess It Up |

I still feel overwhelmed by big messes. People bring me into their homes and draw me back to their most cluttered, panic-inducing corners. Those wall-to-wall, knee-deep, inner sanctums of disorder make even me, a great aficionado of messes, feel feeble.

But then I remember: I can't fail. Because in the words of my mother, directing a room full of children in a Vacation Bible School Craft Project: You can't mess it up.

All you have to do is try. You cannot mess it up.

Where should you start? Anywhere. It just depends on how brave you're feeling.

Choose the space in your home, or life, that is either:

1. **The most distressingly disorganized and impactful.**
2. **Or the least distressing, and therefore the easiest to start.**

It doesn't matter. You can't mess it up.

Make an exhaustive list of your procrastinated tasks, messy corners, and incomplete projects. Then, pick one. Don't worry about prioritizing. Just choose any. If you can't choose, just close your eyes and point at the list. Or flip a coin. You can't mess it up!

If you feel emotionally paralyzed when starting the task, remember to start *tiny*. Identify the tiniest first step of the project and start with that. Sometimes, that's as simple as putting your body in the location where the project would occur.

Sure, you're terrified to renew your car registration. But could you just open your laptop, find the website with the instructions, and call it a day? You can't mess that up.

Sure, you're scared to organize your overflowing closet. But could you put a hula hoop inside the closet, and just clean what's inside the hula hoop? Of course you could!

Remember: Sometimes, there's no magic recipe for fixing a bad situation. There's just putting one foot in front of the other. You can't mess it up.

9 Trash & Recycling

Kicking Out the Garbage

IN THE COURSE OF A LIFE, YOU ACCUMULATE WORK EXPERIENCE, AILMENTS, and ex-lovers. You also accumulate stuff: a personal asteroid belt of clothing, mismatched cutlery, and papers that seem too important to throw away. Each year, the gravitational force of your life sucks in more and more stuff.

After a few years, your stuff starts to constrict. You sit in your home feeling smothered by what you own. *Why?* you ask yourself feebly and also *How? How did I get so much stuff?* Your possessions begin to feel ridiculously nonessential and yet impossible to banish.

After all, where can you send it? You can't in good conscience send it to a landfill, those hells of overconsumption. As the seas rise and the forests burn, it genuinely feels that throwing out that one chipped mug you haven't used in three years may just tip the scales toward environmental destruction. No pressure.

In a burst of organizational zest, you buy a few storage bins and shove all your stuff into them. You stack the bins into a closet and close the door. You experience one shining moment of satisfied serenity.

Then, the earth continues to circle the sun. The accumulation continues.

The new stuff must be imprisoned in new bins. It's frustrating that your onetime effort at organizing didn't solve all tidying problems forever.

The previously packed bins are now inaccessible, covered with unopened mail and a dusty duvet. Your memory of what each bin actually contains, and why you needed to keep it, is vague. But they definitely still feel important to keep!

Time marches forward. Your home does not feel so much organized as it feels populated by containers of beloved junk. The closets are too full to be of any use (probably, you're too scared to look inside). All spare spaces are now storage spaces. You're going to need a bigger house for your junk cubes.

In a moment of clarity, you wonder: Is the plan to just continue collecting more stuff and more bins until you die? Your mind flashes forward into the future: The year is 2100. You're dead! Your loved ones are sifting through your antique bins of stuff. They shake their heads, affectionately yet disapprovingly, at your collection of unused yarn (you did like to knit, but really, one can only use so much yarn in a lifetime). Their grief over losing you takes on a tone of loving exasperation as they dump yet another unused stack of crusty, warped sticky notes into the recycling. But you were so sure those would come in handy one day!

Back in the present moment, you feel lost. **You know what you need: less stuff, more space, ideally a more detail-focused personality. But the process of getting yourself decluttered and organized feels complex, time-consuming, and energy-draining. In other words, impossible.**

THE MAGIC OF TRASH REMOVAL

I know a magic trick, a mystical first step to resolving chaos. Come, lean in as I divulge my secret. It isn't cool or clever or even complicated.

It's trash.

Picking trash out of a pile and throwing it away is easy enough. It requires minimal emotional energy or decision-making.

But when you stand back, the clutter is transformed. The pile is visibly reduced. The room has glimpses of open space—space to work, space to think. Elusive feelings spark in the room—hope, competence, even that trickster spirit: motivation.

When you're overwhelmed with your space, my best advice is and always will be this: Grab a trash bag. Choose a small area of your home—either a single room, wall, or even a few square feet marked off with painter's tape. Then, pick out all the trash.

You don't have to find every bit of trash or recycling. Just pick out what you can clearly see.

Don't devise a great scheme of organization. Just throw shit away. It is really that simple to get started. You'll be delighted by what it can do.

IS IT TRASH?

Do a Trashy Magic Trick

1. Collect everything that's obviously trash and throw it away.
2. Collect everything that's obviously recyclable and put it in the recycling bin.
3. Collect things for donation and put them aside in a box or bag.
4. Enjoy your results and feel immediately smart, brave, and effective.
   - *If you get stuck, keep the item for now.*
   - *Use the following tools to help with decision-making.*

REUSE, REDUCE & RECYCLE

Managing Environmental Angst While Decluttering

Living sustainably is a noble and necessary cause, but it can also be an incredible barrier for people buried in chaos. I have seen homes piled with cardboard boxes, packing paper, defunct electronics, and broken appliances because their owners couldn't bear to send them to the landfill but lacked the executive functioning to repurpose and recycle the items. This can be an agony.

In the context of global climate change, the decision to add to landfills by decluttering your home can involve nauseating ethical calculations. Recycling is easy enough—when it's easy. But if your city doesn't have a good recycling service, if your disability interferes with your ability to get trash out of your home, things can get a little more complicated.

For example, my mom lives in Texas and has to save up her recycling in the garage, then drop it off miles away at a recycling center that keeps dubious hours. My mom can only do this because she has a truck, a garage, the free time of a retired person, and the grim determination of a rural progressive without access to single-stream recycling.

I highly suggest you reuse and recycle what you can. I mean that very literally. Do what YOU, specifically, can.

If you can easily recycle and repurpose lots of stuff that might otherwise end up in a landfill, do that. But if your situation or disability interferes with your capacity to recycle and donate, don't guiltily hang on to stuff. Just let it be trash.

Because if you aren't going to use it, and you can't get it to a recycling center, it's already trash.

It doesn't matter if those rolls of Bubble Wrap are theoretically useful. If you won't, in actual reality, use them, they're just trash waiting to happen. Refusing to accept that some things are trash isn't saving the planet. By saving what you will not use, you only delay the inevitable by turning your house into a mini-landfill of unused stuff.

You can hold on to that stuff for the next fifty years until you die, but then, your grieving family members are sure to send that semiuseful stuff straight to a landfill because they're too busy mourning your death to make use of your nine thousand empty pickle jars. (Note to self: Don't forget to write "Recycle my pickle jars" into will.)

Tidying Tidbit

Reuse and recycle what you have the capability to do. But don't keep things that are beyond your current capacity to repurpose. Just let them be trash.

REDUCING INSTEAD OF REUSING

For the disorganized person, the solution to being environmentally conscious isn't hoarding your trash like a climate-friendly dragon. It's producing less trash overall by *having less stuff.* In the absence of the ability to reuse and recycle, you still have the option to reduce.

Without (too much) guilt, accept where you are now: a person who has probably produced way more trash than you're comfortable with. A person who can't recycle everything that is theoretically recyclable by scientific standards. You are not benefiting the planet by stockpiling your unusable items. You might benefit the planet by setting the intention to buy less—much less—in the future.

DEALING WITH DONATIONS

Balance Good Intentions with Realism

At this stage of the process, you are sure to encounter that cousin of trash and recycling: donations. Donations are items that you don't want, but that others might use.

Beware, reader. If you've gotten this far, you're at a precarious moment of the process. You've climbed out of the abyss, the sun is shining, you have six big blue IKEA bags filled with items for donation. You're glowing with accomplishment! But you don't see what I see: The ground is slippery beneath your feet, and the void pulls at your ankles.

Please, listen to my advice. Get rid of those donations as soon as you possibly can. I know you, reader. You want to be good. You want to get rid of stuff in the most financially profitable, sustainable, ethically responsible way.

Your beautiful brain is full of clever, virtuous ideas. You could sell stuff! Or you could give it to your struggling niece in Ohio! Or you could donate it to a thrift store that absolutely never throws a single thing away (spoiler: It's only open two hours a day every third Wednesday).

I say this with love: I have never once seen someone in chaos successfully do any of these. I'm not saying it can't happen, just that the data don't look promising. You're too tired to pull it off, and that's okay. **Perfectionism—ethical, financial, or aesthetic—is a coconspirator of chaos.** Perfectionism is what lands your donations in your trunk forever, eventually spilling out and re-creating the problem you first sought to solve.

Unflinchingly but compassionately, assess your current level of functioning. If you're barely keeping it together, you don't have the luxury of perfectionism right now. Drop your donations at the morally dubious drive-through donation center. Put them on the curb and see who takes what. You will not single-handedly kill the planet by throwing away your stained, holey socks. At least, I'm pretty sure you won't. Give yourself permission to get rid of things quickly rather than perfectly.

Tidying Tidbit

Give up on finding the "perfect" place to donate your things, especially if you don't have the energy to get them there. Instead, try:

- Dropping them at a mega-donation center
- Putting them on the curb for neighbors
- Listing them online for free

KEEPING TRASH AT BAY

Troubleshooting Barriers to Trash Removal

After dealing with the backlog of trash, it's time to address the root problem: that trash keeps ending up everywhere and isn't leaving the house in a timely manner. Let's troubleshoot barriers to timely trash removal.

PROBLEM: LITTLE MINI-PILES OF TRASH KEEP ENDING UP OUTSIDE THE TRASH CAN

The distance from you to the trash can be physically short but psychologically far.

Observe, like a forest tracker, the debris you leave behind. If little bits of trash keep pooling in a particular zone of your home, such as candy wrappers on your couch, you need to place a trash bin right there.

Oh, but there's a perfectly good trash bin across the room! you say.

Great point, I say, but if the location of that trash can was working, the trash would be in it, not piled up on the couch arm. Wherever trash is, a trash bin needs to be there.

PROBLEM: BAGS OF TRASH/RECYCLING NEVER MAKE IT TO THE OUTSIDE TRASH CANS

If the indoor trash can is psychologically far, the outdoor trash bins seem like they're in another dimension. The transition from inside to outside is necessary for taking out most trash unless you live in a building with a trash chute (and I have found that even then, the problem lingers). But that transition can also be difficult, with unpleasant changes in attire (ugh, where did you leave your outdoor shoes?), temperature (taking the trash out during a snowstorm), and physical exertion (one too many Amazon delivery boxes to carry upstairs, perhaps?).

If you don't already own a pair, slip-on shoes are essential to an easy transition from indoors to the trash world. I have a pair of Crocs just for this purpose, which is how I got admitted to the embarrassing (and liberating!) sisterhood of Crocs wearers.

Assistive Tech: Many issues with trash disposal can also be solved with wheels. A small wagon or cart that lives at your door can help you quickly roll your trash bags to the curb rather than heaving them against your body, hoping they won't split open and baptize you in garbage juice. They even have carts with clever wheels that can climb up stairs. An unboxing station near your door—with a trash can and box cutter—can also help keep delivery boxes broken down and manageable.

PROBLEM: TRASH IS ICKY & YOU DON'T WANT TO TOUCH IT

Speaking of garbage juice. Trash removal (never a favorite activity) has a high potential for sensorial suffering: the weird smell from the trash can, the weight and unwieldiness of the garbage, the unbearable presence of an unknown liquid leaking from the trash bag.

Equip yourself, without embarrassment, with hazmat gear. Keep plastic gloves and surgical masks next to your trash can. Stink Balm is a great product—it's a peppermint-scented balm you rub on your upper lip to block unpleasant smells.

PROBLEM: YOUR HOUSEMATE [INSERT NAME OF THE RASCAL HERE] WON'T TAKE OUT THE TRASH

For some culturally obscure reason, trash management is a traditionally male-coded job. (I assume because lifting stuff and being outdoors are meant to be the realms of men?) But a standoff over who takes out the trash can be bitter indeed. Typically because when someone wants the trash out, they want it out *now* because it's stinky and gross, not at some future undefined time.

No matter who takes out the trash in your house, discussing one unified standard of *when* and *how* the trash should go out can prevent a lot of interpersonal suffering. Try to come to an agreement on your household trash standard.

Tidying Tidbit

- Place trash cans wherever trash accumulates.
- Do whatever you need to do to make the process of taking trash outside easier and smoother.

TRASH SYSTEMS

| Standards & Systems to Keep the Rubbish Rolling |

When it comes to defining a standard for taking out the trash, I feel that only one is easy to enforce: Trash shouldn't exceed the size of the trash can.

Of course, you get to choose the size of the can.

A very small trash can must be emptied frequently, but it requires little physical energy. A huge trash can needs to be emptied more rarely. But it will take a little more physical strength.

No matter the size of the can, taking out the trash is so easy to forget because it can be ignored as easily as you can avert your eyes. **But here's the golden rule with often-forgotten, frequently avoided tasks: Do it more.** Sad, I know. But the more you do a difficult thing, the less difficult it feels. Here are a few ideas for harnessing that inconvenient truth to manage your trash routine.

1. **Use the "No Smoosh" System:** Once your trash reaches the level of the top of the can, it has to go out. No piling it like a Jenga tower. No smooshing it down to make it fit better. A full can is your cue to take it out.
2. **Use the "Trash Day" System:** Choose a day (or days) of the week when you take trash to your outdoor bins. For example, Sunday. On Sundays, you take your trash out, no matter how full it is. The advantage of this system is that it takes decision-making out of it.
3. **Use Motivation Pairing:** Pair taking out the trash with something you do anyway. If you regularly go outside to walk your dog or go to work, take the trash out then. This works best when paired with a task that you *have* to do rather than *want* to do. For example, don't try to pair taking out the trash with an irregular outdoor activity, such as jogging or mowing the lawn, which can be infinitely delayed.

10 Kitchen & Dishes

The Heart of Your Home

OLD FOOD, NOXIOUS DISHES, CRAMMED COUNTERS—A CHAOTIC KITCHEN IS one that you don't want to cook, eat, or even be in. And if you cook, keeping your kitchen out of the danger zone requires constant vigilance. To me, this is the greatest tedium of adulthood.

How many times have I dramatically sworn never to enter my kitchen again? At least dozens. Once, when my cat snuck onto the counter to devour a quarter stick of softened butter, leaving behind a greasy slick of her tortoiseshell fur. Another time, when I dropped a bin of compost scraps on the floor, soaking my socks with wet coffee grounds, old salad, and God knows what else. And frequently, when I think for even a moment about how many hours of my finite life I have spent (and will spend) elbow deep in dishwater.

And yet, I'm stuck with my kitchen because the kitchen is the very center of wellness in my life.

When I'm sad, when I'm sick, when I'm grumpy, where's the first place I wander? The kitchen, to make myself a hot, sugary tea and a life-affirming snack. Because I'm too poor to buy every meal out, the functionality of my kitchen is what holds my life together. If my kitchen is a disaster, I don't eat, and if I don't eat, I'm not Amanda—I'm the human equivalent of my computer's "loading" screen.

An internally organized person must be fed. And to be fed, you need a space to prepare food that doesn't make you want to scream.

DECLUTTERING YOUR KITCHEN

Decreasing the Frustration Factor

A good kitchen organization session starts with an initial declutter.

But we don't need to make a whole meal out of this. We just need to clear out a little space.

Grab a couple of trash bags and boxes. In a very low-pressure, relaxed way, take a look at your counters and cupboards. Is there anything there that you *know* you don't want? Get rid of that thing.

The more your kitchen is stressing you out, the more ruthless you should be. Throw away expired or broken items. Put useful, but not wanted, things in a box for donation. Take the box and put it in your car, destined for the donation center.

ORGANIZING A KITCHEN BY ZONES

Setting Up a Kitchen That's Easy to Keep Organized

It's simple to organize a kitchen: Just go to the store, get organizing products, and arrange your stuff into them!

It becomes much harder, when the forces of fatigue and disillusionment strike, to *keep* a kitchen organized in that same way.

An organizationally sustainable kitchen is one that asks very little from you. There's minimal reaching, bending, or rummaging. I like to organize kitchens into zones with the necessary supplies for each zone (mostly) contained there.

THE FOUR KITCHEN ZONES

FOOD STORAGE ZONE	FOOD PREP ZONE	COOKING ZONE	CLEANUP ZONE
A place to store your ingredients	A place to prepare your ingredients	A place to cook your food	A place to clean up from cooking

Of course, kitchens, like people, aren't designed perfectly, so sometimes zones overlap or break down. Don't go for perfection; go for the kitchen that will accommodate laziness.

Here's an example of a kitchen setup for maximum efficiency (and minimum energy expenditure).

When you're ready to start organizing, designate your kitchen's zones. A roll of painter's tape and a sharpie can help you label and shuffle zones.

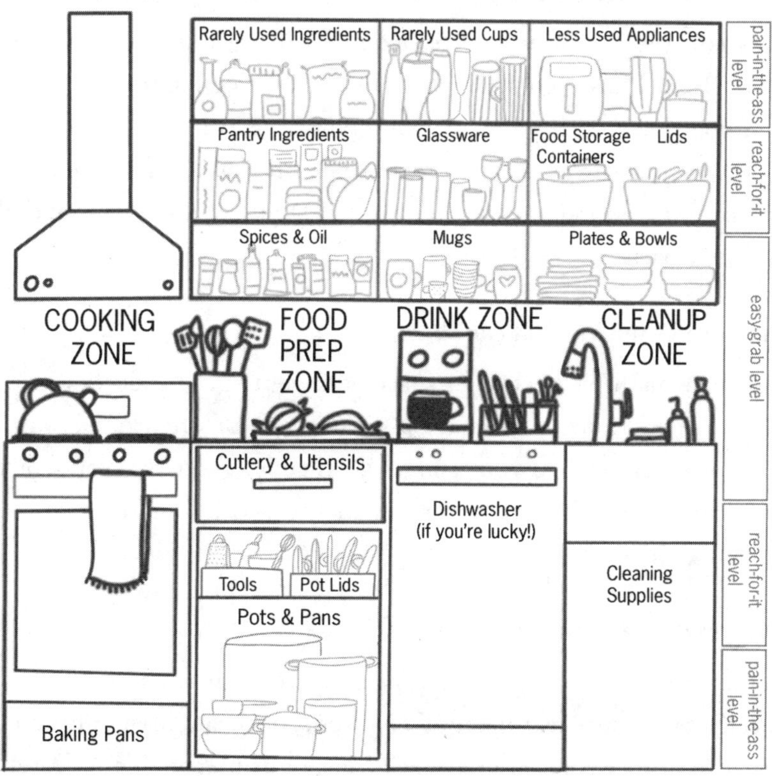

Once you feel good about your arrangement, start moving items into their zones.

Cooking Zone: nearest the stove

Cabinets and countertops in this zone should contain cooking utensils, pots and pans, and often-used cooking ingredients, such as salt and oil.

Food Storage Zone: a cupboard that's easy to access

In a kitchen without a pantry, I suggest keeping food in a cabinet near the cooking zone (I know, I know, the heat can potentially shorten the shelf life of that food, but if a kitchen is running well, food won't stay long on the shelves anyway).

Food Prep Zone: a cutting board-size piece of countertop

This is a section of counter space that you can keep perpetually clear. Reset it after cooking. It should be big enough to hold a cutting board and a few tools. If you don't have at least a little space clear, you will always have to clear up before you can prepare food, and cooking will always be an obstacle. Don't let dishes, food, and mail encroach.

Cleanup Zone: nearest the sink

Devote a small bit of counter space near your sink for dealing with dirty dishes. If you don't have a dishwasher, or often hand wash, a drying rack next to your sink is invaluable. Trust me, you won't want to shuffle your air fryer out of the way to make space for dripping-wet dishes.

Optional Other Zones

Based on your needs, you might need to create more mini-zones for specific tasks, such as a pet food prep zone, medication/vitamin zone, produce storage zone, grab-a-snack zone, or drink/coffee-preparation zone.

USING YOUR LEVELS

Reserving Premium Real Estate for Essential Items

Within each zone, you might find multiple available levels. Using levels helps keep your kitchen from feeling crammed, because it allows you to use *all* of your storage rather than just cramming everything on the countertops.

LEVEL	STORE HERE	LOCATIONS
Easy-Grab	Most-used kitchen items	Countertops, top drawers, eye-level shelving
Reach-for-It	Less-used kitchen items	Mid-upper shelving, lower cabinets, lower drawers
Pain-in-the-Ass	Rarely used kitchen items	Very high and very low shelves

Easy-Grab
Places Between Waist Level and Eye Level

Countertops: for essential items that you use most days

- **What belongs:** coffeemaker, dish soap, large cooking utensils in a vase by the stove
- **What doesn't:** a bread maker that takes up a cubic mile and gets used biannually

Eye-Level Shelving: for most-used items that you'd prefer stored out of the way

- **What belongs:** plates and bowls, spices for cooking, most-used drinking receptacles
- **What doesn't:** dishware you never use, pots and pans

Waist-Level Drawers: for small, oddly shaped items that you use often

- **What belongs:** cutlery and frequently used kitchen tools in drawer dividers
- **What doesn't:** every single dishrag you own, large cooking utensils

Reach-for-It
Places You Can Reach Flat-Footed or Without Crouching

- **Mid-Upper Shelving:** Put your moderately used dishes and glasses here. These shelves are also ideal for storing food if you don't have a pantry.
- **Lower Cabinets:** These are the obvious choice for storing pots and pans, along with moderately used but not counter-worthy appliances.
- **Lower Drawers:** Store your dishrags and potholders here if you don't want to keep them accessible on hooks. If you have a couple of free drawers, store food storage containers—one drawer for bottoms, one for lids—in there.

Pain-in-the-Ass
Very High and Very Low Storage That Can't Be Easily Accessed

- **High Shelves:** Ideal for items you don't mind using a stepladder to grab because you use them so infrequently. Think rarely used ingredients, seasonal serving platters, and special glassware, such as Champagne flutes (though respect if you use those often).
- **Dark Recess of Lower Cabinets:** Use the back of your lower cabinets to store your least-often-used pots and pans, such as your antique turkey roaster (but . . . do you really need that?). This is also a great place to store rarely used specialty appliances, such as that bread maker!

ASSESS THE NEED FOR KITCHEN-ORGANIZING PRODUCTS

| Time to Go Shopping! |

Finally, look for any remaining spots that seem cluttered or awkward. Now is the time to shop for additional organizing products and storage. Choose wisely—not every organizing product works for every kitchen.

Generally, the more complicated the storage, the less useful it is. It doesn't matter whether it organizes your stuff perfectly. If you can't quickly shove your stuff into it on a busy day, it won't work for you. **If it takes more than one second for you to take an item from an organizer or put it back in, it's doomed to fail in the long run.**

But some organizing products can save a kitchen. For example, I can't overstate my love affair with drawer dividers. Drawers without dividers are nightmares—basically like putting a bunch of small objects in a box and shaking it up daily. Drawer dividers—even DIY ones crafted from cardboard, transform drawers into functional spaces.

My Favorite Kitchen Organization Products

- Drawer dividers
- Vases to hold tall kitchen utensils, such as spatulas
- Clear bins to contain small items, such as lids
- Trays to contain small countertop items, such as oil and salt

THE SEVEN DEADLY KITCHEN SINS

| Pitfalls of Kitchen Maintenance |

Setting up an organized kitchen takes about a day. Keeping a kitchen functional is the work of a lifetime.

Like anyone who has lived with anyone, I know that keeping the kitchen clean is the linchpin of domestic harmony. When it breaks down, the entire operation goes off the rails.

Among roommates, families, and couples, there are a few universal complaints—kitchen maintenance habits sure to cause great moaning and gnashing of teeth. I don't tell you about these habits to shame you; I have done these things!

I tell you because, as a cleaning anthropologist (definitely not a real title, definitely just made up), it's my job to report on the facts. Know the offenses so you can prevent them and live in harmony with others.

OFFENSE #1: STACKING PLATES IN THE SINK WITH FOOD ON THEM

Piling dishes in the sink creates a double problem. First, it's really hard to effectively wash dishes in a full sink (*because if no sink, where wash dishes?!*) The dishes must be removed from the sink to wash them, which is annoying and time-consuming.

But now, because the dishes were stacked in a dirty dish sandwich, they aren't just dirty on one side; they're dirty on *both*. You have to vigorously wash both the front *and* the back. Essentially, the benign habit of putting dishes in the sink adds almost twice as much work when it comes time to wash them.

Alternative Household Standard: Scrape or rinse plates before they go in the sink, or place them next to the sink in a defined zone.

OFFENSE #2: PUTTING FOREIGN MATTER IN THE SINK

Dirty dishes and old food are hard enough to face. But sorting through a pile of dirty dishes to find wet paper towels, empty aluminum cans, disposable dishware, or other foreign bodies? Intolerable.

Alternative Household Standard: Make sure you have rubbish bins within reach, so you can scrape plates into the trash. *Only* dishes can go in the sink. No trash. No recycling. And ideally, no large bits of food.

OFFENSE #3: THE INFINITE & DELUSIONAL SOAK

Cooking pans can be genuinely hard to scrub. But "I'm just leaving it to soak!" is so often code for "I'm never ever washing this! Can someone else please do it?" Let's be honest with ourselves. To soak is human, but to forget is also human.

Alternative Household Standard: Set an alarm for the appropriate amount of soaking time. Or just try to clean the pan without soaking. A dish scraper and hot water can take you far. Or prevent the problem before it starts: Keep baking pans from getting extra crusty by lining them with parchment paper or foil.

OFFENSE #4: LOADING THE DISHWASHER LIKE AN ABSTRACT PAINTING

There's no one objectively correct way to load a dishwasher.

Yes, there is, my inner critic says. *It's in the dishwasher manual!* Relax, nerd.

But there are certainly unproductive ways to place things in the dishwasher—namely, in a way that blocks water flow and prevents other stuff from getting clean.

Alternative Household Standard: Remember, the water needs to flow from the bottom to the top of the rack. All bowl-shaped things should be loaded facedown so they don't catch water. Anything big enough to obstruct the running of the dishwasher must be hand washed. Try to load similarly shaped items together, facing the same way, to preserve space.

OFFENSE #5: COUNTERTOP NEGLECT

Wiping the countertops is technically unrelated to washing dishes. But the verdict is in. Wiping the countertops is widely considered to be the final step of "doing the dishes." If the point of dishwashing is to reset the kitchen to baseline function, it doesn't make much sense to leave the countertops puddled and sticky.

Alternative Household Standard: After doing the dishes, give the countertops at least a thirty-second swipe with a wet, soapy rag. No puddles of water on the counter or floor allowed.

OFFENSE #6: LEAVING ALL CABINETS AJAR

As one of my clients, whose partner frequently left cabinet doors open, put it, "When I walk in the kitchen, it looks like it's been burgled."

If you live alone, and you want to leave all your cupboard doors open, more power to you. But for those who cohabitate, this can be a source of great annoyance, bruised knees, and general grumbling.

Alternative Household Standard: If you need to see everything or else you forget it exists, consider removing the cupboard doors altogether and doing open shelving. The doors can be donated to a Habitat for Humanity ReStore (*not* just stacked indefinitely in the corner of your kitchen, friend!). Or, if you're a renter, cram them in the back of a closet until it's time to move out.

OFFENSE #7: PLAYING IT FAST & LOOSE WITH FOOD STORAGE

If someone asks you to put leftovers away, it is indeed implied that those leftovers will be contained and covered. Uncovered food can spoil quickly and attract scary bacteria.

Furthermore, putting a mostly empty yogurt container back in the fridge is just creating a nasty surprise for the next person. *("Not only is there actually no yogurt, but can you also throw this moldy thing away?!")* And even properly stored leftovers will eventually go bad and moldy. Don't neglect them in the fridge.

Alternative Household Standard: Empty containers get discarded if they contain less than a serving. Everything else gets stored with a lid. Make sure you have well-working storage container lids, as well as foil or plastic wrap, at the ready to ensure everything is easily covered. Clean visibly expired food out of the fridge at least monthly.

CLEANING IN PERPETUITY

| Standards & Systems for Kitchen Maintenance |

One thing we must *never tell* children is just how many hours of their adulthood they will spend cleaning dishes. It's untenable. Only hardened adults, calloused by life, can face it.

When I met my husband in college, he lived in a co-op, where all the students pitched in collaboratively to do chores. He must have washed thousands of dishes at the co-op. But when we moved in together, we discovered that his skill set (mass kitchen cleanup with an industrial sprayer hose and autoclave-like dishwasher) didn't translate directly to home kitchen maintenance.

The problem is, I hate washing the dishes too. But I *love* when the dishes are washed. It's a feeling like no other. Sure, sex is great, but have you ever wiped down an empty sink, knowing that you won't have to wash any more dishes for at least twelve more hours? Ecstasy.

To find your own peace with your kitchen, you first need to define what that peace looks like. We need to define standards for dishwashing, putting away clean dishes, and cleaning the kitchen, and choose systems that fit those standards.

DEFINING YOUR DISHWASHING STANDARD

The central question is not "How often should you do the dishes?" It is "How many dirty dishes can you tolerate the presence of without spontaneously combusting?" That will depend on your personal preference and habits.

But it really is important to find your standards. If you don't have a household standard for dishwashing, the dishes will always be hanging over your head (metaphorically, of course, as they're actually hanging out in the sink). **By defining a household standard for dishwashing, and sticking to it as best as you can, you neutralize emotional energy around the dishes.** You know you have a set time when they will be done, which takes off the moment-by-moment pressure to wash the dishes.

The two simplest standards for dishwashing use time and space to define frequency.

- **Standards by Time:** Do dishes daily, or on defined days of the week. I suggest doing dishes at least twice per week at a minimum for a one-person household, and daily for a multiperson household.
- **Standards by Space:** Define a zone that can be filled by dirty dishes—such as a section of the countertop or a bussing bin. Once that space

is full, no more stacking. Dishes must be washed. I suggest that this space isn't the sink because it's difficult to wash dishes in a sink full of dishes.

DEALING WITH CLEAN DISHES

Often, the biggest barrier to a functional kitchen is putting away clean dishes. It seems like the least urgent job of kitchen maintenance. Yet it creates a cascade of problems. The cascade goes like this:

1. Dishwasher or dish rack is full of clean dishes.
2. Dirty dishes can't be washed because there's nowhere to put the clean dishes to dry.
3. Because dirty dishes can't be washed, the sink and countertops are blocked.
4. Because the sink and countertops are blocked, they can't be wiped down or cleaned.
5. Because there is no clean or open space, the kitchen can't be used for cooking.
6. Because the kitchen can't be used for cooking, your choices are starvation or takeout—again!

As you see, there's a lot riding on unloading the dishwasher. Many of my clients struggle with this troublesome task and its associated potential for chaos. **Here are a few of my favorite hacks for unloading the dishwasher:**

- **Streamline your process:** Instead of unloading each item and walking it to its location, one at a time, unload all clean dishes onto the countertop at once, stacked by type. Put them away in groups. Keep your dish storage as close as possible to your dishwasher or dishrack, so you don't have to go far.
- **Declutter to prevent barriers:** Jammed drawers and precariously crammed shelves can make putting away dishes hazardous. Declutter your drawers and cabinets until you have enough space to easily and quickly put dishes away.

- **Use the walk-by method:** Leave the dishwasher open. Any time you walk through the kitchen, grab one clean item and put it away. This works best only if you frequently walk through your kitchen to get somewhere else.
- **Pair it with an idle activity:** If you find yourself in the kitchen waiting on something—such as a kettle or a microwave—use that moment to unload as many dishes as possible. Sure, this is sort of an antimindfulness practice, but we have to make concessions to practicality.
- **Set a daily deadline:** Set a deadline each day for dealing with the dishes. You can use alarms to remind yourself. My deadline is five p.m., so that dishes don't interfere with making dinner.

CHIP AWAY AT DEEP CLEANING

Even a well-run kitchen will, inevitably, get very dirty with crumbs and food spills. But finding time to do the inevitable deep clean isn't so easy, especially because deep cleaning your kitchen usually requires removing everything from the countertops, which is inconvenient if you want to use your kitchen to eat anytime soon (and I do!).

My method for keeping the kitchen clean is to pair small deep-cleaning tasks with what you're already doing in the kitchen. These can be done sporadically, in one- to five-minute increments, when the opportunity strikes. For example, when you've just finished washing dishes. Or you're waiting for your dinner to finish in the oven. Or you're standing around while your coffee is brewing. Throw in one of these cleaning tasks:

Kitchen Mini-Cleaning Tasks

Most of these tasks can be done with an all-purpose kitchen cleaner, such as Simple Green:

Scrub and rinse the sink.

Spray and wipe a section of countertop.

Spray and wipe a section of the stovetop.

Spray and wipe a single appliance.
Sweep the floor beneath the cabinets.
Throw away some expired food.

Doing these tasks a little at a time will delay the necessity of doing them all at once. If you struggle with remembering small tasks like these, print out a list and tape it on your fridge, or next to your sink. Make sure you have all the supplies you need—such as cleaning rags and an all-purpose cleaning spray—within arm's reach.

AMANDA'S KITCHEN MAINTENANCE SYSTEM

Here's an example of my kitchen maintenance system, to give you an idea of what these tasks can look like in real time.

Stats: Two people use the kitchen.
Preference Level: Clean/tidy

Daily Kitchen Maintenance

- **Afternoon Clean:** Put away clean dishes; wash breakfast and lunch dishes; clear space for cooking dinner.
- **Kitchen Bedtime:** Clean dinner dishes; throw away any trash/recycling; put away any cooking supplies; quickly wipe visible countertops and stove with an all-purpose cleaning spray.

Monthly Kitchen Maintenance

- Spray and wipe behind appliances (at least half-assed); wipe any visible drips and smudges from cabinets; scrub stove; remove old food from fridge.

CONSIDERING YOUR BARRIERS

Cleaning the kitchen is the source of many small, peripheral sufferings. There's no use denying your barriers. Assess capabilities and put an accommodation in place if needed.

BARRIER	SOLUTION
Sensory: the feeling of wet, squishy food	Wear a waterproof apron and dish gloves. Look for cotton-lined ones with elastic cuffs to prevent water trickling down your forearms.
Sensory: smell of old food or cleansers	Put on a mask sprinkled with peppermint oil or Stink Balm.
Sensory: sound of splashing or clanging	Wear noise-canceling or -reducing headphones.
Sensory: bright lights	Instead of using the overhead light, put a lamp in the kitchen (away from splashes) for ambient light. Bonus points: Light a candle each time you do the dishes.
Physical: sensitivity to scents and chemicals in cleaning products	Seek out natural cleansers with a minimal scent, and use as little as gets the job done.
Physical: pain or fatigue while standing at the sink	Adjust the level of the sink with a collapsible dish tub so you don't have to bend over. Only load the top rack of the dishwasher. Or sit on a stool. Office chairs with wheels and adjustable height are great for zipping around the kitchen to put dishes away.
Executive functioning: difficulty getting started doing the dishes	Break the seal. Wash one dish on the way to the bathroom. Just one! Or, make it a game. See how many you can wash while waiting for the coffee to brew.

11 Laundry & Clothing

Making Peace with a Lifelong Chore

I STILL HAVE VISCERAL FLASHBACKS OF DOING LAUNDRY IN WINTER IN BOSTON. Weekly, I half carried, half fell with my inconceivably heavy hampers down three flights of narrow apartment stairs (that always smelled powerfully of fried fish and were built, I imagine, sometime before the Colonial War).

While I awkwardly heaved my laundry up the icy sidewalk, my face went painfully numb from the sleet while my body grew unbearably sweaty beneath my parka. Everyone I passed looked equally filled with despair and rage (was it laundry day for them too?).

In the dingy refuge of the neighborhood laundromat, the coin machine was invariably broken, and there was always a murky puddle on the floor, drawing my clean socks toward it with an evil magnetic force. In those moments, I would think of my grandmother in her dusty Texas yard, hand-cranking the laundry of seven people in a tub filled with scalding water. How could I be so far from her suffering but still so close?

And yet, laundry can be beautiful: burying your face in a heap of deliciously warm towels the moment they come out of the dryer, lifting a clean sheet onto the bed in a light-filled sail, pulling on your favorite T-shirt after a long separation while it languished in the dirty hamper.

Laundry is our compulsory lifelong companion, our unwanted roommate. If it isn't contained (and it so rarely is), it morphs into a formless, tangled blob, overtaking your walkways, your furniture, your sense of sanity. As one of my clients described it, "I have laundry dripping from every surface like surrealist Salvador Dalí clocks."

Existing solutions for laundry are based on the assumption that you've got the basics down and now only want luxurious variations on the theme: scented sprays, aesthetically pleasing hampers, and special compartments designed to painstakingly split your clothes into more and more minutely defined categories.

But money can't buy the motivation to fold your laundry into that beautiful system when your back hurts, the kids are screaming, and your inbox is overflowing with approximately nine million emails. Worst of all, laundry is never actually complete. Rather, it's like a relay race that you can never stop running, unless you make peace with permanent nakedness. And there are laws against that.

To create laundry harmony in your life, you need three things: to have less of it, a place to put it, and time to do it. You need to declutter and organize your clothes into a system that you can maintain. My philosophy on this subject is simple: Throw out rules and aesthetics and focus on what works.

DECLUTTERING YOUR LAUNDRY COLLECTION

Making Your Life More Manageable by Having Less

A too-full wardrobe is like a traffic circle with no entrance or exit.

You have a huge pile of clothes. It needs to be contained in the closet, but the closet is blocked by the huge pile of clothes. There are too many clothes and you need to get rid of some. But there's no place to sort your clothes—there are clothes everywhere! With no obvious way to enter the organizing process, you bitterly accept chaos as the nature of your wardrobe.

I have solved this sequencing problem many times with many clients.

It can be done in a few days or a few weeks, depending on your pace and needs.

Steps to Laundry Decluttering

Step 1: Just clean everything.
Step 2: Create temporary storage.
Step 3: Emotionally prepare to declutter.
Step 4: Actively and bravely declutter.
Step 5: Create permanent laundry storage systems (Chapter 13).

STEP ZERO: IF YOU'RE NOT READY

Most Common Barrier: "I Haven't Even Started Yet and I Already Want to Cry."

If the prospect of decluttering your wardrobe is giving you nausea, pause here for a moment. Decluttering will give you maximum benefits, but only if you are able to do it. If you can't, that is okay.

Instead, grab your favorite clothes and put them in a single bag or bin. Imagine you're packing for a trip. Contain the rest of your scattered clothes—dirty and clean—in bags (big contractor trash bags are ugly but work great) and put them as far away from you as possible. Then, skip ahead to the organization section. Return to decluttering when you are ready.

STEP ONE: JUST CLEAN EVERYTHING

Most Common Barrier: "I Don't Know What's Clean and What's Dirty."

Consider your dirty laundry. Maybe it's just a few baskets. Maybe it has invaded your entire house, forcefully occupying your couch, doorway, and bed. Staring into the laundry heap's dark heart, you are filled with confusion. What's clean? What's dirty? You have a vague idea but can't exactly remember, and in any case, remembering would cost you all the energy you have to spend.

Confusion is the enemy of progress. We must kill confusion. To do that, we're going to make a broad generalization: All that laundry sitting on the floor is dirty. Or rather, if it's been brewing in a pile on the floor for more than a week, it's dirty enough to get washed again. There: No decisions necessary!

HOW TO CLEAN A TERRIFYING AMOUNT OF LAUNDRY

Method	Cost
Wash and dry as many loads of laundry as you can. Pair with a movie marathon. Use a 1-hour timer after each load to keep you on track.	*1–2 full days* *Physical energy* *Sustained focus*
Wash and dry a load of laundry every day until your pile of dirty laundry is depleted.	*5–14 days* *Sustained focus over multiple days*
Load as much laundry as you can into trash bags and take it to the laundromat at a low-traffic time. If you can't take it all, take what you can. Wash and dry everything simultaneously.	*3–4 hours* *Physical energy* *Approx. $4 per load*
Pay to have all your laundry cleaned at a local wash-and-fold laundromat. Some services even pick up from your home. This is the most expensive option but worth it if you are overwhelmed and can afford it.	*2–3 days (Inactive)* *Approx. $10–20 per load*

STEP TWO: CREATE TEMPORARY & IMPERFECT STORAGE

Most Common Barrier: "I Don't Know Where to Put the Clean Clothes."

You've cleaned (or are cleaning) all your laundry: Look at you go!

But you're already anxiously anticipating the next hurdle of the process:

where to put the rapidly growing pile of clean clothes. Your closet, dresser, and brain may still feel hopelessly disorganized, and you don't want to re-create the chaos you tried to solve by just shoving clothes anywhere.

"Where is the organizational system this book was supposed to give me?!" you wail. Patience, reader. You are exhausted from washing and drying a metric ton of laundry. Pace yourself.

You *cannot* create a functional storage scheme yet. With all your clean clothes mixed up and jumbled, you don't have big-picture clarity on what you own. You can't decide how many drawers to allot to T-shirts because you don't know:

1. How many T-shirts you have
2. Whether they fit
3. Whether you actually like them
4. What to do with your ex's Pink Floyd T-shirt (My solution: I never gave it back.)

There is a common pitfall here. Unable to make the perfect system, we get stuck and make no system at all. After all, why waste the energy to make something ineffective? But remember: Unattainable perfection and total chaos aren't our only options. A medium-good solution is better than no solution at all.

For now, make a temporary place for your clean clothes to live. This is especially necessary if you are cleaning your laundry over days or weeks. That way, you won't be buried by clean laundry piles while you declutter and reorganize. **Here are two methods for temporarily containing your clothes in a semi-organized state.**

Capsule Method: Put a few of your most worn items in a bin, basket, single dresser drawer, or on a garment rack. This is your wardrobe for now. See what it's like to cope with less. Pack the remainder away in bins or large trash bags until you are ready to deal with them.

Hamper Method: Buy a few cheap mesh pop-up hampers. Designate one for tops, one for bottoms, and one for underwear/socks. As your laundry comes out of the dryer, sort it into the clean hampers.

Keep your clothes in the temporary system until you are ready to begin actively decluttering—whether that takes days, weeks, or months. Some of my clients like their temporary system so much that they decide to keep it forever. Go at your pace.

STEP THREE: GET YOUR MIND RIGHT (INTERNALLY PREPARE TO DECLUTTER)

Most Common Barrier: "My Clothes Are Intertwined with My Self-Worth."

I once had a perfect pair of jeans. They were so perfect they deserve to be capitalized. The Jeans cost $75, which was for me, a child of the recession, a luxurious extravagance. I wore them (while feeling amazing and looking objectively hot) for a few glorious months before circumstances intervened.

The circumstances: I got older and fatter, as one does, and developed a quarantine-era sensorial aversion to buttoned-up, coarsely stitched pants. This was, if not an emotional trial, at least a logistical one. The Jeans, once blissfully comfortable, had become a restrictive denim torment. Unable to tolerate anything but elastic, I felt myself prematurely barreling toward my biological destiny: a stooped grandma in stretchy pants and a flannel housecoat.

I was stuck. A former eating disorder therapist, I would not undertake an effortful weight-loss campaign to wear The Jeans again, on principle. But I was pained when I thought about relinquishing the youth and sexiness The Jeans represented. My only hope was that they, or I, would magically resize overnight.

Instead, they sat untouched in my drawer for two years, squished behind less exciting pants that actually fit me. It was finally time to let The Jeans go. But they were surprisingly difficult to give away. My friends couldn't take The Jeans, because they didn't fit them, either, like some cursed reversal of the *Sisterhood of the Traveling Pants*. In a final anticlimax, a slick teenager at Buffalo Exchange bought The Jeans for a paltry $9 legal US tender—a sum that did not atone for the $75 (plus two years of hand-wringing) they had cost me.

I wish I had just dumped The Jeans in a donation box the moment I realized they didn't fit. But they were a teacher—an opportunity to annihilate my old self, that very small, very good girl, furiously clinging to her glamour, terrified that life would snatch it away, wielding a pair of unworn jeans as a protective talisman against aging, unwilling to open her eyes and see that her youth was already dissolving, despite her most diligent effort.

Take this as your guiding principle for decluttering your wardrobe: *Your clothes have nothing to do with your body.* Your body is a complex marvel of skin, hair, specialized organs, mineral-rich bones, and yes, fat, all powered by electrical pulses and animated by your spirit. Your body experiences, it ages, and most of all, it changes. It is never not changing. But your clothes are just fabric.

Clothes adorn you, they express you, but they are not you. They can't compel you, through their silent presence in your drawer, to get thinner, better with money, or less burdensome to our injured planet. At the end of the day, clothes can protect you from nothing except nakedness. And if you don't wear them, they don't even do that.

We fear we will lose so much by letting go of clothes: our money, our beauty, our identity. But in the end, those things are lost, or at least transformed, without our permission, whether we keep the clothes or not. You can't recover who you were or what you had by holding on to the things you no longer need. You can only unburden yourself by shedding what no longer serves.

STEP FOUR: ACTIVELY & BRAVELY DECLUTTER

Most Common Barrier: "I'm Worried This Will Feel Awful."

Having been transformed into a creature of blissful nonattachment, you're ready for the organizing rite of passage: decluttering your clothes.

As with all difficult tasks, prepare yourself appropriately. Make sure you are maximally rested, fed, calm, and if possible, accompanied by a compassionate helper. Good vibes are essential: Set a positive mood with a TV show, music, or podcast. Declutter in the least chaotic place in your house, whether that is a patch of floor, a made bed, or a cleared table. Start with one basket or bin of clothes at a time, and sort into the following categories.

Keep	**Clothes you would wear in the next six months** These are the clothes you will eventually organize in your closet. For now, return them to your temporary system.
Storage	**Clothes that are out of season or sentimental** These should be stored out of your way, so they don't interfere with your everyday systems or block your prime storage real estate. In a bin on a high shelf or under the bed is ideal.
Donation	**Clothes you don't like, don't need, or can't wear** These can be contained in a box or bag for the final step. Very damaged clothing can be recycled or thrown away if recycling is unavailable (I know it hurts, but sometimes we have no choice).
Alterations and Repairs	**Clothes that you like but don't fit or are damaged** If you want to keep an item that needs alterations, consider first whether you have the time and energy to enlist a tailor or tailor them yourself. Be ruthless in your self-assessment.
Mystery Pile	**Clothes that you aren't sure about** Don't get stuck. Set these aside and try them on after you've sorted the others. Many people find it very difficult to decide on the first few items, then the decisions are surprisingly easy after that.

If you get tired or overwhelmed, feel free to sort one basket at a time, and spread the process out over days. Try as much as possible to contain your sorted clothes between sessions so they don't creep back into the general population to wreak havoc. Then, enjoy the feeling of lightness that letting go brings.

One of my clients once called me after cleaning out her wardrobe. At the back of her closet, she had found a tub of too-small clothes. She had saved them years ago, she explained, in the expectation that they would someday fit again. They didn't.

"Well, what did you do with them?" I asked.

"I just laughed and laughed," she said. "Then, I dumped them all in the trash! I've never felt so free."

> **Now What?**
>
> Now that all your clothes are clean, you need to know where to put them! For guidance on permanent clothing storage systems, see Chapter 13.

TROUBLESHOOTING LAUNDRY BARRIERS

Now that you've dug out of laundry chaos, let's figure out what went wrong in the first place, so it doesn't happen again. Nonjudgmentally assess where your laundry process breaks down. Consider smoothing that barrier with a clever accommodation. Throw out the rules and go wild. There is no frustration too silly, no solution too excessive.

COMMON BARRIER #1: CARRYING LAUNDRY

Lugging laundry up and down stairs, bending to pick it up, and navigating around sprawling piles can be a real barrier for people with chronic pain, fatigue, or mobility concerns. Even for the able-bodied who are functionally able to carry laundry, it can simply suck. Luckily, there are plenty of accessibility gadgets designed to ease the physical burden.

Stair-climbing carts, hamper backpacks, and mesh laundry bags (throw 'em down the stairs, kick 'em down the hall!) can transport laundry without lifting. Reacher-grabber tools, coat hanger reaching hooks, and laundry turtles can help you gather laundry without the need to bend. Remember, even if you don't physically *need* these devices, they can still be helpful.

COMMON BARRIER #2: DIRTY LAUNDRY CHAOS

Look at your house. Where are the dirty clothes? Not where *should they be*, but *where are they?* **Wherever dirty laundry pools, that's where a hamper should be. Your hampers work for you, and you tell them where to go!**

You might find enclaves of specific dirty laundry that need their own container. If your hamper is too stuffed with linens to add any clothes, take it as a sign that you need a separate hamper for linens. If your Purgatory Clothes (you know, the ones that aren't exactly clean or dirty, that you just tried on before discarding) are piled everywhere, you need a Purgatory Hamper. A basket or an over-the-door coatrack also works great for those. Wall-mounted hampers can help keep the floor clear in tight spaces.

COMMON BARRIER #3: WASHING & DRYING LAUNDRY

When it comes to washing laundry, keep it simple or, rather, *make it* simple. If sorting your laundry by color is a barrier, just don't. I give you permission to just throw it all in at once and wash on COLD. It's not illegal! Color-catching sheets can be added to the laundry to prevent colors from bleeding. But I've been washing lights with darks with colors for years. No bad results yet. It's my little version of gambling.

Fabrics that require delicate handwashing, dry cleaning, or air-drying might simply be too much work right now. Banish them from your home, or put them away until you have more energy to deal with them. If you must have fragile clothes, add a mesh bag to your laundry hamper for delicates, so you don't have to fish them out each time you wash. Or throw caution to the wind and treat them a little badly. They'll wear out faster, but at least you will get to enjoy them in the meantime.

COMMON BARRIER #4: PUTTING LAUNDRY AWAY

This step is, by a wide margin, the most loathed part of the laundry process. To make it less time-consuming, sort laundry into categories before putting it away instead of putting away each individual item, one at a time.

Do less. Stop folding. You hate it anyway. You'll be rumpled, but it's

better to be rumpled and happy than crisp and bitter. Stop matching socks. Put them all in a drawer and figure it out later. Don't save all those single socks, waiting for a mate who is never coming back. I give you permission to let go. Better yet, just get one brand and kind of sock; no more matching needed!

Only hang the essentials. Banish clothes that are hard to hang up (begone, one-shouldered top). Get plenty of coat hangers, so you don't have to hunt for them.

Tidying Tidbit

- Use assistive tech to help with carrying laundry.
- Put a hamper wherever dirty laundry pools.
- Keep only laundry that's easy to wash and dry.
- Give up on folding.

TROUBLESHOOTING LAUNDRY ROUTINES

Figuring Out Frequency

For people with tricky brains, the main problem with laundry is that it isn't urgent until it is *very urgent.* There is no external pressure at all to wash, dry, or put away laundry until you're suddenly out of underwear, and now can't present yourself in society. And by that time, the laundry pile is massive.

Doing laundry more frequently equals smaller laundry piles, less time, and less work. But it's difficult for laundry haters to force themselves, with no outside pressure, to do laundry more frequently. That's why many of my clients find it most effective to create artificial pressure in their laundry routine by self-imposing structure and rules. Everyone has a structure sweet spot: enough rules to make you do stuff, but not so many rules that you burn out and rebel against the system. My clients like to center their laundry structure around rules, such as:

Full Hamper Rule: When your (reasonably sized) dirty laundry basket is full, what's in it has to be washed. No squishing down or overflowing allowed.

Designated Laundry Days: Create multiple designated days each week for washing, drying, and folding, depending on your schedule.

Laundry also requires the ability to hold an inactive task in your working memory while performing multiple transitions to other activities. It's so easy to forget that you started a load of laundry, only to find it desiccated and mildewy two days later. **Auditory alarms, such as timers or visual cues (e.g., a laundry basket in the doorway of the room you're in), can help keep you on track.**

EXPECT THINGS TO FALL APART

It's a Normal Part of the Process

My dear sweet chaotic friend, you've made it. You have survived the physically strenuous and emotionally poignant journey out of the laundry abyss. Rest, relax, and continue to test drive your new system. Delight in its clever, orderly solutions. But please, do not expect it to stay perfect.

Even the best system will occasionally devolve into chaos. That doesn't mean you failed at a system; that just means that your system needs to be reset or adjusted. Expect laundry to pile up when you're busy, traveling, or unwell (those unpreventable trials of adulthood). **When your system falls apart, don't panic. Slowly deal with the backlog as you are able, then gently return to your original routine. Remember, your system isn't busted just because it was disrupted.**

12 Decluttering & Organizing

Taming Your Clutter

CLUTTER HOLDS YOU IN CHAOS. NOT BECAUSE IT'S BAD OR UGLY. BUT because the more stuff you own, the more you have to take care of. And you, who are very tired, need less to take care of.

Humans have two opposing impulses: toward security and toward freedom. Security drives you to gather and nest, to build up your little collection of stuff. But when the impulse for freedom comes, your collections start to constrict. They turn into clutter. And just as you shed old habits, old lovers, old lives, you must shed old clutter too.

HERE'S THE DEAL WITH CLUTTER

Clutter is subjective. One person's clutter is another person's collection. Clutter is just stuff plus negative emotion. Only you can decide what's clutter and what's treasure.

Clutter is in the wrong place. Papers neatly organized in a filing cabinet aren't clutter. But those same papers scattered over your dining table, seasoned with crumbs and coffee rings? That's clutter.

Clutter is too much. It exceeds your available space. When you own the "right amount," you don't feel cluttered. But the "right amount" varies hugely from person to person, year to year, space to space, as circumstances change.

Clutter is in the way. If stuff prevents you from entering doorways, opening windows, or sitting on your furniture, that's clutter. If Grandma can't walk through it without risking a fall, it's clutter. If it keeps you from being able to clean your space easily, it's clutter.

Clutter conceals. It hides horrors and treasures alike. While decluttering various spaces, I have found a collection of eight hundred gel pens, hundreds of dollars in cash, and an old container of wonton soup in an armoire. Antique jewelry. Sex toys. Court summonses. You name it, I've probably found it.

Clutter tends to accumulate in Doom Piles. The term "Doom Piles" originated on the internet, a colloquial name for the heaps of stuff you Didn't Organize, Only Moved. These piles are small colonies of items that don't have clear homes, so end up heaped in one place: the closet floor, the kitchen counter, the opaque boxes from your move five years ago.

Doom Piles seem to multiply in the dark, kind of like fungus, when chaos overwhelms your life. They thrive on your inattention. The more sick and tired you feel, the easier it is for a single pile to consume an entire room.

There's only one way to dismantle a Doom Pile: by making a home for one item at a time. (Or by tossing the entire pile into the garbage, a radical choice I won't judge you for.) First, we'll declutter. And then, organize.

HOW TO MAKE HOMES FOR ALL YOUR STUFF

First: Decluttering

1. Choose a pile to declutter.
2. Sort items into categories.
3. Get categories to the right (general) location.

Next: Organizing

1. Divide rooms into storage zones and shuffle stuff into the right zone.
2. Micro-organize each zone.
3. Prevent clutter with new Drop Zones (see page 168).

FIRST: DECLUTTERING A DOOM PILE

STEP ONE: CHOOSE A PILE TO DECLUTTER

You can't declutter your entire house at once. You don't have that many hands. Choose one area at a time. Start small. An entire room is too much. One box, corner, or table is a better goal.

If you get overwhelmed by choices (because the clutter is everywhere!), start with the area that causes you the most inconvenience. For example, decluttering your desk is probably more crucial than the top shelf of your linen closet.

Try not to let emotion-related avoidance derail you. Decluttering can be emotional, but it shouldn't be painful. You may feel guilt, anxiety, and/or regret, but they will also pass. I don't think I've seen a single person cry while decluttering (okay, maybe a tear or two, but no sobbing). More often, decluttering makes people smile and laugh at themselves. Here's a guide to managing difficult emotions along the way.

AN EMOTIONAL GUIDE TO DECLUTTERING

Guilt	Being confronted with overshopping, wasted purchases, and unsent gifts can give you a guilty conscience. Remember, it's just stuff, and everyone makes shopping mistakes. Use your guilt to help you make thoughtful shopping choices in the future.
Shame	If your Doom Piles contain some gross or grubby material, try not to let shame overtake you. Shame is a sign that our behavior isn't in line with our societal expectations. Reconsider whether those expectations are working for you. And if they are, remember that you are currently working toward living with new standards.
Fear	Fear of being completely overwhelmed—that you will fail any attempt to clean up—is common. Luckily, the only way you can fail is by not attempting. Start small. Start so small, starting doesn't feel scary anymore.
Confusion	Decluttering involves dozens of tiny decisions. Suddenly, there are so many chances to get it wrong! If you feel confused or unsure, just set aside the offending item and move on to the next one. Things usually get clearer as the project progresses.
Frustration	It's easy to resent decluttering. That's especially true if you're clearing someone else's mess, or don't recognize the version of yourself who made the mess because you were so unwell. Remember, patience and compassion are your most powerful tools. Take breaks and keep your sense of humor.
Sadness	You might run into items that remind you of loss—lost people, lost careers, lost possessions. Allow yourself to feel sad and grieve what the object represents. Give yourself permission to save anything that's too painful to get rid of.

STEP TWO: SORT ITEMS INTO CATEGORIES

Now, we need to put related items together. Clear a little working space near your pile. If there is no clear space (hence, the clutter), throw the clutter into a box and take it to the clearest area of your home. I like to sort piles on the floor, a big table, or a made bed.

Don't get stuck. If you aren't sure whether you want to keep something, set it aside in the Mystery Pile for now. We'll deal with those later.

If you aren't sure what category an item belongs to, here are a few ways to categorize tricky items and a visual guide of what it looks like to sort a Doom Pile into categories.

How to Categorize Tricky Items

By Location: Put an item in the room where it's most likely to be used or enjoyed.

Examples: Put your nighttime facial moisturizer on your nightstand. Put your sketchbook on the couch where you can pick it up and draw. Put the book you're currently reading in your purse, so you can read it on the bus.

By Function: Put the item with other things it's likely to be used with.

Examples: Put your heating pad with your first aid supplies. Put your pocket knife with your office supplies, to help open boxes. Put your extra phone charger with your toiletries bag in your suitcase, for overnight trips.

For Display: Put items meant for looking (not using) where they can be easily seen.

Examples: Put a knickknack on your bookshelf. Hang art on the wall. Put your printed photos in an album.

STEP THREE: GET STUFF TO THE RIGHT LOCATION

FIRST, DECIDE ON MYSTERY ITEMS

Pick up each item, one by one, from the Mystery Pile.

Ask yourself: Do I want or need this thing?

You might find it easy, now that you've looked at everything in your pile, to know whether you want something or not. But if it's still not easy to decide, use the upcoming guide (Should You Keep It).

If, after using the guide, you *still* can't decide, just keep it for now. It's better to keep a little more than you need than to get stuck.

NEXT, GET RID OF TRASH, RECYCLING & DONATIONS

Get rid of the stuff you don't want quickly, and by any means necessary. If you don't, it will inevitably creep back and wreak havoc.

Put it in the trunk of your car, destined for a drive-through donation center. Post it for free online. Put it on the curb. Bottom line: Make it leave your house, now.

Above all, don't turn every discarded item into a new task for your

to-do list. Don't try to sell it unless you need money badly. Don't save it as a gift for your twelve-year-old cousin. Don't make art out of it. Disappear it, fast.

FINALLY, MAKE (TENTATIVE) HOMES FOR THE STUFF YOU WANT TO KEEP

Take all the items you're keeping to their new homes—or at least, their *tentative* new homes. **That tentative new home does not need to be organized yet!**

If you want your pens in your desk drawer, but your desk drawer is horribly jumbled, don't worry. Just shove the pens in there. *For now.*

Right now, all you need to do is get the stuff you're keeping to the right *general* location. We'll deal with organizing small spaces (micro-organizing) later.

The main reason I do things this way is to keep you from getting sidetracked.

Your most urgent job at the moment is dismantling Doom Piles. You can't do that if you get distracted by micro-organizing your desk drawers. **Stay on mission. Put your decluttered items in the room or area where they are most likely to be used, for now.** We'll organize them into a system later.

If you're exhausted, you could stop here. Just continue dismantling Doom Piles and getting things to the right general location. Your rooms might be disorganized, but they'll only contain items that you need in that room, which is a big improvement on a bunch of functionally opaque, heterogeneous doom piles. **But if you're still feeling zesty, move on to the next step: organizing.**

WHEN THE DOOM PILE IS AN ENTIRE CLOSET

Unsure what to do if your Doom Pile has grown so large that it fills an entire closet?

Never fear—it's a common problem.

Here's a guide to dealing with an overstuffed closet.

Step 1: Prepare Supplies

- 1 trash bag
- 1 bag for recycling
- 1 box/bag for donations
- 1 box/bag for items that will stay in the closet
- 1 box/bag for items that go elsewhere in the house
- 1 box/bag for items you don't know where to put

Step 2: Clear Floor Space

Sort items that are on the floor of the closet into categories. Take items going elsewhere to their new homes. If you're stopping for the day, neatly arrange items that are staying in the closet back into the closet.

Step 3: Clear Doom Containers

One by one, open miscellaneous bags and storage bins. Sort them, using the earlier-discussed method.

Step 4: Clear Shelf/Hanging Space
One by one, remove items from shelves, sort, and replace, using the earlier-discussed method. The closet is now decluttered and is ready to be organized.

Step 5: Pause & Assess Your Storage (Optional)
Take a look at your closet and decide whether your current storage system is working. Do you need additional shelves, hanging space, or floor baskets? Now's the time to adjust your closet storage system.

Step 6: Organize Remaining Items by Zone
Decide on locations for any remaining items using the three-zones method (see page 164). Reorganize everything back into the closet.

NEXT: ORGANIZING ANY SPACE

Creating Permanent Homes for Your Stuff

Organizing

1. Divide rooms into storage zones and shuffle stuff into the right zone.
2. Micro-organize each zone.
3. Prevent clutter with new Drop Zones (see page 168).

Think of organization as making homes for your stuff. Each item in your house needs a designated location: one where it can be put back, over and over. The floor doesn't count!

The reason functional homes work on this standard is that it makes cleaning easy. **When your possessions don't have designated homes, you can't effectively tidy or clean because every item you pick up poses an existential question. ("Where would a competent adult put batteries, and am I indeed a competent adult?")**

Not all designated locations need to be perfectly organized. For example, if you have a load of books, you just need a bookshelf to put them on. The bookshelf doesn't need to be color coordinated or alphabetized. It just needs to hold books.

As long as an item fits and can be found, it's organized enough. If you aren't sure where an item should belong, use the guide included at the end of this chapter. Then, organize one room at a time.

Start by choosing a room—any room—you want to organize. Then, you can use the steps below to put it in order.

STEP ONE: DIVIDE THE ROOM INTO STORAGE ZONES

I like to organize by zones (easy-grab, reach-for-it, pain-in-the-ass), as we did in the kitchen chapter. This ensures that your most-used items are

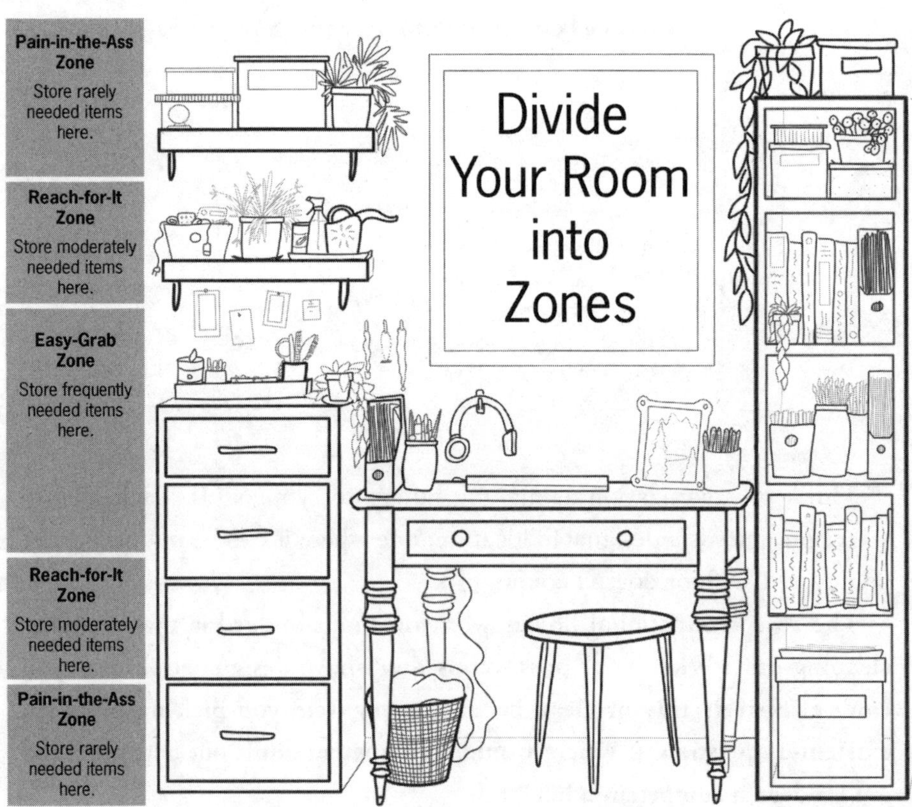

accessible, and your rarely used stuff isn't in your way. First, take a look around your room and designate your storage zones.

STORAGE ZONES

EASY-GRAB	REACH-FOR-IT	PAIN-IN-THE-ASS
Store your most-used items (about once a day) here. Contain small items in cups, baskets, or bowls.	*Store your moderately used items (about once a week) in places it takes a few moments or steps to reach.*	*Store rarely used items (monthly or less) in places that are inconvenient to access.*
Flat surfaces (e.g., tables, dressers, or desks)	Waist-to-eye-level shelves	Very high and low shelves
Top drawers	Middle drawers	Bottom drawers
	Middle shelves in closet	Underneath furniture
		High shelves in closets

Map out your zones roughly. In your head is fine. If you can't hold the plan in your head, do a quick sketch on scrap paper. Or use sticky notes to indicate your zones.

Move Your Stuff to the Right Zone: Reflect on your stuff, and determine which zone it should belong in. This works best if you've already decluttered your Doom Piles and roughly sorted your stuff by category, first.

Slowly, begin moving your stuff into the right zone.

Take your rarely used quilt from the floor and put it up on a high shelf.

Rescue your jewelry from the half-buried box in the corner and put it on your dresser top.

Move your old puzzles, which you'll never do again, to the bottom of your bookshelf. Move your favorite books to pride of place on an eye-level shelf. Get the idea?

This process can involve a lot of shuffling, moving around, and pulling out stuff just to put it back. This is definitely an "it looks worse before it looks better" situation. That is normal. Just try to trust the process.

Adding Storage

If, even after decluttering, there's no space for your stuff except the floor or an overstuffed flat surface, you probably need more storage. Storage can be added in the form of:

Easy-Grab Storage	Reach-for-It Storage	Pain-in-the-Ass Storage
If you have frequently used items that need a place Side tables Nightstands Rolling carts Open shelving *(Use the eye-level shelves.)*	*If you have moderately used items that need a place* Dressers Sideboard/buffet tables Wardrobes Bookshelves & floating shelves *(Use shelves below waist level.)*	*If you have rarely used items that need a place* Underbed bins Storage bins A high shelf in a closet Bookshelves or floating shelves *(Use highest shelves.)*

STEP TWO: MICRO-ORGANIZE EACH ZONE

Once you've got your stuff into the right zones, it's time to organize the small spaces you've been cramming everything into, such as single shelves, drawers, or tables. I call this micro-organizing.

Thank goodness, the fun part! Reaching this step of the process is what will truly make your space look organized to the untrained eye. The principle for this is pretty simple. Just contain small, related items in containers.

Time to Shop: Now is the moment to buy those cute little drawer dividers and storage cups. Organizers can be expensive, so check thrift stores or social media resale/gifting marketplaces for discounted organizing items. They are frequently donated due to our collective striving and failure to get organized. Others' loss is your gain!

Contain Small Items: Keep small items—pens, cosmetics, or small toys—neatly contained. If you don't contain them, they'll jumble together with other categories and foil your attempts at organization. Contain similar small items by category in containers, such as little baskets, bowls, or trays. A pile of writing implements? Horrifying. But a pencil cup? Adorable and responsible!

Use Geometry: Items in a heap will always take up more space than items placed neatly and squarely. It's science! You've played Tetris, right? Imagine that while you're organizing your desk, dresser, or bookshelf, you're playing a three-dimensional game of Tetris. Stack similarly shaped items together. Don't stack things at odd angles; try to put items together at neat, perpendicular angles. Not only is this a great organizational method, it's also a great tidying method.

Containers for Micro-Organizing

Here are some of my favorite things for keeping small spaces organized.

Storage Bins & Boxes: These can be placed on shelves or flat surfaces to contain related items. I like bins without a top best—anything with a top will just get buried. Only use bins with a top if you're storing something away for the long term. Use clear boxes if you tend to forget what you can't see!

Cups, Mugs & Vases: These are perfect for containing tall, skinny items—e.g., pens, paintbrushes, or kitchen tools. These are ideal for art and craft spaces, workspaces, and the kitchen.

Trinket Dishes: Small dishes and bowls can help contain teeny items—e.g., jewelry, hair ties, small charging cords, or your collection of lip balm.

Jars: Jars are ideal for storing multiples of a single identical item—e.g., cotton swabs or coins. Or you can use them for display—e.g., your collection of cool rocks (just me?).

Trays: You can use a tray to corral several smaller containers and keep them neat on a flat surface. They're also great for storing paper.

Magazine Holders: These are basically upright, hard-sided file folders. They're excellent for holding paper or mail waiting for your attention.

Baskets: Large baskets are ideal for containing fabric items—e.g., blankets or clothes.

Drawer Dividers: I can't say enough good things about drawer dividers! They make drawers functioning spaces rather than black holes of tangled, jumbled panic. I believe all drawers need dividers to work unless your drawer only contains multiples of a single item (e.g., socks).

STEP THREE: PREVENT CLUTTER WITH DROP ZONES

Because life is busy and tiring, very few of us, even organized people, have the fortitude to put something away exactly in the place we intended every single time. Work with this nature rather than against it.

Keep clutter at bay by creating intentional Drop Zones. Drop Zones are basically disorganized piles but on purpose. Drop Zones are places to dump your stuff, where it can still look organized. This method of chaos prevention, once set up, requires very little from you. And it is easily reset, even when the forces of fatigue and disillusionment strike.

Example: Front Door Drop Zone

The area next to your front door is a common clutter zone. It's the first place you arrive after a long day, drop all your stuff, and take off your bra (just me?). Prevent front-door chaos by creating intentional, low-maintenance spaces for your frequently dumped items.

Here are a few of my favorite Drop Zone features:

Flat Space: You're going to want some form of flat space by your door—whether it's a table, shelf, or bench. Without it, everything will just end up on the floor, or on your nearest piece of furniture (dining table that's no longer a dining table, I'm looking at you!).

Hooks: Over-the-door hooks or wall-mount hooks are a lifesaver! They can be used to hang keys, bags, and coats. Get more than you think you'll need. Arrange them near your door.

Trinket Dishes: Small cups, bowls, or bins can also be used to corral pens, keys, coins, and small tools that inevitably end up near the door, where you empty them from your pockets or purse.

Shoe Storage: Keep it simple, sweetie! Shoe cabinets with dozens of tiny cubbies seem like a great idea, until you're too frustrated to put your shoes in them. Instead, put a big basket on the floor where you can dump your shoes fast.

Mystery Item Bin: I like having a table or bench with a small basket to contain in-and-out-of-the-house junk. Papers, shopping bags, the bouncy ball you found on your walk: These things are sure to accumulate next to the door. Instead of creating a new Doom Pile, contain them in a designated basket, to be cleared out and organized with the aforementioned methods when it gets full.

Recommended Drop Zones

Here are a few more potential Drop Zones for your consideration. Keep your clutter under control by setting up a customized Drop Zone in a chaotic place.

Mail Drop Zone: Create this zone in the place mail already accumulates. Use a tray to contain mail. When the tray gets full, you have to clean it out. Keep a cardboard cutter nearby for breaking down packages.

Kitchen Counter Drop Zone: Keep the miscellaneous items that always end up on the kitchen counter contained in a tray. (Mine has my dog's medicine, my fiber powder, and my houseplant watering can.)

Nightstand Drop Zone: A small basket on your nightstand can help contain your lip balm, medication bottle, TV remote, and whatever else you reach for on your way to sleep.

Coffee Table Drop Zone: Use a tray to hold coasters, remotes, candles, and other living room miscellany.

TIDYING THE ABYSS: KEEPING YOUR HOME ORGANIZED

Tidying is the perpetual final step of organization. After decluttering, I suggest sustaining your progress by taking a few minutes in each day to tidy your house.

When your house is in chaos, tidying up is a nauseating prospect. But the funny thing is, once you've gone through the painful process of decluttering and organizing, tidying is transformed into a pleasure.

By decluttering and organizing, you turn your home from a resented stranger into a beloved friend. You are intimate with its quirks and qualities. And so tidying it feels like an act of love rather than an act of punishment.

Like any friend, don't expect your home to be perfect. Even best friends take a trip off the deep end occasionally, and a good friendship can survive this. Expect the same from your home. If needed, return to the basics: identifying clutter, decluttering, and organizing in new ways. When your home challenges you, give it affectionate attention.

FAVORITE METHODS FOR TIDYING UP

Temporal	Spatial
Weekly Routine: Tidy a different zone of the house on designated days of the week. **Tornado Cleanup:** Set a timer for 5 minutes. Put as many scattered things back in their places as you can, as fast as you can. **Motivation Pairing:** Pair tidying up with another idle task. While the coffee brews, or the microwave nukes, or during a commercial break, spend a few minutes putting items back in their homes.	**Clutter Containers:** Have a few baskets and bowls around the house on tables to contain clutter. When those are full, the rule is you have to clean them out. **Room Inboxes and Outboxes:** Keep two baskets near the door of each room. One is the outbox: Items you find in the room that need to go elsewhere. Another is the inbox: Items you find elsewhere in the house that need to be put away in the room. When they're full, clear them out.

Remove & Replace: Resetting Your Flat Surfaces (as Needed)

If your Drop Zones are feeling cluttered, reset them quickly with a technique I call Remove and Replace. Simply take everything off the surface. Sort it by category. Then, place the remaining items back in their original location. Remember to place things at right angles—they take up less space and look neater!

WHERE TO PUT EVERYTHING: A GUIDE

LAUNDRY	Clothes	**High Use:** In a bedroom dresser or closet On hooks in bedroom **Low Use:** In storage bins under the bed In storage bins on a high closet shelf
	Linens	In a hallway closet In a designated linen drawer or dresser In underbed bins
HYGIENE	Toiletries	**High Use:** In the shower On the bathroom counter **Low Use:** In bathroom cabinet or drawers In a travel kit for your car, bag, or suitcase
	Cosmetics/Hair	**High Use** *(use organizers to contain small items)*: On a bathroom countertop or in a top drawer On a dressing table or in a top drawer In a makeup or hair bag **Low Use:** In harder-to-reach bathroom drawers or a bin on a low bathroom shelf
MEDICAL	Medication & Medical Supplies	**High Use:** On a kitchen counter, nightstand, or wherever you will remember to take them **Low Use:** In a bathroom cabinet or medicine cabinet, hallway closet, or bin on top of the fridge
BOOKS	Books & Journals	On a bookshelf On a wide windowsill

WHERE TO PUT EVERYTHING: A GUIDE

ADMIN	Mail & Papers	**High Use:** In a basket near your front door In an upright folder or tray on your desk **Low Use:** In a filing cabinet or file box
	Office Supplies	**High Use:** On a desk in cups or bins In a top drawer (use dividers) **Low Use:** In a bin on a shelf or in a closet
ELECTRONICS	Charger Cords & Devices	In a basket on a shelf In a designated electronics drawer near your desk Hanging on hooks
HOUSEHOLD	Hardware & Supplies	In a tool bag or box In a drawer or box to contain batteries, scissors, and other frequently used supplies
	Cleaning Supplies	Under a sink or in a high cabinet In a basket near where they will be used
KITCHEN	Food	In the kitchen pantry In a location where you're likely to need snacks
	Cooking & Dishes	In the kitchen cabinets or on shelves or a pot rack
TOYS/HOBBY	Toys	In the children's room In a playroom or play corner
	Hobby/Art	In a craft room or studio At a designated hobby/art desk On a designated hobby/art shelf, with bins to contain small items

WHERE TO PUT EVERYTHING: A GUIDE

SENTIMENTAL	Photos & Memorabilia	In albums on a shelf In a box on a shelf in a closet
	Art & Knickknacks	Hung on the wall (don't worry about hanging it perfectly, just get it up there!) On a bookshelf

13 The Bedroom

Building a Retreat from Chaos

MEDICAL EXPERTS AGREE: FOR A HEALTHY PERSON, THE BED IS FOR SEX and sleep. For the rest of us, the bed is also for snacking. And when you're sick, suffering.

The early days of my chronic illness left me bedbound for days at a time, in a twilight of not-quite-sleep, not-quite-consciousness. I lay perfectly still, braced by six ergonomic pillows, watching old episodes of *Frasier*. My logic was that, if I moved as little as possible, I could forget, not only that I was sick, but that I lived in a body at all! Thanks, bed.

Going to bed is a daily occurrence but *taking to the bed* is a life choice you make when you run out of better choices. There's a reason that depressed people take to the bed. It is a zone where you can hide from the world outside, undone and unseen. So that you can recharge and feel better.

But when the bedroom becomes a little rat's nest of suffering, swamped by clothes, electronics, empty Diet Coke cans, and all the junk (physical and psychological) you don't want visitors to see, it doesn't make you feel better. It's just another load of crap in the larger load of crap in life. When that happens, you have no place to retreat from chaos, even in sleep.

Undoing a chaotic bedroom and transforming it into a retreat can be a

deeply cathartic process. The bedroom should be a core of serenity in your home where you can feel unburdened by chaos, completely at ease. It can be a place of illness and isolation but also a place of rest and healing. Let's treat it seriously.

Up Next: Creating a Serene Bedroom

1. Organizing your clothing storage
2. Setting up strategic Drop Zones
3. Making the perfect bed (for you)
4. Keeping the bedroom clean

ORGANIZING YOUR CLOTHING STORAGE

Setting Up a Clothing Storage System

1. Sorting your clothes by category
2. Organizing your closet by level
3. Dressers and dresser alternatives

Traditionally, clean clothes live in our bedroom, neatly contained in closets and dressers. This works great until chaos strikes: You can't open the closet door because it's blocked by laundry, and you develop a powerful emotional aversion to the tedious work of putting clothes on hangers.

To make an effective organization system, you must work with your chaotic nature rather than against it. I have a client who solved her lifelong laundry struggle by storing her clothes in clear plastic drawers next to her washer and dryer. No more carrying clothes across the house to her bedroom—something she was rarely able to do even though it seemed, on the surface, straightforward. Instead, she simply had to open the dryer and sort the clothes into bins one step away. Chaos resolved.

Remember: You are not planning an organizational system for your aspirational self. You are storing your clothes in a place that accommodates the sickest, laziest, saddest, and most stressed and fatigued version of Future You. You are shrinking the distance, physically and mentally, that Future You has to traverse for clean clothes. This is how you create sustainable change—by planning to fail.

STEP ONE: SORTING YOUR CLOTHES BY CATEGORY

Sorting your clothes into categories is the first step of organizing them. You need categories because, without them, you have to suffer the indignity of rummaging nude through a tangle of unsorted laundry, like a possum in a Dumpster, desperately seeking an elusive pair of underwear (though, if that's your thing, you go, possum!).

But don't go overboard by sorting your clothes into a kaleidoscope of tiny, narrowly defined categories. Give up on color-coding your closet. That kind of organizing may flood your brain with a sugar rush of satisfying neurochemicals, but where is that energy when you're folding laundry at eleven thirty p.m. after the kids are in bed? Nowhere to be found. You're too tired.

I find it more sustainable to sort clothes by broad categories. Here's a guide to broadly categorizing your clothes, and figuring out where they should live.

CLOTHING CATEGORIES & WHERE TO PUT THEM

Dresser or Shelves *Items that are okay(ish) wrinkled*	Casual tops (long- or short-sleeved) Casual bottoms (long or short) Undies and socks Pajamas Activewear Sweats

CLOTHING CATEGORIES & WHERE TO PUT THEM (continued)

Hanging in the Closet *Items that are not okay wrinkled; items too big for a drawer*	Dresses, skirts, and jumpsuits Blouses and slacks Jackets
In Storage *Bin on a high closet shelf; bin under the bed*	Out-of-season clothes Out-of-size clothes Sentimental but unworn clothes

CATEGORIZING REBELLIOUS ITEMS

Some items are sent to test us. They defy categorization and disrupt the organizing process. But don't worry: We just need to place these items with their closest relations.

Sweaters, Sweatshirts & Hoodies: These can hang in a closet or live in a roomy drawer or shelf. Hanging may slowly warp the shoulders of knit sweaters but, truthfully, my sanity is worth more than pointy shoulders.

Bathing Suits, Stockings & Long Johns: Store them with your underwear, your activewear, or in your seasonal clothing storage.

Accessories (Hats, Gloves, Scarves, Bags): Frequently used accessories can be stored on hooks, for easy access, near the entryway of your home. All others can be put away on a high shelf with seasonal storage, or displayed on wall hooks if they're fun to look at.

STEP TWO: ORGANIZING YOUR CLOSET BY LEVEL

Bedroom closets can be a hive-inducing jumble of clothes, shoes, and God-knows-what-else. Not all closets are created equal. Some are as spacious as studio apartments. Some are just glorified cabinets. But they all need to work because anything that isn't stored in the closet is sure to end up on your bedroom floor.

If your closet is relatively decluttered, organizing it is simple. It all can be put in order in the same way: from the ground up. We'll organize, as before, into three zones.

GROUND LEVEL	EASY-GRAB STORAGE	REACH-FOR-IT STORAGE
Try to keep the floor of your closet as clear as possible. Shoes and hampers	*Waist-to-eye-level storage is reserved for your most-worn clothes.* Closet rods Easy access shelves with bins	*Keep rarely used items out of your way.* Top shelves for out-of-season clothes and accessories

CLOSET STORAGE LEVELS

Closet Decluttering Tips

If Your Closet Is Already Crammed Full

Follow directions for decluttering a closet in Chapter 12.

If You Have Way Too Many Clothes

Follow directions for decluttering your laundry in Chapter 11.

Ground Level: The Closet Floor

What Belongs: Shoes & Hampers

Start by clearing the floor of the closet and remedying any large piles of clothes. Then, designate an area of the floor for shoe storage. Unless you're very fastidious about shoes, inevitably, they're going to end up kicked off on the bottom of the closet. So do that, but on purpose! An open shoe rack, or just a few baskets, in the "kick off" radius can be a great shoe storage option.

The closet floor is the ideal place for a clothing hamper. It's not the ideal place for piles of clothes, which will render your closet unusable. This is bound to happen to everyone at some point, so make sure to go through your closet every couple of weeks to remedy any fallen clothes.

Tip: Try-On Drop Zone

Much clothing clutter results from trying on and discarding outfits. Prevent this by designating a Drop Zone for those clothes, either in a basket or on hooks. Put clean clothes in there, rather than on the floor, when you're done with them. Put all clothes away when the basket gets full (about once per week).

Easy-Grab Level: The Hanging Space

What Belongs: Clothes That Are Too Big or Fancy to Store in Drawers

Hanging clothes is the most labor-intensive part of the laundry process. Unless you love it, for some mystifying reason, you'll want to minimize what you have to hang. Only hang up items that *need* it and seriously interrogate that need.

My policy is to hang clothes that are big or fancy. Big clothes, such as dresses, jumpsuits, and jackets, are impossible to fold. Fancy clothes, such as blouses, suits, and slacks, are a nightmare to unwrinkle. They can be hung in the closet (old school), on a garment rack (accessible), or even on over-the-door hooks (easiest).

Make sure you have about 10 percent more hangers than you have clothes. Store rarely worn clothes on the farthest reaches of the clothing rod, near the back of the closet. Don't be seduced by hanging organizers for your shoes or sweaters—just trust me. They sound nice and look cute, but aren't worth the effort it takes to cram your stuff into them, where it's likely to topple off onto your closet floor.

Reach-for-It Level: The Storage Space

What Belongs: Clothing Storage & Accessories

Reserve the least accessible part of your closet for items you rarely grab. If your closet is equipped with shelves above eye level, line them with baskets and bins. Use those bins to hold clothes that can't be worn in the near future. The bins will prevent the clothes from slumping and sliding all over the shelves and falling on your head—a situation sure to drive anyone mad.

These shelves can also be used to store bedsheets, accessories, and luggage. What can't fit here can go in the back corners of your closet floor or under your bed.

STEP THREE: DRESSERS & DRESSER ALTERNATIVES

Give the rest of your clothes (underwear, socks, bras, tops, bottoms, activewear, and loungewear) easy-to-reach homes. Dressers are traditional. If you use a dresser, try to designate a drawer for each type of item: T-shirts, jeans, underwear. If you want to have multiple categories in one drawer, drawer dividers are really worth it.

Try to store fewer items in your drawer than it can hold. If your drawers won't close easily, you'll never want to use your dresser, and you'll end up piling your clothes on top of it. Declutter (or add additional storage) until drawers can easily close even when everything is put away. If your drawers stick, not from being overfull but because the tracks are off, slide the drawer out and rub a little bit of bar soap on the tracks to make it run more smoothly.

DRESSER ALTERNATIVES: FATIGUE-FRIENDLY CLOTHING STORAGE

Dressers aren't for everyone. The small suffering of opening a creaking, too-stuffed drawer, then shoving it closed, only to forget what you put inside it, can be a significant barrier to wanting to put your clothes away.

Many of my clients love using cube shelves with cubbies instead. Your clothes can be either folded, rolled, or tossed into the cubbies, depending on your energy level. Clothes can also be stored on hooks or in rolling under-the-bed storage bins.

If you hate, or historically struggle with, folding laundry, I give you permission to simply stop folding. Wrinkles are the worst that can happen, and wrinkles can be quickly solved by wrinkle spray, a trip through the dryer, or a steamer (or an iron, of course, if you have the energy).

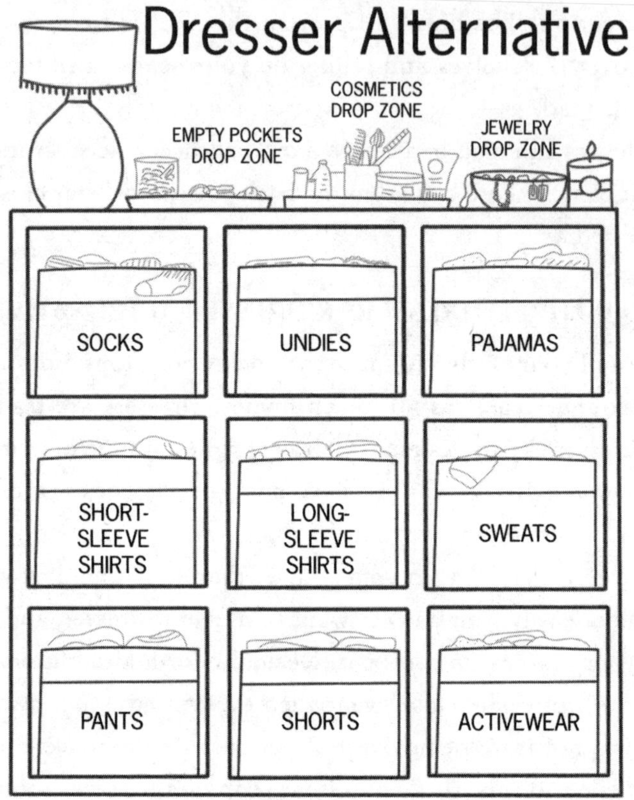

SETTING UP STRATEGIC BEDROOM DROP ZONES

| Keeping Nightstands & Dresser Tops Clutter-Free |

Once your clothes are neatly stored away (or as neatly as you can manage), it's time to turn your attention to the flat surfaces in your bedroom, which can quickly get very cluttered. Just as in the rest of your house, setting up a few strategic Drop Zones can help keep that clutter manageable.

NIGHTSTAND DROP ZONES

The nightstand is the dumping ground for everything you're too tired to get out of bed and put away. This is as it should be. You deserve a little nook to completely surrender to the forces of sloth. So, that nightstand needs to work hard to stay in order.

First, if you don't have a nightstand but rather a pile of stuff on the floor next to your bed, can I please recommend the virtues of a bedside table? It can (but doesn't have to) have a drawer to hide your unmentionables (which I will not mention). Nightstands can be oddly expensive, so check thrift stores. For years, I used an old wood wine crate, turned on one end, which I got for free at a liquor store. Resourceful! All a functional nightstand needs is a lamp and a Drop Zone.

Go shop, or just look around your house, for a small container for your bedside table. A small bowl, basket, or tray will work. This container can hold all those tidbits that will inevitably clutter your table—such as lip balm, phone charger, and medication bottles.

Try to keep *all* bedside clutter in this container. If your clutter outgrows that container, it's time to go through and edit. If you keep outgrowing your storage, you might need to add an additional kit under your nightstand or in its drawer. Just make sure it's worthy of your serene bedroom. I once organized a bedroom that had, in lieu of a bedside table, a box full of crumpled business receipts, and I don't wish that life for you.

Bedside Kits

Use small trays or boxes to contain your relaxation-promoting bedside supplies.

Hygiene Kit: for when you're too tired to go to the shower

Face wipes, bath wipes, deodorant, disposable toothbrushes, moisturizer

Hobby Kit: for when you need a little healthy distraction

Puzzles, a nonmessy craft project, a game, a book, headphones, etc.

Chronic Illness Kit: for when you need to tend your body carefully

Bottle of water, rescue meds, snacks, pain-relief ointments, heating pad

DRESSER-TOP DROP ZONES

When you open your eyes in the morning, ideally you'll be greeted by an orderly space. In the real world, you open your eyes and see the top of your dresser, which attracts clutter like a magnet. And so you wake up to the sight of dusty mail, empty energy drink bottles, foreign coins, all hidden under three pairs of unwashed pajamas. Well, you're only human.

The secret to a serene dresser top is relentless editing. Objects need to earn a place in your inner sanctum, and the dresser top is prime real estate. Try to limit the dresser top to items that are either aesthetically pleasing, meaningful, or useful. After an initial declutter (directions in Chapter 12), set up a few thoughtful Drop Zones to manage the influx of clutter.

Possible Drop Zones for Your Dresser Tops

Empty Pockets Drop Zone

Designate a zone to contain whatever you take out of your pockets when you undress. A basket can hold your wallet or glasses. A jar can hold paper currency or coins. A small wastebasket nearby can help keep old receipts and gum wrappers out of the dresser top mainstream.

Jewelry Drop Zone

After many long arduous years of searching, I have concluded that there is no perfect jewelry storage method that doesn't cost a fortune. Instead, I keep a small bowl on my dresser top, into which I drop often-worn jewelry. I keep less frequently worn items in a drawer (with dividers!).

Electronics Drop Zone

Contain all your charging cords and electronics in one drawer-top basket. This is also a great place to put your phone if you don't want to be tempted to use it in bed.

MAKING THE PERFECT BED (FOR YOU)

| Creating (and Maintaining) Cozy Vibes |

A bedroom can be functional without being comfortable. But you deserve comfort! Make your bedroom feel like home with this trifecta: drapes, a rug, and a lamp. Drapes will control the light level in the room and will also dampen sound, along with the rug. A rug will prevent the shock of moving your feet from toasty bed to chilly floor, so get a rug that's bigger than the bed. A lamp fills the room with ambient lighting, which sets a cozy atmosphere. Equip your nightstand with a lamp, so you don't have to get out of bed to turn out the light, a universally dispiriting experience.

And finally, most important, give serious attention to the comfort of the bed.

Having a bed frame and a headboard for your mattress isn't essential, but it does make you feel like an adult. Use cotton sheets in warm weather, and in the cooler months, flannel sheets. Have at least two pillows per person sleeping in the bed. Most people sleep on only one pillow, but it's nice to have an extra to prop yourself up. Personally, a fluffy comforter is crucial to my emotional well-being. Get curious about what brings you comfort, and imbue your bed with that comfort. Troubleshoot any disrupter to your bed environment.

BED PROBLEMS & SOLUTIONS

Pain	Extra pillows can help brace your body into a semicomfortable position while you sleep.
Anxiety	Adding a weighted blanket to your bed can help with nervous restlessness.
Temperature	If you get cold, add a heating pad to your bed near your feet. If you get hot, try cooling sheets and a fan.
Sound	Block out sounds with a white noise machine or earplugs. You will still be able to hear nearby sounds, but they will block out ambient noise outside.

BED PROBLEMS & SOLUTIONS (continued)	
Light	Use blackout drapes or a sleep mask to block out light. Put a small piece of electrical tape over lights from electronics. If you get scared in the dark but don't want to use bright lighting, you can get a nursing lamp from the baby department (no one has to know whether it's for babies!).

CHANGING THE BEDSHEETS

Changing your sheets every one to two weeks is ideal. Err on the side of changing them more often if you are a sweaty sleeper, eat in bed, share the bed with pets, or don't shower before bed. Generally, your top blankets and duvets can be washed a little less often than your sheets and pillowcases.

Sheet changing is commonly known as the most difficult household task among my clients, because it is physically and cognitively demanding for people with disabilities. Luckily, a few hacks can help ease the burden so you can have clean sheets more often.

PHYSICAL DIFFICULTIES: PAIN & FATIGUE

Changing the sheets requires a lot of physical energy, bending, and even lifting. If possible, try to enlist the help of another person when it comes time to change the sheets. If you can't do that, there are a few products that could help, such as bed levers to help lift the mattress to put on the fitted sheet. Or bed bands—large elastic bands that fit around a mattress—can be used to secure sheets to the bed without needing to tuck them into the corners.

When my pain and fatigue are bad, I take this chore very slowly, with the strategic help of a stool so I don't have to crouch and bend as much. And remember, it's okay to take the job in stages with breaks in between. If you put the fitted sheet on in the morning, the covers in the afternoon, and the pillows in the evening, no one will know or judge.

COGNITIVE DIFFICULTIES: TIMING & MEMORY

It's so easy to put sheets in the wash, forget to put them into the dryer until midnight, and bam, you're sleeping on a bare mattress that night. Even the possibility of getting into that pickle can prevent people from washing sheets. The timing is too precarious.

To eliminate that problem, I got a duplicate set of sheets and blankets for my bed, which I store on a high shelf in a hallway closet. The moment I put my sheets in the wash, I just put the duplicate set on the bed, so I'm not racing the clock. Changing the bedsheets is turned from a multistep marathon into a single task.

SPATIAL DIFFICULTIES: BEDSHEET CONFIGURATION

Unless you sleep in a twin bed, getting your sheets correctly configured on your bed can be a little mysterious. You're just supposed to glance at a crumpled sheet and know which side is the top or bottom?! Help yourself by labeling the bottom end of your fitted and flat sheets—the one by your feet—with a permanent marker, large safety pin, or bedsheet label (available online). Some sheets even come prelabeled. If you can find a tag on your sheets, that typically belongs at the bottom right corner of the bed.

This problem is multiplied when it comes to duvet covers, which are delightful to sleep under but absolutely maddening to put on the comforter. If this is the case for you, consider changing from a duvet to a simple bedspread that can be washed and dried on its own.

KEEPING THE BEDROOM CLEAN & TIDY

| Maintaining Your Retreat |

Giving your bedroom a little love and attention each week should keep it tidy and harmonious. **Decluttering and organizing the bedroom is the most labor-intensive part of the process. After that, it only needs to be reset periodically.** Lots of my clients prefer to do this before they go to bed at night. Here are a couple of methods for resetting your clothing storage and Drop Zones.

Bedroom Reset Methods

Weekly (or Nightly) Bedroom Reset

Throw away any trash/recycling. Put away scattered clothes.
Straighten Drop Zones by returning items to small organizers.

For Bonus Points:

Vacuum the floor (especially if you have pets) and change the sheets.

Monthly Bedroom Reset

Remove items from flat surfaces and dust. Vacuum the floor.
Tidy the closet by pairing up shoes. Put clothes back on hangers.
Air out your room by opening the windows if climate allows.

For Bonus Points:

Declutter any Doom Piles that may have accumulated.

A NOTE ON BEDMAKING: A MATTER OF PERSONAL PREFERENCE

I don't think making the bed is the emotional panacea it's cracked up to be. I have made my bed every day for my entire adulthood and managed not to become very healthy, wealthy, or wise. But there are a few logistical reasons to make your bed each day.

First, it makes your bedroom look visually harmonious by creating an anchor of order. It is an excellent base camp for sorting laundry, organizing piles, and tidying up. At the end of the day, getting into a made bed just feels nice, which is why I neurotically make it five minutes before going to sleep.

Your relationship with your bedsheets is a question of personal style. Make the bed in the morning and start your day with a small accomplishment. Half-ass make it by pulling the bedspread over it to form a semi-orderly surface. Or leave it as a warm little mouse's nest of tangled sheets. It will make little difference in your organizational life!

14 Bathrooms & Personal Hygiene

A Clean Place to Get Clean

I HAVE SEEN SOME *REALLY FUNKY* BATHROOMS. A TIME OR TWO IN MY LIFE, I'VE been the owner of a really funky bathroom. Bathrooms, by their nature, create funk.

For the exhausted person—whether ill, depressed, or overworked—the bathroom can quickly spiral out of control. It only takes a few weeks of inattention to transform the bathroom from a retreat of cleanliness into a den of disgust, brimming with mold, soap scum, hair (why so much hair?!), and empty containers of embarrassing products you'd rather no one know you use.

And the most natural response to a funky bathroom? Avoid, avoid, avoid.

But avoidance creates a second cascade of problems. Because if you can't stand the sight of your dirty shower, you don't shower. And if you don't shower, people start to worry.

Unfortunately, that worry, offered from care, often only increases shame. Because people feel shame when they detect their behavior isn't in line with social norms. Bathing is certainly a social norm, as is clearing the unmentionable stains from your bathroom. That puts people in a bind when they're too sick and exhausted to care.

Your relationship with your bathroom is closely related to your relationship with your body and its less glamorous workings. So, if you're going to go through the effort of resetting a chaotic bathroom, you might as well give some thought to how your bathroom could accommodate your particular needs. There are so many sensorial and psychological barriers to bathing. Yet people often feel so ashamed of their barriers that they can't bear to give any thought to solving them.

Because the bathroom is the smallest room of the house, it is also one of the most easily wrangled back into order. Here's how.

UNCOVERING BATHROOM BARRIERS

Understanding What You Need from Your Bathroom

If you find yourself out of step with the social norms on cleanliness and hygiene, I encourage you to take a step back from your shame. Instead of isolating yourself and hiding your difficulties to prevent rejection, reach out for support where you can. Compassionately and nonjudgmentally assess your barriers. Then, fill your bathroom with solutions.

EMOTIONAL BARRIERS

If you're really suffering emotionally, getting yourself clean and bathed can feel so overwhelming. Bathing requires caring: caring whether you look nice, whether you smell bad, and whether your body is worth the attention. If you're in the pit of despair, you might find caring in short supply.

Bathing requires you to be alone with your nakedness as well as your naked thoughts. That's why bathrooms can be really triggering spaces for people recovering from eating disorders and sexual trauma. Their thoughts aren't usually pleasant companions, and nakedness does not always feel safe.

The internal experience of a shower is less like, *Yay, I'm getting clean!*

and more like, *I hate my body and, in addition, I'm pretty sure everybody hates me!*

The most important thing is to assert ownership over the bathroom, to *make it* a place you can be safe by filling it with comforting sights and sensations.

Practice a little strategic avoidance by equipping your bathroom with pleasant distractions. Hook up a waterproof speaker to play an audiobook or music while you bathe. If being naked is a trigger, get a bathrobe to wrap up in right before and after bathing. Offer yourself a few neutral affirmations, such as "This bathroom is gross, but I am not!"

Making the Bathroom Feel Emotionally Safe

- Use a speaker to play music you like.
- Put a lock on the door.
- Temporarily cover or remove your mirrors if you avoid bathing to avoid seeing yourself.
- If you have natural light, add plants to your bathroom—alive things to keep you company! Pothos are easy to take care of and love bathroom steam. Water weekly.
- Get luxurious lotion and use it to moisturize any parts of your body you feel insecure about, to practice interacting with your body in a compassionate way.

SENSORY BARRIERS

For most of us, showering is a pleasant or at least neutral activity. **For people with sensory issues, the bathroom can be filled with unpleasant, even painful, sensations.**

Sensory issues can lead to hygiene avoidance. That can be hard for people to understand because it seems like being unbathed must also be an unpleasant sensory experience.

But for hygiene-avoiders, being unbathed is *familiar and predictable.* Feeling grubby is a fixed state. Even if it's unpleasant, it's still preferable to gritting your teeth through the shifting, unpredictable, unpleasant sensory input of showering. That's why sensory barriers need to be carefully identified and accommodated to reduce hygiene avoidance.

Sensory Icks & Accommodations

(Remember, any electric appliances used in the bathroom should be splash-safe!)

Wet Hair: A shower cap or claw clip can keep your wet hair off your neck and shoulders.

Slimy Skin: Instead of regular lotion, try Nivea In-Shower Body Lotion as a moisturizer. You can apply and rinse it in the shower to get rid of the feeling of slimy skin while keeping your skin moisturized to prevent itchy, flaky patches.

Brushing Teeth: Use a sensory-friendly toothbrush, such as a three-sided brush or a U-shaped electric toothbrush. Both are gentler on the teeth.

Bright Lights: Use a water-safe lamp for mood lighting. They even make dim lights specifically for the shower!

Roaring Sound: Use waterproof earplugs or use a speaker for music.

Temperature Transitions: Getting too hot or cold can be solved by using a fan or splash-safe space heater in the bathroom.

EXECUTIVE FUNCTIONING

For people who struggle with time management and task initiation, figuring out when to shower can be complex.

When to fit in a shower today? Before bed? But you don't want to go to bed with wet hair. You could shower before work in the morning, but then you'll be all sticky and damp on your commute. Better to shower after work. But wait! You exercise in the evening after work. What's the point of showering if you'll just get immediately sweaty afterward? Better shower after exercising. But wait! Can't go to bed with wet hair— and so on and so forth. For an extra-fun complication, throw into the mix an infant child who needs constant supervision. You may never shower again!

Showering at a set time of day, especially bedtime, is the easiest to manage logistically. The process of showering transitions more easily into sleep than it does into any other activity. And you can plan your evening hours around it.

But washing hair can still be a barrier because many people don't want to go to sleep with wet hair. Luckily, your hair can go a lot longer between washes than your body.

Use a shower cap to keep your hair dry while bathing on regular days.

Then, designate a day of the week for washing your hair. You might need multiple days, depending on your hair type. On those days, take your shower earlier to give your hair time to dry before bed.

(Or just go bald—now, there's a solution!)

Time Blindness Tip

One of my clients struggled with showering because they could never accurately estimate how much time it would take. They added a waterproof clock to their shower wall, and ta-da! No more time blindness. It was easy for them to see that showering took very little time.

PHYSICAL BARRIERS

For people living with chronic illness, often the desire to shower remains, but the ability to do so is compromised. Accessibility devices, such as shower stools, can make showering less fatiguing. All the comfort of a bath with the convenience of a shower! Use a handheld fan or box fan to control any issues with overheating.

If you are unable to easily wash your own hair because of issues with lifting your arms over your head, some hair salons will wash and dry your hair weekly for a small fee. For people with curly hair, hair washing can be especially laborious. Keeping your hair in braids can help keep it manageable for longer periods of time.

Nonshower Hygiene Kit

If your disability prevents you from being able to shower as often as you'd like, there are some products that can help you feel fresh between baths.

Face Wipes: Use wipes specifically designed for the face to prevent irritation or breakouts.

Bath Wipes: These large, moisturizing wipes (different from baby wipes) can be used to clean yourself bit by bit as you lie in bed.

Disposable Toothbrushes: These single-use toothbrushes can help freshen your mouth in between brushing. U-shaped autobrushes are a more eco-friendly (if pricey) alternative.

SETTING UP A SERENE BATHROOM

Decluttering & Organizing

Steps to a Serene Bathroom

1. Doing an initial declutter
2. Organizing your shower
3. Organizing your storage by zones
4. Keeping the bathroom clean

Once you understand what you need from your bathroom, all you need to do is put it in order. And that means decluttering, organizing, and cleaning.

Start with an initial declutter. Decluttering the bathroom is pretty simple. Grab a trash bag and go shelf by shelf. You are sure to find empty containers, expired products, or things that you will never use that can't be donated because they're too yucky, broken, or embarrassing.

Throw away expired products. Throw away products you know you won't use. Throw away stray tiny objects, such as single cotton swabs or press-on nails. It's more trouble than it's worth to reunite them with their comrades. Once you've thoroughly (or even half-assedly) decluttered, move on to organizing.

A FEW BATHROOM ITEMS THAT CAN BE DONATED

Unwanted Medication
Many pharmacies have large metal boxes where you can discard unwanted medication (like a mailbox, but for pharmaceuticals). Search for "Pharmacies with Drug Take-Back Programs" online to find one in your area.

Unopened Bath & Beauty Products
If your local thrift store doesn't take bath products, try homeless shelters or family crisis centers.

Old Towels
Old towels are often needed at animal shelters or animal hospitals for cleaning and bedding. Your loss is a puppy's gain!

ORGANIZING YOUR SHOWER

Whether you have a tub, shower stall, or some combo of the two, you need storage for bath supplies. Shower storage should be free-draining to prevent mold buildup. Choose the shower storage that fits your needs best. They make all kinds: those that go over the showerhead, wedge in the corner, or suction to tile walls.

Follow the same principles we've been using: Keep your most-used products in the easiest-to-grab location. Rarely used products can go on higher shelves. Don't forget to go through your shower every once in a while to get rid of empty and expired products.

ORGANIZING YOUR BATHROOM STORAGE

Bathroom clutter is, I'll admit, my least favorite kind of clutter. Sorry, bathroom clutter!

It's made up of dozens of teeny tiny objects: nail polish bottles, crushed Band-Aid boxes, oddly shaped hair tools. These objects have a tendency to crowd your flat spaces, tangling together, jamming your drawers, toppling into the sink when you're just trying to brush your teeth.

That's why we need storage—*organized* storage. If you don't have any bathroom storage, now is a good time to add it. Then, as usual, we'll organize by zones.

Bathroom Storage Zones

Places to put stuff, other than the bathroom countertop, the sink, and the floor:

Easy-Grab Storage	Reach-for-It Storage	Pain-in-the-Ass Storage
For frequently used items Countertop Medicine cabinet Eye-to-waist-level open shelving	*For moderately used items* Upper drawers Bathroom shelves Towel racks and hooks	*For rarely used items* High shelves Adjacent closets The back of cabinets

Storage That's Easy to Add if You Need It

- Narrow shelving units
- Over-the-toilet shelving units
- Three-tiered carts
- Over-the-door towel racks

EASY-GRAB: COUNTERTOP, MEDICINE CABINET & SHELVES OVER THE SINK

This is the most valuable real estate in your bathroom. Reserve it for essential items that you use daily, such as hand soap, toothbrushes, and frequently used skin care. Keeping this space minimal will help make it easy to clean because you don't have to remove sixty tiny objects before wiping the sink.

Small countertop organizers can help keep tiny products in check. Just remember: the simpler, the better. A fiddly, multilevel organizer with fifty tiny compartments seems like a good idea until you're the one who has to squeeze your products into those tiny compartments every day. It's much easier to chuck them into a basket. If you have too many high-use products to store on your countertop, adding a couple of open bathroom shelves near your sink can expand your easy-grab real estate.

REACH-FOR-IT: UPPER DRAWERS, BATHROOM SHELVES & HOOKS

Items that you use every few days, or weekly, can be stored within arm's reach. Towels that are in use can be stored on towel racks. If you don't have a towel rack, add hooks—either wall-mount hooks or over-the-door hooks. Frequently used cosmetics, hygiene supplies, or hair products can be stored in upper drawers or shelves. Medical supplies can also be stored here if you use them frequently.

This is one moment where I implore you to use organizers! Drawer dividers will keep your drawers from getting jumbled. Small baskets for your shelves will keep tiny products from spilling everywhere.

PAIN-IN-THE-ASS: HIGH SHELVES, ADJACENT CLOSETS & LOWER CABINETS

Relegate infrequently used items to places that are harder to reach—the places you have to stretch or crouch to access. This is one of the areas where it is semi-important to keep things sorted and contained by category, not for aesthetics, but for your own sanity. It's already frustrating enough to find a rarely needed item in dark, hard-to-reach areas. Make your life a little easier by keeping like items together, contained in baskets.

You might have to do a bit of creative shopping to find containers that fit your space. I like to go to the store with measurements of the space and a tape measure in hand to see whether containers will fit well.

C-String Bathroom Categories to Keep in Storage

Contain these items in baskets in storage, since they won't be needed often.

- First aid supplies and medical ointments
- Manicure supplies
- Hair tools and less-used hair products
- Spare towels and toilet paper
- Large medical devices, such as braces, heating pads, and humidifiers

KEEPING THE BATHROOM CLEAN

As we've discussed, standards for cleanliness vary widely from house to house. But I do find that the generally accepted standard for bathroom cleanliness is this: All the fixtures should be accessible and body excretions should not be visible. Hair, spit, fingernail clippings, urine—I don't need to go on, do I? You get it.

But cleaning the bathroom can be very labor-intensive and, frankly, kind of yucky, making it a highly avoided task. Everyone loves having a clean bathroom, but few of us enjoy sweeping up small hairs and scrubbing pink slime while sweating and inhaling chemicals.

The important thing to keep in mind is that not every bathroom cleaning experience needs to be an ambitious deep clean. Don't make yourself miserable and exhausted every time you clean. That doesn't build positive associations with cleaning in your brain. Create lasting motivation by breaking your cleaning sessions into small chunks. Cleaning the bathroom in small steps can help keep the task manageable.

A Note on Cleaning Products

Because you're tired, let's not overcomplicate things.

There are hundreds of bathroom cleaning products designed to do specific jobs in optimal ways. But an all-purpose disinfecting bathroom cleaner plus a few rags will clean almost anything. Just remember to read the directions, ventilate the room, and don't mix cleaners. You never know what kind of chemical reactions you might set off.

THREE LEVELS OF FATIGUE-FRIENDLY BATHROOM CLEANING

| Itty-Bitty, Quick & Deep |

If you are overwhelmed, feeling pressure to deep-clean the bathroom, every time you clean it at all, is likely to create avoidance. Here are three levels of bathroom cleaning: itty-bitty, quick, and deep, so you can do what you have the time and energy for.

Itty-Bitty Bathroom Cleaning	Quick Bathroom Cleaning	Deep(er) Bathroom Cleaning
Energy Level: Slim to none	**Energy Level:** A little juice in the tank	**Energy Level:** Having a good day
Time Investment: 1 minute	**Time Investment:** 5 to 10 minutes	**Time Investment:** 15 to 30 minutes
Frequency: Whenever you can bear it	**Frequency:** Once per week, or divided between two days per week	**Frequency:** Once per month, or one deep-cleaning task per week

ITTY-BITTY BATHROOM CLEANING

Energy Level: Slim to none

Time Investment: 1 minute

Frequency: Whenever you can bear it

Keep an itty-bitty cleaning kit (disinfectant wipes and disinfectant spray) near your bathroom sink. Take one wipe and choose the dirtiest-looking surface: sink, toilet seat, or tub rim. Quickly wipe that with the disinfectant wipe. No need to get every nook and cranny; just focus on improving the overall look of the surface. You're done! For bonus points, haphazardly spray disinfectant mist on fixtures to make them feel less germy. Your bathroom won't be superclean, but it will be cleaner than when you started.

Tip: Clean the Shower While You're in the Shower

This genius idea comes from professional cleaner Vanesa Amaro.

- Buy a dish-cleaning brush with a reservoir for soap.
- Fill it with equal parts dish soap and white vinegar.
- Put the dish brush in your shower.
- The next time you're in the shower, waiting for your hair conditioner to soak in, use the brush to scrub your shower. Either rinse the suds with a handheld showerhead or keep a cup in the shower to fill with water and rinse the walls.

QUICK BATHROOM CLEANING

Energy Level: A little juice in the tank

Time Investment: 5 to 10 minutes

Frequency: Once per week, or divided between two days per week

Spray and wipe any visible portions of the sink and countertop. Clean the toilet as fast as you can, just focusing on the most offensive stains. Spray the shower with cleaner. Let sit per its instructions, then rinse. For bonus points, change out the towels or sweep the floor.

DEEP(ER) BATHROOM CLEANING

Energy Level: Having a pretty good day

Time Investment: 15 to 30 minutes

Frequency: Once per month, or one deep-cleaning task per week

Dust or vacuum any dust or hairs from surfaces first. Remove items from the sink and countertop. Spray the sink and countertop with cleaner and wipe them down. Thoroughly scrub the toilet bowl with cleaner. Spray and wipe the exterior of the toilet with disinfectant cleaner. Spray the shower with cleaner and scrub it from high to low. Rinse. Sweep or vacuum the floors, then mop.

HOW OFTEN SHOULD I CLEAN THE BATHROOM?

The Unanswerable Question

I have almost broken the old therapist's habit of being maddeningly vague about advice. But I still find the question of cleaning frequency impossible to answer because it depends on so many factors. **In general, if pressed, I will tell you that you need to clean the bathroom as often as it takes for body excretions, mold, hair, and soap scum to become visible to you (or to others if you have bad vision). Generally, that means most people will have to give their bathroom a bit of attention about once a week.**

Note on Preference: Some people are more easily disgusted by body excretions or mold than others are. They will find dirty bathrooms extra distressing. Disgust is an innate human emotion, and it isn't easy to talk yourself out of feeling disgusted. If you're one of those people (or live with one of those people), you may need to clean your bathroom a bit more often. These people may only feel comfortable in bathrooms that are disinfected, even if the actual risk of disease transmission in an illness-free household is relatively low.

FACTORS THAT MAKE BATHROOMS MORE DIRTY, MORE OFTEN

These bathrooms may need to be cleaned more frequently and intensively.

High Usage: If your bathroom is used by more than two people, especially if it is used by children who haven't quite mastered the art of potty training yet, it will need to be disinfected more frequently. This is especially true if any of your household members easily get sick.

Pets: If your bathroom doubles as a litterbox zone for your kitty cat friend, you will need to be extra vigilant about sweeping tracked litter and managing litterbox odor. Houses with lots of pets can also benefit from keeping a mini-vacuum in the bathroom to deal with drifts of hair.

Climate: If your climate is humid and more susceptible to mold, clean more frequently with a mold-specific cleaner, and make sure to ventilate the bathroom so fixtures dry as quickly as possible. If your local water is mineral rich, you may have to use a decalcifying cleaner to treat hard water deposits.

15 Rooms to Live In

Living Rooms, Dining Rooms & Workspaces

While writing this book, I helped my mom host a memorial for her sister, who died suddenly of cancer. Devastated and exhausted, we spent two days scrubbing my childhood home, with obsessive attention to the public-facing rooms. I mopped the living room into oblivion, filled it with cut flowers, and artfully arranged the throw pillows.

Aware that we were overdoing it a bit in our haze of grief, we both kept trying to intentionally lower our standards for hosting guests.

"This is good enough!" we kept saying, holding back the hysteria. "No one will care whether the house is clean."

Then, silently agreeing that it wasn't good enough, we proceeded to attack the porch with brooms, sweeping Texas-size spiders out of the eaves. God forbid anyone might spot a cobweb at the wake—we have standards, after all, and can't be caught slipping in front of dozens of equally stunned family members who probably wouldn't have noticed were the house on fire, much less whether the floors were clean.

But we couldn't help it. The impulse to prepare the living room for guests was so strong, even grief couldn't drown it. The ritual was too powerful.

Your loved ones have seen you in many states of embarrassing personal

disarray. And yet, when the public-facing rooms of your home are in chaos, you feel unable to invite your loved ones to visit without hours of furious, sweaty cleaning. When I interviewed people about these random bursts of intense motivation, their opinion was unanimous.

"I only clean the living room or dining room when people are coming over," people told me. "And I only clean my home office if I have a video call, but just the bit that you can see on camera. It's only embarrassment that drives me."

Okay, right, good, I thought, trying to figure out how to spin public shaming as a valid motivator to my readers.

When I was a therapist going on home visits, I often found my clients energetically cleaning their living room in preparation for my visit (ironically, a visit that usually involved them volunteering their deepest darkest secrets).

My favorite thing was getting to know clients so well that they stopped the presession cleaning routine and instead just threw open the door to their untidied living room, saying, "Make yourself at home!"

On a couch covered with laundry, with a strange dog curled up in my lap, and my client in their house slippers, I knew we were getting somewhere.

We need to find a way to walk that middle path with the remaining rooms in the house. Ideally, they should be presentable enough that a friend could come over without your having a meltdown. But they should also be cozy and comfortable, whether it's a living room, dining room, home office, or creative space. Let's find that in-between standard.

Semipublic Rooms of Your House to Get Semi-Organized

- The living room
- The dining room
- Spaces for work and play: craft rooms, home gyms, and home offices

MAKING A LIVING ROOM THAT WORKS FOR YOU

How Clean Is Clean Enough?

How to Set Up Your Living Room

1. Define a standard for hosting.
2. Organize your major zones.
    - Coffee table
    - Seating
    - Storage

The living room is a tricky room to organize. Mainly because you own it, but it's also for other people. And there's a lot of pressure to create the perfect space for hosting—so much pressure that you might be tempted never to invite anyone over. *Ever.*

Instead of trying to live up to some ambiguous standard of hosting, let's set a few concrete ground rules for a clean-enough living room.

First, at the minimum, remove any offensive stimuli, such as litterbox leavings, dirty socks, old food, or stinky trash. **Some clutter on the floor and surfaces is totally okay.** You don't need to create a new Doom Pile by shoving it all under your bed. Even very neat people can tolerate clutter in someone else's house.

Make sure, though, that the clutter doesn't pose any functional barriers. The floor should be clear enough for walking without tripping hazards. There should be enough open seats for guests (scooch over, laundry pile!). And your flat surfaces should have enough clear space to put down a drink.

Remember to treat yourself with hospitality too. If these things are good enough for guests, they're good enough for you. And remember, if you're in total despair, it's better to let someone see your substandard living room than to isolate yourself forever. Sometimes, hospitality means showing trust by letting people see and help you.

CLEANING UP FOR GUESTS BY PERSONALITY TYPE

We're returning to our four cleaning personality types from Chapter 3. Find a cleanup method that works for your style and needs.

Type 1: Tidy & Clean
Your living room will already be immaculate, so your job is to add warmth. People feel uneasy in a too-clean room (they're scared of messing it up!), so add a bit of artful disarray with throw blankets, books, and snacks. Set a timer with a maximum limit for how long you can spend cleaning for guests, so you don't overdo it.

Type 2: Tidy & Natural
Your living room is sure to be neat already. So, instead of tidying, give a bit of extra attention to grime. Wipe down your coffee table. Clear any dust bunnies or dog hair drifts from the corner. Take a detour to quickly wipe down the bathroom sink. Guests love a clean bathroom.

Type 3: Messy & Clean
Everything is already so lovely and sanitary. Turn your attention to tidying. Do a quick tour around your living room to throw away trash and recycling. Tidy papers into neat stacks and straighten up the couch. Set a timer to start cleaning a few hours before guests arrive, so you don't feel frenzied at the last moment.

Type 4: Messy & Natural
Focus on function. Clear enough space that your guests can sit down without crunching a pile of papers. Make sure there's enough open flat space for people to put down a drink, and enough sink space to manage dishes. Address the living room one quadrant at a time, so you don't get overwhelmed.

ORGANIZING YOUR LIVING ROOM

Keep your living room manageable by creating a few anchors of order. These spaces can be reset to their default level of tidiness over and over. When you need to clean up quickly, focus your attention on these zones. They're sure to make the most impact.

THE COFFEE TABLE

In theory, it's a place to put a coffee cup. In practice, it's a place to put everything.

The coffee table is the nightstand of the day. (Daystand?) It's the place where you dump stuff when you're too cozy to get up.

Solve coffee table chaos by creating a well-edited Drop Zone. I prefer a tray for this job. It can hold remotes, a few coasters, a candle, and whatever necessary supplies you need at the ready. Relentlessly edit this tray each time you tidy up, as random tidbits are sure to pool here.

Or be radical. My friend solved coffee table chaos by just getting rid of her coffee table.

"I'll just fill it up with empty cups," she said. "No coffee table, no cups." She just holds her beverage in her hands and when she's done, she takes it to the sink. I can't do this because I have at least three beverages going at any given time, and only two hands, but I still admire a clever solution.

THE COUCH & OTHER SEATING

I vow to remain neutral. I shall not judge you for using your couch to store paperwork or laundry. But can't we agree: Isn't it nicer to use a couch for sitting rather than storage?

At a minimum, make sure there is enough open couch space for everyone in your household to sit comfortably. If your couch keeps getting filled with stuff, you might need a Drop Zone nearby in the form of a shelf or side table.

Possible Living Room Drop Zones

(See Chapter 12 for instructions on setting up a Drop Zone.)

- Toy/Play Drop Zone
- Electronics/Gaming Drop Zone
- Reading Material Drop Zone
- Art Project Drop Zone

LIVING ROOM STORAGE

You will need some sort of storage to make your living room work—otherwise everything will end up on the couch, coffee table, and floor.

Bookcases, sideboards, and TV tables are great options for living room storage. Side tables with drawers or shelves also come in handy. No matter what sort of storage you have, follow the general guideline of storing infrequently used supplies (games, books, electronics) in the hardest-to-reach places.

But living rooms are meant to be used! Keep your favorite items in arm's reach by using activity kits. Examine your living room for activity supplies that are scattered about, whether it's drawing, knitting, gaming, or yoga. Load a basket with the minimum supplies you need for that hobby. Store it under your coffee table or side table, or on an accessible shelf.

Possible Activity Kits for Your Living Room

(A small bin of supplies you use for one hobby)

Crochet Activity Kit: A crochet hook, yarn, and one in-progress project to work on while watching movies

Journaling Activity Kit: A notebook and a few pens, so you can doodle or jot down your thoughts (or to-do lists!)

Yoga Activity Kit: A basket with a mat, block, and strap

THE DINING ROOM

Discerning the Purpose of Your Dining Table

One of my clients had a dining table that was overflowing with clutter. Noticing that a large portion of the clutter was reusable shopping bags, I suggested he add some hooks next to the dining table to hang the bags.

"I already have hooks for bags," he said, leading me ten paces away to a beautifully designed storage closet. On the inside of the door, there were indeed several dusty hooks intended for shopping bags.

"Okay," I said. "And how long have the shopping bags been on the dining table instead?"

He thought for a moment. "How many months ago was Christmas?" It was autumn.

The dining table is where things end up when other storage systems fail. Dining tables are conveniently located in the center of the home, on the footpath between the front door, living room, and kitchen. So, they become a de facto Drop Zone for shopping, paperwork, and any item in the category of "I'll deal with this later."

That's fine until you actually want to eat at your dining table. Then, the pile of clutter might become a barrier. But that really depends on your household. The dining table only needs to function as what you need it for. That doesn't mean it *has* to be pristine all the time.

I grew up in a big family that ate every meal—breakfast, lunch, and dinner—at the kitchen table. My parents, married for decades, still share every meal at the table. As such, that table is ruthlessly decluttered because it needs to hold a lot of food and a lot of people.

My cousin, an only child, also shared daily meals with her parents. "There were three of us, and four chairs," she told me. "So, the fourth chair was for the clutter!"

Now that I'm an adult, I have a dining table, but I use it only for company. At all other times, I eat every single meal on the couch. (Sorry, Mom!) My dining table is just there to look cute and hold a vase of flowers—a motivation compelling enough to make me tidy it once a week.

Throw expectations out the window and consider: What do you actually need from your dining table? Do you want to be the kind of person who eats meals at the table? If so, declutter and decorate until it entices you to sit there.

If not, get creative. What would serve your household best? A dining table could be a desk for homework, a worktable for art, or a household command center. A dining table can also be removed to add more cozy seating, a play area, a plant nook, or anything you like. Instead of feeling sheepish about your dining table clutter, get radical about how you use your space. It's your house, after all.

ORGANIZING THE DINING TABLE

The dining table, by its nature, resists all organizational systems. It's almost as if its job is to attract clutter. Just know and accept this.

If your dining table is piled unfunctionally high with clutter, return to Chapter 12, and follow the steps for decluttering. When that's done, you might want to set up a dining table Drop Zone. Mine is a wicker tray in the center of the table that holds all the bits and bobs that accumulate there: salt and pepper shakers, hot sauce, a vase of flowers, a few pieces of mail.

Something about having those items contained in a tray, rather than a pile, makes it feel like a purposeful design choice rather than an accidental Doom Pile.

Declutter the dining room table weekly to keep it manageable. And while decluttering, pay attention to what pools there. Use this guide to find more permanent homes for frequently found items.

WHERE TO PUT EVERYTHING (INSTEAD OF THE DINING TABLE)

Takeout Paraphernalia	There are two camps on this. My husband's camp, which is to save all of this in a designated space because it may someday be useful. Or my camp, which is to immediately throw it away because I know I won't use it. Find a happy medium by requesting takeout without extra cutlery and condiment packets.
Shopping	If your shopping often pools on your table and never gets unpacked, you might be chasing the high of shopping without the bandwidth to enjoy your purchases. Make a weekly habit of putting away any shopping. The obvious exception is, of course, groceries, which you need! Put away perishable items immediately. Nonperishable items conceivably can wait until you're less exhausted.

Packages	If possible, set up a Drop Zone for dealing with packages in a place that's near your door, but not necessarily the dining room table. Include a trash bin for unrecyclable plastic and a box cutter to break down boxes. If there's a fair distance between your house and the recycling bins, consider using rolling carts to contain broken-down cardboard boxes until you are ready to discard them.
Homework	The kitchen table is ideal for kids completing homework, since you can keep an eye on them as you cook dinner. Keep the space manageable with a homework caddy to contain school supplies. Magazine holders can contain spare paper, as well as homework papers for each child. These can be put away on a shelf or sideboard next to the table when homework is done, or neatly contained at one end of the table.

SPACES FOR WORK & PLAY

Craft Rooms, Home Gyms & Offices

There are a final few semipublic areas of your home: those where you work. Art studios, home gyms, and offices, whether it's an entire room, or just a tiny corner, have one thing in common: a high potential for chaos. And when those spaces get overwhelming, you don't want to use them anymore.

Decluttering is the essential first step of getting these rooms into working shape. It's hard to form an effective organization system without an accurate idea of what you actually have. Once the Doom Piles are (mostly) gone, you can organize by using the same general framework.

Organizing a Workspace by Zones

Any functional workspace—whether it's for business, art, or exercise—can be organized using these three zones.

Clear Zone

Choose a section of workspace or floor that always stays clear—like a no-fly zone, but for clutter. Reset it to default each time you're done using the space. This will act as an anchor of order, and ensure you always have space to work (without shoving stuff out of the way first).

Easy-Grab Zone

Keep frequently used items in accessible places, within arm's reach of your Clear Zone.

Reach-for-It Zone

Keep less-used supplies in harder-to-reach locations, within a few steps of your Clear Zone.

CREATIVE SPACES: ART STUDIOS & CRAFT CORNERS

Creative spaces are my favorite to organize (don't tell any of the other rooms). I've set up a pottery studio in a barn. A remote control car workbench in a garage. A gaming corner. A yoga studio. And many, many craft corners.

Creativity is chaotic by nature. When you have a creative passion, you develop an equal, and sometimes greater, passion for new supplies. Hobby supplies are like little glimpses into your possible future. You could be a person who paints! Or knits! Or welds little circuit boards into electronic creations!

But not all supplies get used, because not all supplies stay fun. Creativity is fickle. Having a cool art supply doesn't guarantee you'll complete a cool project. Capability doesn't equal action, and skill doesn't equal passion. But boy, can those unused supplies really bring on a crisis of failed self-actualization.

We look at them and think, *I really should use my watercolor supplies. Wouldn't it be cool to be a person who does watercolor? Why don't I ever use them? I should keep the supplies, so I'll definitely paint.* And then proceed to never paint one single time in seven years.

Hobbies are meant to be fun. If you start a hobby-related sentence with "I should," the magic is already gone. Give yourself permission to be delightfully capricious and pass on hobby supplies that no longer light you up.

Setting Up a Creative Space by Zone

Clear Zone

You will need a desk, table, or workbench. Designate a section, at least 2 square feet large, that will get cleared and reset after every creative session. You can define this space with washi tape or a drawing board. Sitting down to a craft only to realize you have no clear space to work stymies creativity.

Easy-Grab Zone

Start collecting mugs, vases, and other small open containers. Line them up on the borders of your table, within arm's reach of your Clear Zone. Use those to store pens, paintbrushes, tools, and any other small, frequently used supplies by category. If you run out of space, you can expand into a top drawer on your desk (use drawer dividers!) or expand your flat space by putting a shelf next to your desk.

Reach-for-It Zone

A shelf or cabinet can contain less-used supplies, such as fabric, big tools, or canvases. Most shelves are built for books, not art supplies, so start stocking up on baskets and containers that fit your shelves, which will store items by category and keep them from jumbling with one another.

TROUBLESHOOTING CREATIVE SPACES

ALMOST-DONE PROJECTS

You don't have to keep that project that's been 90 percent done for three years. It's okay to lose passion before the finish line. If you donate it, someone else might finish it. Or, if you have a burst of motivation, do a tour of your studio to find all unfinished projects, and finish them all at once. Satisfying!

BAD RESULTS

Good artists produce much more quantity than quality. You don't have to keep art you dislike, just because you spent time on it. I spent a lot of time with my ex-boyfriends, but that doesn't mean I kept them! Let subpar projects go, and clear space for new projects you love.

SALVAGED ITEMS WITH POTENTIAL

Repeat after me: "Just because I *can* make art with it doesn't mean I *will* make art with it." Artsy items salvaged from thrift stores, Dumpster dives, or your friend's decluttered studio can make great art. But if they've gone unused for longer than a year or two, they're not fueling your creativity. They're just taking up space.

LOTS OF ART SUPPLIES, NO CREATIVE SPACE

I've set up my own art studios in closets, laundry rooms, sheds, and my generous neighbor's attic. But, sometimes, there's just no space at all. Three-tiered carts are a great substitute for a proper studio. Fill the top with an active project, the middle with easy-grab supplies, and the bottom with storage. Wheel it wherever you work.

EXERCISE SPACES: HOME GYMS & YOGA NOOKS

For people with a passion for exercise, home equipment can build up fast. It's big, it's heavy, it's weirdly shaped. And when you get overwhelmed and don't use it, it's transformed from a stationary bike into a reproachful presence.

Generally, you need a very compelling reason to do something as inconvenient as exercise. (I exercise at home in my pajamas, at nine p.m., while watching TV in my living room, because it's the only way convenient enough for me.) Guilt isn't going to be a compelling enough reason, and even when it is, it isn't healthy. Instead, set up an exercise space with choice and enjoyment at its center.

Setting Up Your Exercise Space by Zone

Clear Zone

Clear a section of the floor, big enough to fit a yoga mat or exercise machine. Reset this zone to default after every workout session. Or, if it doesn't inconvenience anyone, just leave the yoga mat unrolled there.

Easy-Grab Zone

Large floor baskets are ideal for holding blocks, bands, and light weights. When you're done, just chuck them back in the basket. If you're near a door, an over-the-door coatrack can also contain exercise bands or bags full of light equipment.

Reach-for-It Zone

A strong shelf or rack can contain heavier equipment. For equipment that's large but not tall (e.g., large blocks, steps, or medicine balls), utilize space under furniture. Storing bulky equipment under the bed, under the couch, or on the floor of a closet can help keep it grabbable but out of footpaths.

TROUBLESHOOTING EXERCISE SPACES

EXERCISE AVOIDANCE

Be honest with yourself about why you're avoiding and try to honor that reason. Set up your exercise spaces for maximum novelty, convenience, and comfort, so that the psychological and physical space between you and exercise is as short as possible. Move your equipment as close as you can to the place you *actually* hang out, without inconveniencing yourself or others. If you can, don't change clothes to exercise—sometimes, that's just another barrier. Remember, a little is better than none. If you can't get yourself to work out for an hour, one minute is better than zero minutes.

EQUIPMENT GUILT

Don't let your exercise spaces become a source of shame. If you don't want to use your equipment anymore, you don't have to keep it. If you know you get bored easily, don't invest in expensive stuff. Remember, your equipment works for you, not the other way around.

WORKSPACES: HOME OFFICES & DESKS

If you work from home, it's hard to maintain work-life boundaries. Video meetings, unloading the dishwasher, doing spreadsheets on the couch, and walking the dog all get mashed together into a work-life soup. Setting up a designated workspace can help physically separate your work life from your home life.

The trick is to make your workspace at least as attractive as your bed or couch—a tall order! Otherwise, you'll never want to work there. You don't have to drop thousands on a custom home workspace to do that. But make sure you have a comfortable chair, adequate warm lighting, and enough storage to contain the chaos.

Setting Up Your Workspace by Zone

Clear Zone

Choose a desk that's comfortable for you. Designate a space large enough for your computer, any other essential work items, a few papers, and a drink—at least 2 square feet. Most important, this space should be reset at the end of each work session. You can designate it with tape or a desk mat. This will help act as an anchor of order when you sit down to work each day.

Easy-Grab Zone

Line up your easy-grab storage along the perimeter of your Clear Zone. You'll need at least a cup or two for pens and tools. A small organizer to hold frequently used electronics and chargers is also handy. A magazine folder or tray can help contain a few paper action items. This is a great place to sort mail or paperwork when you need to deal with it.

Reach-for-It Zone

Use desk drawers to hold office supplies and infrequently needed electronics. If you have more than your desk can hold, add a shelf nearby—especially if you need a printer, shredder, or extra storage space for equipment. You will need some sort of filing system nearby, as well: either file boxes on a shelf or a filing cabinet.

TROUBLESHOOTING OFFICE SPACES

OFFICE OVERSTIMULATION

If the prospect of sitting at your desk nauseates you, and each item on your desk starts to meld with the psychological pressure of your to-do list, you might be overstimulated. Or you might just hate your job, which is a different book. In any case, you will need to make your office more minimal than most. Store supplies and papers away in drawers and baskets on shelves, and keep your desktop completely clear except for your absolutely essential work supplies. If you easily forget what you've stored, label the baskets. Use noise-canceling headphones to reduce sounds, and a weighted lap pad to settle your body.

OFFICE UNDERSTIMULATION

If you feel distracted, tired, or fidgety at your desk, it might not have enough stimulation for you. Everyone has an individual, optimal level of stimulation where they feel able to focus. Increase stimulation by playing music through a speaker or headphones. Switching to a chair (or footrest) that can spin or rock is an old occupational therapist's trick. Keep a basket of small toys or putty for fidgeting. Use a fan or heating pad to keep yourself at an optimal temperature.

ELECTRONIC CORD HELL

Once, on the internet, I suggested that people get rid of their unused power cords. People *really* didn't like that, and one commenter even suggested that I should strip the cords for the valuable copper wire and sell it instead. Flattering that they thought I have the capabilities for a copper resale racket!

If you're an electronics buff, this isn't for you. But if you're just a regular person who is scared to throw away an aux cord you haven't used in six years, it's probably okay to let it go. Follow this guideline: If you don't know what a cord does, it's okay to get rid of it. Old electronics and cords can be dropped off at electronics stores, such as Best Buy, which most American cities have. Some will take them for no fee. Beyond that, I suggest designating a basket, drawer, or pegboard for electronics cords and devices.

PAPER OVERLOAD

If you're underwater with papers (underpaper?) and have no idea what to do, don't despair. Proceed to the next chapter for dealing with paper and other burdensome life skills.

ADDING WARMTH

| Hang Your Art |

If you want your home to feel cozy, you have to fill it with a bit of personality.

The trifecta of a rug, lamp, and drapes will help soften the space. But more than anything, wall decor helps a room feel inviting. Are you one of those with a secret stockpile of unhung art, stuffed in the back of a closet? I implore you to hang that art!

Let me banish your hand-wringing about hanging art.

Don't know how to get it framed? Most art stores have cheap, premade frames.

Don't know how to hang it without damaging the walls? Use a monkey hook, which makes one tiny nail-hole in the wall, but will hold 25 pounds. When you take down the art, fill the hole with a dab of spackle from the hardware store. It will be invisible (so says every single deposit I've gotten back as a renter).

Worried that you don't know how to arrange a gallery wall? I work in an art studio, frequently hang gallery walls, and can tell you that it's a much more slapdash affair than you'd ever imagine. Just slap that art up there. It will be okay.

Tidying Tidbit

Don't let your art be floor clutter. Art is better hung crookedly than it is collecting dust in the back of your closet.

16 Papers, Admin & Life Skills

Building Your Confidence

PILES OF MAIL, MISSED DOCTORS' APPOINTMENTS, UNANSWERED EMAILS. We can organize our physical homes without even touching the internal chaos caused by life skills deficits.

I'm used to getting sheepish looks from my clients after we physically organize their homes. "Now that the closets are done," they say, "can I admit to you that I haven't renewed my car registration in seven years?"

Just because your home is organized doesn't mean your life is in order. Having a messy house, with stacks of papers, can take the wind out of your sails. Forgetting to pay your electricity bill, hidden somewhere in that paper, is what will really sink the ship. Because those tasks are such a part of adulthood, we feel that we should just know how to do them. And when we don't, we're too embarrassed to tell anyone, much less ask for help.

We want to be mature, competent, and formidable, but we're just grown-up, misguided children. Fearing some cosmic retribution if we throw away an important paper, we insist on saving the ten expired Pep Boys coupons stacked up on our dining table for three years. In this chapter, I provide guidance on managing files, mail, communication, appointments, and other onerous life tasks.

SETTING UP A SYSTEM TO MANAGE PAPER

| Decluttering & Organization |

Let's start with the great scourge of adulthood: papers. Whether it's paperwork or mail, paper clutter is the most nauseating of all clutter. **A large stack of papers implies the existence of a large stack of undone tasks, getting embarrassingly more overdue by the second.**

If you have a mountain of papers waiting to be dealt with, gather them into one location. We're going to set up a system to contain those papers.

This paper system closely mirrors your behavior. It's divided into four "stations" that help you deal with paper in stages. Imagine that this is an administrative assembly line in your house.

The Four Paper Stations

1. **Paper Drop Zone:** where new papers live
2. **The Workstation:** where papers get dealt with
3. **The Waiting Room:** where papers wait to get filed
4. **The Files:** where papers are stored permanently

CATEGORIZING PAPERS: A GUIDE

USE THIS GUIDE TO HELP MAKE DECISIONS ABOUT PAPERS IN THE UPCOMING STEPS.

DON'T KEEP	DEAL WITH	KEEP FOR FILING
Paid bills	Unpaid bills	Vehicle records
Junk mail	Letters that require answers	Education records
Papers from your days in school	Paperwork to complete	Financial records
		Identification documents

Don't Keep	Deal With	Keep for Filing
Coupons you won't use in the next 60 days Any documents from the third column that has an electronic copy	Coupons you'll use soon	Health records Home/rent records Professional documents Warranties Sentimental *(more on this later)*

STATION #1: THE PAPER DROP ZONE: AN UNFILTERED INBOX

Find the spot in your house where you already dump your papers—for me, next to my front door. There's the location for your Paper Drop Zone. This will require minimal changes to your behavior. Put a tray or magazine holder there. Drop your mail and papers in there as they come into the house.

How big should the Drop Zone be? That depends: How scary do you find piles of paper, and how hard is it for you to deal with them? If you're very avoidant, choose a smaller container. Smaller piles of paper are less scary.

Moving Your Papers to the Next Station

Once your Drop Zone is full (no piling or smooshing allowed), it's time to deal with the papers inside.

Sort your papers into two categories:

Papers You Don't Need (Junk Mail, Etc.)	Papers You Need to Deal With (or Save)
Recycle promptly.	Keep and move to the next station.

STATION #2: THE WORKSTATION: PAPERS YOU NEED TO DEAL WITH (OR SAVE)

Move the papers you need to keep/save from your Drop Zone to your Workstation.

Your Paper Workstation should be set up as near to your natural workstation as possible. If you use a desk, do it there. You can use a magazine holder to contain your papers until you're ready to deal with them. A tray will work, too, but I like standing folders because you can't easily pile stuff on top of them.

Alternatively, if you don't work at a desk, sandwich your papers in your laptop, so you'll see them next time you sit down to work. (Beware this method if you're likely to just set the papers aside and forget about them.)

Moving Your Papers to the Next Station

Once every week or two, deal with papers at your Workstation. Sort your papers into two categories:

PAPERS TO DEAL WITH	PAPERS TO FILE
Papers that require action Do those tasks promptly and discard the papers. If you struggle with this, we'll work on that later in the chapter.	*Papers that don't require action but need to be saved* These papers will need to be filed. Move them to the Filing Waiting Room.

STATION #3: THE FILING WAITING ROOM: PAPERS THAT NEED TO BE FILED (SOON)

If you can promptly file your papers right after dealing with them, you don't really need this step. But if you're like me, and prefer to file in

batches, a Filing Waiting Room will keep papers tidy until their appointed time.

Set up a tray or folder on top of, or conveniently near, your filing location. Dump papers in there when you've finished with them at your Workstation. File them when the folder gets full. If you feel psychological pain about filing, you've waited too long: Strike now before it gets worse! We'll set up that filing location in the next step.

STATION #4 THE FILING SYSTEM: FUNCTIONAL PAPER STORAGE

Only about 5 percent of the papers from your Paper Drop Zone typically make it to permanent storage. **Before permanently storing a paper, really consider if you will ever conceivably need to reference that paper again, or whether a digital photo of the paper would suffice.**

Here's a hard truth for the new adults: You need files. An accordion folder might have worked okay in college, but adults have too much administrative baggage for one flimsy folder. At minimum, you need a large filing box. More realistically, you need at least a small filing cabinet. Store it in a corner or closet where access will never be blocked; if you can't get to it easily, you'll never file those papers.

Now file! Sort your papers into files by category, using the "Keep for filing" column of the table on page 222. No need for elaborate alphabetical systems or fancy labels; if the folder has a name on it, and the stuff inside fits that category, it's organized enough.

A NOTE ON DIGITIZING

Digitizing your paper files is a wonderful way to reduce paper clutter. To make that work, you will need a scanner (or a scanner app on your phone). But remember, scanning papers does add another task to your to-do list. Make sure your scanner is set up and very easy to access. Be honest with yourself about your capacity to keep up with a digitizing system. If you do decide to digitize, make sure to store the scans in a specific file on your computer and give each item a distinctive name.

TROUBLESHOOTING YOUR PAPER SYSTEM

To keep chaos at bay, you'll need to conduct regular paper-sorting sessions. Depending on the influx of papers, it works well to do this every one to two weeks. Most people in chaos loathe this task because it's a huge undertaking with a ton of papers. But with small stacks of papers sorted regularly, it doesn't feel like such a big deal.

Look out for barriers to maintaining your paper system. If you notice that you're consistently avoiding dealing with papers, get curious about what's causing the avoidance. Be nonjudgmental and look for solutions.

THE BARRIER: YOU NEED TO DEAL WITH A HUGE BACKLOG OF PAPERS

You might have a monstrously large collection of papers—too much for that cute little filing system! But no matter how many papers you have, they get dealt with in the same way: one at a time. (Or by throwing them all in the recycling bin and damning the consequences.)

Gather a stack of papers and take it to a comfortable spot. A dining table, couch, or (my favorite) a stretch of open floor is ideal. Get cozy, and remember, you are a strong and competent adult! Or if you aren't yet, you're getting stronger and more competent with each paper you deal with.

Sort your papers, one by one, into the categories we discussed a few pages ago. If you have lots of papers, it's helpful to keep a few boxes (one for recycling, one for dealing with, one for filing) to keep papers contained while you work. You might need to do multiple sessions of this. Just be patient with yourself.

ENVIRONMENTAL BARRIERS

We love an environmentally conscious person. And tearing every bit of plastic out of an envelope so it can be recycled—very responsible! But you have nine hundred envelopes to shred. It will take you days to separate out all the plastic, and you're already crying. Give it up, baby. Throw away anything that can't be easily recycled and move on. You can recycle envelopes when you're not up to your ears in credit card statements.

SHREDDING BARRIERS

Shredding your mail so your identity doesn't get stolen—great idea! But do you even have a shredder? And if so, do you have the bandwidth to sit in front of it for an hour while you slowly shred everything with your initials? Do you have the emotional fortitude to not throw the shredder across the room when it gets jammed? Be honest.

I don't want your personal information to be stolen and exploited. I really don't want that. But let's be realistic. What are the chances someone will break into your trash, rip open the bags, find your name on your Old Navy coupon, and do something with that name? Only you know how dangerous your life is, so only you could say.

If your life doesn't seem that dangerous, it's probably safe to take the usual precautions. Cut up old credit cards. Shred or black out anything with your social security number, your bank account number, or any other highly sensitive information.

I take my chances with the rest, so I guess my identity is open to being stolen. I can't imagine why they'd want it. If you're still nervous, throw everything into a trash bag and take it to your local package shipping store, such as UPS. Often, they offer industrial shredding services by the pound.

INITIATION BARRIERS

If you just can't seem to get started on sorting your papers, don't despair. It is a highly nonpreferred task. You may need to reward yourself each time you sort your papers, with whatever floats your boat. Or associate paper sorting with a pleasurable activity, such as a fun snack or watching an episode of your favorite show.

Above all, don't "should" all over yourself. It doesn't work. Try sorting just one single paper and see how you feel. One is better than none.

SENTIMENTAL BARRIERS

If you're an especially sentimental person (guilty!), you might find yourself with more sentimental papers than you have room for. But you have options. Very precious sentimental papers can be framed and displayed as decor.

If an item is only of moderate sentimental value, consider taking a picture of it on your phone. Then, place the paper in the recycling bin. How does it feel? Sometimes, having a digital copy to honor the paper is enough to help you feel okay letting it go.

COGNITIVE BARRIERS

Brain fog—which we can define as powerful mental fatigue—is a common accompaniment to illness. At times, my brain fog is so severe that I can barely read, much less interpret complex information. I have developed a few helpful (if a little weird) strategies for managing administrative tasks with brain fog.

Strategies for Managing Brain Fog

Wake Up Your Brain by Waking Your Body

Briefly stimulate your mind by giving your body invigorating sensory input. Eat something crunchy. Drink something cold and fizzy. Go out in the chilly air. Splash cold water, or spray cold mist, on your face. Sing *la, la, la* loudly. Spin around in your office chair. Or my favorite: Gently but firmly pat your own face as if you're trying to wake up someone who's passed out. Sometimes, this is enough to help me feel focused for a few moments.

Sprint Focus, Then Take Breaks

Sometimes, the prospect of playing a game can focus me. I will set a timer for three minutes, then try to sort as many papers (or emails) as I can during that time, racing the clock. Then, I will set a timer for five minutes and take a mini-nap. Repeat.

Read Out Loud (Loudly)

If you're alone, try reading out loud. Not quietly; loudly. You don't have to scream, but read in a fully audible voice. Repeat until the information makes sense to you. Sometimes, getting the information audibly and visually at the same time helps. There are also programs that will read digital information out loud to you.

Enlist a Helper

Ask a trusted friend with good focus (or, at least, better than yours) to come over and help you do some administrative work. They can sort papers and only hand you the important ones. They can also highlight important information for you with a marker.

UNDONE TASKS: PAPER'S EVIL COUSIN

Oftentimes, people aren't really avoiding their paper clutter. They're avoiding the tasks associated with paper clutter. Bills, doctors' appointments, car registration renewal: Those are the tasks likely to send me voluntarily packing into the abyss to hide in the dark.

It's said the only things we can be sure of are death and taxes. At times, I thought I would rather have the former than the latter. Administrative tasks can feel like insurmountable obstacles, especially for people in early adulthood. They are part of the warm, mystical world of adult competence, and you are outside in the cold wind of childlike confusion.

Remember that no one knows how to do *anything* until they do it. At one point, you didn't know how to tie your shoes, and you felt incompetent watching everybody swish their hands over a shoe and tie it with ease. It seemed impossible, until you learned. And now, you do it just as easily.

Administrative tasks are the same. You feel incompetent simply because you don't have enough practice. Once you get over the learning curve, you'll be just as competent as anyone else. Maybe more! Maybe you have a secret, undiscovered talent for canceling unwanted subscriptions by phone. Let's find out.

HOW TO CATCH UP ON AN OVERWHELMING TO-DO LIST

STEP ONE: MAKE A (STRATEGIC) LIST

Undone tasks seem more threatening while free-floating in the ether of your brain, only surfacing when you're trying to fall asleep. Instead of letting them float around and terrorize you, contain them in a list. I know, a list is conventional advice. And a list won't fix things. But it is a starting place. List every single undone task you can think of, as if it were a cathartic brain dump.

STEP TWO: PRIORITIZE THE LIST

Now, take a moment to banish panic. Emotions are like a wave. They start slow, reach a peak, then taper off. If you turn away from your to-do list now, at the moment of greatest panic, you'll never get a chance to feel the fear recede. **Try to sit with your anxiety for a moment, if you can, and begin sorting the list by priority.**

First: Prioritize Needs over Wants

Go through your list. Tasks that **need** to be done (e.g., paying a bill) should stay on the list.

If the task is only something you **want** to do (e.g., using a coupon), eliminate it for now.

Optional: Rewrite the List

Rewrite the list with only tasks that **need** to be done.

This will help you feel less overwhelmed by choices.

(If you like, put the tasks you **want** to do on a second list for when you have more capacity.)

Next: Circle Anything Urgent

Urgent Tasks Are:

Time Sensitive: They have an upcoming deadline or are already overdue.

Impactful: They have a serious impact on your health or quality of life, such as a doctor's appointment.

> **Consequential:** There will be trouble if they go undone, such as an unpaid bill or nonrenewed driver's license.
>
> **Barrier Tasks:** These tasks are holding up another task. For example, you need to order your transcripts before you can register for school.

STEP THREE: YOU CAN DO IT, BABY

Of those urgent tasks, choose the one that is easiest to do. If none of them is easy, try randomizing your choice by flipping a coin to choose between two. Or write them all on small pieces of paper and pick one out of the bowl. Or assign each one a number from 1 to 12, and roll a pair of dice to choose.

Once you've completed your most urgent tasks, return to your to-do list and use the same method to complete nonurgent tasks. When you've done those, move on to your wanted tasks. Pay attention to any barriers that come up.

TROUBLESHOOTING TASK AVOIDANCE

| Why You're Always Behind |

Just because the method for knocking out a to-do list is simple doesn't mean you are simple! You are psychologically complex, and your brain is likely to throw some roadblocks in your way. Let's take a nonjudgmental look at those barriers to see where accommodations can help.

EMOTIONAL BARRIERS

When you think, "I've got to deal with that task," what emotion comes up? Emotions aren't always rational, but they do give you valuable information about your inner state, which gives you information to create a solution.

If you feel scared, try to identify, specifically, what you're afraid of.

Are you afraid of making a mistake? Missing a deadline? Facing the consequences of inattention? Often, fears are more intense in the periphery. When you face your fear squarely by naming it, you usually feel a flash of intense anxiety, followed by relief as you recognize the fear is manageable.

If you feel confused about how to do a task, go on a fact-finding mission. Confusion and ambiguity are the fuel of anxiety. Information is the antidote. Phone a trusted friend and ask their advice. Look up "how to do [hated task]" online. Go to any websites associated with the task, and do some sleuthing. The more information you have, the more confident you'll feel.

If you feel embarrassed that you haven't done the task already, you're in good company! I once had a client with a grossly expired driver's license. She was too humiliated to renew it because she was sure she'd be ridiculed by the clerks at the city office. Come to find out, the clerks didn't even care that her license was overdue. They just wanted to get their job done and were very generous in helping her navigate the process.

INITIATION & CLOSING BARRIERS

The two hardest parts of doing a boring admin task? Getting started and finishing. The middle is easy. If you struggle to start a task, start by identifying the first, tiniest step to beginning. For example, if you need to run an errand to a place you've never been, start by mapping the route.

If you struggle with finishing the final steps of a task, do a "Closing Tour" where you clump a few undone tasks together and knock them out. However, beware of our old enemy, false optimization! Don't wait so long to finish a few tasks at once, in an optimally efficient route, that you don't even do the tasks at all. A task done inefficiently is better than a task not done at all.

INADEQUATE SUPPORT

Some people with executive dysfunction just aren't able to easily execute lots of nonpreferred tasks on their own. They might want the task done, but they just can't get started. That's part of the disability.

If that's you, it's important not to berate yourself. Shame will only isolate you. Ideally, enlist a helper to assist you regularly. Ask a friend, family member, or professional whether they can meet with you monthly to review your undone tasks and help you knock them out. This is a very reasonable accommodation for people with executive dysfunction.

BABY STEPS TO HELP INITIATE TASKS	
Calls/ Emails	Look up the phone number of the person you need to call and save it in your phone.
	Write a script of what you will say on a phone call.
	After reading an email you're not ready to deal with, mark it as unread, so you'll have a visual signal that it's still unanswered.
	Designate a "communications" block of time to knock out emails, calls, and texts all at once.
Errands	Look up on a map the place that you need to visit.
	Drive by the place you need to visit, as reconnaissance.
	Call the place you need to visit to get information on what to do when you arrive. Or look up FAQs on its website.
	Bring a friend to run errands together.
	Make follow-up appointments in person, ideally recurring so you don't need to remember to call and schedule again.
Admin/ Paperwork	Put the paperwork in the place where you will complete it, with no pressure to fill it out yet.
	Just start by opening the paperwork and filling out no-brainer information, such as your name and address.

MAINTAINING COMPETENCE OVER TIME

Systems for Managing Admin in the Long Run

The sad fact about knocking out a to-do list is that tasks will just start piling up again. That's administrative entropy, darlin'. What's done doesn't stay done forever.

Instead of waiting for the dark to close in again, create a system for managing tasks as they come up. And remember, it's normal for your workload to get overwhelming at times. Sometimes, lots of tasks just come in batches. It's not necessarily your fault. (And even if it is, you can fix it.)

SYSTEM #1: THEMED WEEKDAYS

Choose an administrative "theme" for each day of the week. On that day, deal with one of the logistical categories of adulthood. Try to make it fit your schedule. For example, if you're already out and about on Tuesdays, make that your errand day. If you're already home with your computer on Thursdays, make that your admin day. This is the most structured option, and as such is the hardest to maintain over time, so choose wisely.

Themed Weekdays Example

Monday: Communications (answer calls, texts, and emails)
Tuesday: Errands (shopping, in-person tasks, and appointments)
Wednesday: House tasks (cleaning and lingering house projects)
Thursday: Admin (tasks to complete on a computer)
Friday: Paper (sorting mail and filing)

SYSTEM #2: THE WEEKLY SPRINT

Designate an hour each week to knock out as many avoided tasks as possible. The principle is the same as walking over hot coals: If you go fast, you won't feel it. By the time it starts stinging, it's already done. The benefit of this system is that you never have to wonder or plan when you'll knock out a hated task; you already know you have a designated fail-safe in your schedule. Ideally, it works best to do this at the beginning or end of your workweek.

SYSTEM #3: THE MONTHLY MARATHON

This is the same as the weekly sprint but less often and more intense. **Let your lingering tasks build up until a designated day of the month; then,**

deal with them all at once. If you have a weekday off work, that day is ideal. Knock out all your lingering tasks that day—from calls to paperwork to getting your car's oil changed. This option takes quite a bit of focus and stamina, but you get a huge payoff.

KEEPING TRACK OF TASKS & APPOINTMENTS

| There Is No Perfect System |

There is no perfect planner, calendar, or to-do list keeper. Or rather, there is only one: the one you'll use.

If you have a tricky brain, the chances are pretty low that you will find one perfect method for tracking your time and tasks in perpetuity. That doesn't mean you're doomed. You just need to be flexible.

This is how it will go. You will find a new system, have a glorious honeymoon with it, and it will work for a while.

Then, that system will get stale, boring, or overwhelming. And you'll start to avoid it.

Instead of hating yourself at that moment, just say good-bye to the old system, with a kiss. Then, switch to a new method. Generally, my clients like to switch back and forth between electronic and paper methods—it keeps things fresh.

Above all, keep it simple. Elaborate setups with color coding and sticky notes can be fun at first. But the system will only last as long as they remain fun. Release the pressure to find the perfect system and use the imperfect one, whatever that is.

Don't Overdo It:
Minimal Requirements for Life Organization

1. A digital calendar (e.g., Google calendar or Outlook) accessible by your computer and phone
2. Something on/in which to write to-do lists (e.g., a

notebook or a dry-erase board posted near your door, so you can see tasks as you leave the house)

3. Nice to have while they work for you:

    - A digital to-do list (e.g., Notion, Microsoft OneNote, or the Notes App)
    - A paper calendar that can fit in your purse or backpack

17 Routines That Work

Building Home Care Habits

IT'S TIME TO PUT IT ALL TOGETHER.

We've tackled every area of disorganization in your life, one by one. But cleaning problems don't come one by one, do they? They come all at once.

There are dozens of chores to remember, not just one. Maddeningly, they all need to be handled at different intervals. Managing every single chore over time, with their overlapping frequencies and varying levels of priority, is the real trial of home care. Holding it all in your brain isn't easy, especially if your brain doesn't work too well in the first place, or it used to but no longer does.

Enter the home care routine. Wait, don't run away! Home care routines are pretty boring stuff, which is why I'm a staunch moderate on routine. Not all functional adults have, or need, home care routines. Some people simply:

1. Notice a thing is dirty.
2. Clean it.
3. Notice a task is undone.
4. Do it.

If that works for you, feel free to disregard this chapter. But if you're like the people I work with, in the absence of routine, you:

1. Will not notice.
2. Will not clean.
3. Or you will notice and desperately want to clean, but will be too tired to get out of bed.

If home care doesn't come naturally to you, a routine can be a safeguard. It's a strategic plan that prevents forgetting. It takes the guesswork out of what and when to clean. You don't have to spontaneously remember to do chores, or agonize about when to do them. You just follow the plan, doing chores at the appointed time.

Coming Up

Why You're Bad at Routine

- Memory difficulties
- Trusting experts over experiences
- Good habit overload
- Routinus interruptus
- Insufficient structure

WHY YOU'RE BAD AT ROUTINE

Troubleshooting Barriers

Grappling for a sense of control over your life, it's easy to resolve to *get into a* routine. I love that phrase: get into a routine. As though routine is a bus or a car, something that you can just put your body inside and be carried away. That said, when a routine works, that is what it's like. You're carried away by its purpose, along for the ride.

But on the front end, forming a routine isn't so simple. Many people

who crave routine find it devilishly tricky to stick to. If you struggle with routine, let's troubleshoot your barriers first.

BARRIER #1: YOU CAN'T REMEMBER NEW HABITS

I'm going to vastly oversimplify (look away, scientists).

There are two kinds of memory: working and long-term. Your working memory is like a waiting room for your long-term memory. New tasks and desired habits live in your working memory. Once you repeat a new habit enough times, it is admitted to your long-term memory.

Once something enters your long-term memory, recalling it becomes mostly automatic. That's when a routine feels like a routine, not a to-do list that you're struggling to follow.

Neurotypical, healthy people might find it fairly easy, after a week or two, to remember a new habit. But if you struggle with memory, you might find it takes weeks or even months for a routine to feel automatic.

It's important to be patient with yourself during the routine-building process, and surround yourself with as many reminders as possible to decrease your cognitive load.

METHODS TO HELP YOU REMEMBER A NEW ROUTINE

Visual	Print your new routine on bright paper, with a large font, and post it in several highly visible places in the house. Screenshot your new routine and save it as your phone's background.
Auditory	Set your phone, smart speaker, or smart watch with auditory or buzzing reminders at strategic times.
Kinesthetic	Put a piece of string or a rubber band around your wrist. Put something in the doorway of the room where you're supposed to do the task (e.g., an obstacle or a strip of painter's tape on the floor), to remind your body to stop and do the new habit.
Active	Print and laminate your routine so you can check off the tasks with a dry-erase marker each day. Record your routine in a spreadsheet and track your progress each day to keep score.
Supportive	Enlist a friend to help you remember your new tasks and, if necessary, do them with you until you've gotten the hang of it.

BEWARE HABITUATION!

HABITUATION IS YOUR BRAIN'S SUPERPOWER: STRATEGIC IGNORING

If you noticed every sight, smell, and sound, every second of the day, you would be absolutely overwhelmed with information. To help you focus, your brain automatically filters out familiar information. The longer you see, hear, or smell something, the less you'll notice it.

In this way, you learn not to hear the fridge running, or the weird thumping sound the dryer makes, or the fire alarm beeping at you every ninety seconds to change its batteries. You learn not to see the box of clutter sitting in the corner. You learn not to smell the malodorous reek of your beloved dog's breath. Because it's so familiar, your brain thinks it isn't noteworthy.

HABITUATION WORKS AGAINST YOU WHEN YOU WANT TO MAKE AN INTENTIONAL REMINDER

After you hear the alarm a few times, your brain is like, *Great, got it, we can ignore that now.*

After you see the sticky note on your mirror for a few days, your brain is like, *Hasn't that sticky note been there since before I moved in?*

To fight habituation, you need to be flexible with your reminder method. If you notice—well, that you're *not* noticing—it's time to change it up. Switch to a new alarm sound. Make the visual reminder bigger and more obnoxious and change its location. Do whatever you need to do to show your brain *Hey, this reminder is new and exciting and worthy of attention!*

BARRIER #2: TRUSTING EXPERTS OVER LIFE EXPERIENCE

Creating a routine from scratch is no easy task for an addled brain. That's why we turn to the glamorous higher powers of cleaning—such as experts, magazines, and influencers—for their routines. If it's good enough for them, it's good enough for you!

The problem is, the lifestyle these sources present are aspirational, aimed at getting your home as clean as possible. Those routines will have you dusting your baseboards and degreasing your stove hood once per week. (When was the last time you even thought about the necessity of degreasing your stove hood? I bet it wasn't this week. Or last.)

Taking advice about developing a cleaning routine from professional cleaners is like taking advice on an exercise regimen from Olympic athletes. The advice is not bad. In fact, it's really good.

But you are not a professional. You are an amateur, and that's okay! You need an amateur routine: one that acknowledges your barriers, gives you just enough structure to get by, and keeps the house from falling down around your ears.

BARRIER #3: GOOD HABIT OVERLOAD

When creating a new routine, you might be tempted to slip in every single good habit you've neglected over the years. One of my clients, tempted by the siren song of "New Year, New Me," brought me her handwritten New Year Self-Improvement Plan.

It contained no less than sixty items, ranging from mopping to exercise to journaling to clean eating to sustainability to healthy relationships. I felt stressed just looking at it.

"This is so well intentioned," I said, trying to be gentle. "But, realistically, you might be able to do, like, three of these things, *maybe*."

"But I really need to get it together!" she insisted. "And I'm really motivated."

But it isn't just about motivation. Motivation isn't that powerful. Relying on motivation to fuel tons of new habits results in the classic January phenomenon, in which you perform thirty-one days of glorious new healthy habits, followed by a crash, and then eleven months of the same old shit.

We just aren't built to change all at once. When we see people pull off massive behavioral changes, it's usually accompanied by a total change in life circumstances, such as going to rehab, joining the military, or experiencing a life-threatening illness. The circumstances force the change, not the motivation.

My client was able to start with her highest-priority new habits: cooking *most* meals at home, going to therapy, and maintaining the minimum standard of cleanliness at her house. After three months, those habits were locked in. She was able to add a few more: daily walks, buying less, and writing a journal entry at least once per week. **By slowly, gently building new habits, she was able to change sustainably over time.**

When life is challenging, you don't need to drink lemon water and meditate for thirty minutes every morning in the immediate future. You need clean underwear and food in your fridge. Focus on what really matters. Leave the ambitious extras to a future, better-equipped version of yourself.

BARRIER #4: ROUTINUS INTERRUPTUS

We've all been there. You've got a good routine going for a few days, then boom. Disruption hits. It doesn't matter what it is: You go on vacation, or get a sore throat, or switch to a different work schedule. Or you just get bored of doing the same thing. And suddenly, your winning streak is over, and you feel like a failure.

Luckily, a good routine isn't like a spaceship leaving for a distant universe. If you miss it, your chance isn't gone forever. A functional routine is more like a train running on a circular route. You can hop off and hop on at any time. It's flexible. If you miss it—even for a long period of time—your opportunity to board is going to come around again, and again, and again.

When I was young, I thought a successful routine meant I would do the same thing every day for my entire life until (I guess) I died. I still haven't managed that yet.

But I've had very helpful routines that lasted only a few weeks. They were no less helpful because they were temporary.

Routines will change as your preferences, your schedule, and your interests change too. Deal with interrupted routines without judgment. Assess what you liked about your old routine. Salvage what was working and adjust what wasn't.

BARRIER #5: INSUFFICIENT STRUCTURE

Counterintuitively, it's easier to add routine to a life that's already full and busy than it is to add it to a life that's very open and free. Cleaning tasks can be easily piggybacked onto existing schedules: work, school, bedtime, and meals.

But for people who work for themselves, work from home, or don't (or can't) work at all, especially those who have very loose, irregular schedules, imposing a cleaning routine is actually very difficult because there's no external structure to attach it to. All the structure has to be self-motivated. Creating and sticking to each hour of your personal daily itinerary is no easy feat for people living in chaos.

If that's you, it might be time to consider adding a little external structure to your life. External structure is any commitment that requires you to be somewhere at a specific time. Here are a few factors that can add structure to your life.

Factors That Add Structure to Your Life

Classes

Whether you attend school as a full-time student, or just take a weekly class on a subject that interests you, you will be forced to create a routine around the timing of your classes. Think beyond the academic. It doesn't matter if the class is on accounting, yoga, or pottery. If it's at the same time every week, it can give your life structure.

Work

Set work hours are the best—and most conventional way—to create natural structure around your time, especially sleep, meals, and errands. This works best when your work hours occur on the same days, and at the same times, every week.

Appointments

If you attend regular appointments for your health, see how many can be set at regular recurring times. You can piggyback crucial errands onto that schedule. For example, if you have to leave the house to go to therapy, you might be able to pick up groceries at the store on the way home.

If you're worried that you look like you've been crying, just wear sunglasses into the store, like a movie star!

Social

A weekly social event can also serve the same purpose as long as it's recurring and regular. This could be anything: a trivia night, a volunteer gig, or looking after an ailing relative.

Pet Care

I don't advise getting a pet just to pull yourself out of chaos. But if you have the capacity, caring for a pet is a wonderful way to add structure to your life. Feeding them and walking them at regular times provides a framework from which to plan your day. Just be thoughtful in your decision to get a pet. There's always a chance that they'll bring more chaos, not less! (See next chapter.)

These structure makers aren't effortless. They require time and energy (both mental and physical) and, in many cases, money. As such, they may be beyond your current capabilities. But if you feel like your main problem isn't a lack of resources, but that you're floundering in a structureless existence, it really is worth considering adding one of these commitments to your life.

BARRIER #6: INSUFFICIENT SUPPORT

If you feel hopeless at forming habits because you fail over and over, it's possible that you're just inadequately supported. Some people need, in addition to many visual and auditory reminders, helpers. Helpers come in the form of people in your life whose job it is to remind you about the habit you're supposed to be doing, and, if necessary, to do that thing with you until you've truly gotten the hang of it. Consider adding some helpers to safeguard your new routine.

Routine Helpers

Mental Health Therapists

If your mental health is a major barrier to forming new routines, a therapist can help diagnose the cause of your distress, assist you in recovering, and support you as you form new habits.

Occupational Therapists

An OT's job is to help develop and maintain life skills through illness and disability. They can support you in identifying barriers, developing routines, and using assistive technology.

Partners, Friends & Family

It can be uncomfortable to think of yourself as someone who needs caregiving, and vulnerable to let your loved ones help you. Even so, the people you see the most are the best positioned to support you in forming new routines. Be specific when asking for their assistance: How can they support you? Reminders? Doing the routine with you? Make sure to specify what is and isn't helpful.

Tidying Tidbit

- Surround yourself with plenty of reminders to keep your new habits in mind.
- Expert-endorsed cleaning routines might not be the best fit for exhausted people.
- Don't cram your new routine with tons of good habits; just pick a few.
- Don't abandon a routine just because it got offtrack. You can always restart.
- Adding external structure to your life can help prop up your routines.
- Make sure you have enough support to make new habits happen.

MINIMAL ROUTINE OPTIONS

Four Methods for Keeping Up with Your Home

Following are four options for putting domestic routine into your life, with increasing levels of structure. None of these options aims for perfection. They prioritize function. Browse these options and choose which seems best for you. Customize it. Abandon it when it stops working and choose a new one. Above all, stay flexible.

ROUTINE #1: THE BASICS METHOD

Best for Times of Great Struggle, when You're Just Keeping Things from Getting Worse

This method is best for you if you're struggling, not only with home care, but with basic self-care, such as eating, sleeping, and showering. As we've discussed, if your basic needs aren't met, you don't have much of a chance of keeping a functional home (and even if you do, it isn't very healthy!). Think of this method as a disaster recovery plan to help stabilize you—and your home.

How to Do It: Create natural structure in your day with sleep and meals. Keep it simple by scheduling two-hour windows for waking up, eating meals, and going to bed. Then, piggyback your crucial home care and self-care tasks onto that structure.

Time	Routine	Add One Task
6 to 8 a.m.	Get out of bed.	Brush teeth.
8 to 10 a.m.	Eat breakfast.	Put away clean dishes.
Noon to 2 p.m.	Eat lunch.	Take out trash *or* do a little laundry.
7 to 9 p.m.	Eat dinner.	Wash dirty dishes.
9 to 11 p.m.	Go to bed.	Shower.

Go at your own pace. This method doesn't include everything it takes to keep a well-functioning home. That's a problem for Future You. But it does cover the most urgent needs of home and self-care. It will help you establish a baseline level of functioning. Once you have your baseline down, you can start adding more household tasks to your routine.

Add new habits, one by one, as you're ready, such as:

Cleaning the bathroom, *a little*
Cleaning the kitchen, *somewhat*
Cleaning the floors, *one small section at a time*
Decluttering Doom Piles, *even itty-bitty ones, a bit at a time*

Remember, a little cleaning is better than no cleaning at all! All-or-nothing thinking is a barrier to getting things done.

ROUTINE #2: THE MENU METHOD: BASICS + CHORE MENU

Best for People Who Can Handle a Little More Than the Basics but Still Need Flexibility

This method is best for you if your basic needs are met, but you're still struggling to keep up with your home. Because choice is at the center of this plan, it's a good option for people who don't like to feel too constricted by routine. If you find yourself internally rebelling against demands and obligations (even if it was you who created the obligation!), this menu method could be a good fit for you.

How to Do It: Keep the basics under control with a daily routine, in the left column. Then, each day, choose one task from the menu on the right. The menu is a list of more intensive home care tasks. Remember, it's a menu, not a to-do list, so it preserves your sense of personal choice every day. You get to choose. If you can't choose one (or don't want to), randomize your choice by flipping a coin, rolling dice, or picking one task out of a jar.

Daily Tasks	Home Care Menu
Daily self-care (food and hygiene) Unload, load, and run dishwasher at some point before bedtime. Choose one task from menu.	Wash, dry, or fold laundry. Throw away trash or recycling. Clean one bathroom fixture. Tidy up a room. Wipe kitchen counters. Declutter a surface. Vacuum one room. Clean something random (baseboards, windowsills, windows, appliances, etc.).

ROUTINE #3: THE DAILY THEME METHOD

| Best for People with Too Little Structure & Too Much to Do |

This method is great for those who don't have a lot of structure in their lives but still feel overwhelmed with lots to do—like freelance workers or people who work from home. **It's the opposite of multitasking. Instead of jumping from task to task and getting overwhelmed, you group related tasks on a single day of the week.**

How to Do It: Designate a day of the week and choose a domestic theme. Try to tailor this around your schedule. For example, tasks that are more time-consuming are best done on days when you're usually home all day. If you miss a day of the week, just pick it up again in the following week.

Day	Theme	Options
Sunday	Kitchen	Clean out fridge, deal with dirty dishes, or clean sink and countertops.
Monday	Admin	Deal with papers, mail, or digital communications.
Tuesday	Trash	Search your house for trash and recycling or take out the trash.
Wednesday	Tidying	Declutter a Doom Pile or tidy up a room.

DAY	THEME	OPTIONS (continued)
Thursday	Floors	Sweep, vacuum, and/or mop floors.
Friday	Bathroom	Clean a bathroom sink, toilet, or bathtub.
Saturday	Laundry	Wash, dry, fold, or put away laundry.

Anxiety Relief Bonus: I find that this method helps overwhelmed people feel less anxious because it builds confidence and self-trust. When your brain is full of a free-floating, anxious swarm of undone tasks, it can be easy to lose confidence in your ability to get any of them done. But when people follow this routine, they have designated times to handle each task.

So, if on Tuesday, you notice your bathroom is dirty, no need to feel anxious about when you will be able to clean it. You already know you will handle bathroom cleaning on Friday. You can trust yourself to do it. It's off your mental to-do list for now.

ROUTINE #4: THE CALENDAR METHOD

Best for People Who Thrive on Structure but Struggle to Remember Unscheduled Tasks

This is the most labor-intensive, demanding routine option. It's best for people who already have the everyday basics of home care and self-care under control. **If you know you thrive on routine, but struggle to remember incidental, infrequent deep-cleaning tasks, this is a good option for you. It tracks tasks on a daily, weekly, monthly, and annual basis.** Experiment with scheduling crucial home care tasks on your calendar to help keep track of them.

DAILY TASKS	WEEKLY TASKS
Take care of these tasks at mealtimes each day.	*Do one task each weekday, or a big session on the weekend.*
Daily self-care (food and hygiene)	Deal with mail, papers, shopping, or admin tasks.
Unload, load, and run dishwasher every evening.	Bathroom mini-clean

Daily Tasks	Weekly Tasks
Pet care (food and walking) Mini-tidy (take 5 minutes to throw away trash and put items away)	Kitchen mini-clean Laundry Vacuum
Monthly Tasks	**Annual/Biannual Tasks**
Every weekend, do one monthly task. Thorough kitchen clean Thorough bathroom clean Thorough floor clean (vacuum and mop) Doom Pile resolution Wipe surfaces.	*Do these tasks as needed.* Home maintenance (e.g., repairs) Clean appliances. Clean a weird thing (under the stove, under the fridge, behind the couch, baseboards, windowsills, etc.).

Keep It Flexible: If you manage to follow this routine, your home will be very well cared for! So, it's not a big deal to skip a weekly or monthly task every now and then. That's what makes this routine resistant to disruption. It's not a calendar to be followed; it's just a tracking method to keep chores from passing beyond your realm of awareness.

GOOD ROUTINES AREN'T PERFECT

Remember, routines aren't about doing things perfectly. Even though it can feel like it, they aren't about winning (what would you even win?!).

Routines are about making tasks automatic so your exhausted brain can rest. Experiment until you find a routine that's just structured enough to help you get by—for now.

Give up the expectation that this routine will last forever. Just as time will change you, it will change your routine too. In the rest of the book, we'll tackle the forces most likely to interrupt and transform your routine: pets, illness, and children.

PART III

Beware the Backslide

Troubleshooting Your Domestic Harmony

18 Expanding the Nest

Troubleshooting Pet-Related Chaos

ONCE, ON A ROAD TRIP THROUGH TEXAS, I RESCUED A SCRUFFY ORANGE kitten from behind a Luby's Cafeteria. He was so small, he could've easily gone unnoticed, except that he was meowing at me as loudly as a tiny kitten conceivably could.

I picked him up, climbed back into the driver's seat, and continued on my way. The kitten purred in my lap the entire drive home while I tried to choose a name for him.

Once I got him home, his name became immediately clear: *Rascal.*

He was a tiny terror. He scratched the furniture, chewed through my laptop charger, and peed in my roommate's purse for no discernable reason. He kicked litter out of the litterbox with gusto. He could smell turkey, his favorite food, in a closed refrigerator. He stalked me, waiting for me to open the fridge door a crack, then torpedoed his head through the opening, wrecking the fridge's contents with teeth and claws until he found the lunch meat. I adored him.

When you bring home an adorable, fluffy little companion, you rarely think about the unseen cost of pet ownership: cleaning. Many, many hours of cleaning. Animals produce large amounts of hair, urine, and feces.

Fingers crossed that it all ends up in the right place! When it doesn't, you're on the hook for cleanup. Because unlike children, pets can't be taught to clean up after themselves.

I've worked in a lot of houses with out-of-control pet situations. Once, at the end of an hour-long social work visit in a house that smelled so strongly of cat pee that my sinuses burned from the ammonia, I dropped my pen, bent down to pick it up, and discovered a litter of newborn puppies, their squinty eyes barely open. They had been under the couch the entire time. The chaos of the house was such that the puppies were barely noticeable.

When pet messes start to pile up, a house can quickly go from "living with an animal" to "living like an animal." When that happens, it's hard to know where to turn for help. There's a lot of judgment out there. Out of a desire to protect animals, we've developed some strong moral beliefs about pet ownership. Mainly, that pet ownership is only for the mature, responsible, and financially secure. Which it is, in a perfect world.

Do you live in a perfect world? *Me neither, babe.*

The tension of pet ownership is this: On one hand, a pet brings you companionship, joy, and structure. On the other hand, you have to keep rubber gloves and cleaning supplies constantly available because your dear furry friend just dropped a deuce on the kitchen floor. *Again.*

When we acquire or inherit a pet, we're gambling on the hope that the pet will be easy to care for. And sometimes we gamble incorrectly, which puts us in an impossible position, unable to protect our household from the chaos of pets we dearly love.

If your pet's messes have gotten away from you, don't let the taboo prevent you from finding solutions. You can't easily moralize yourself out of a stinky pet house situation. I've seen people try very hard, and it doesn't work.

Telling yourself that you're irresponsible, and your house is disgusting, and you've failed your pet isn't helpful. Those beliefs will only intensify your shame, which will increase your avoidance of the problem, and lead you to even greater despair.

Instead, simply accept, without judgment, that you live in a stinky pet house. Stinky pet houses happen when your pet's ability to make a mess outpaces your ability to clean, whether because you're ill, depressed, overworked, or simply aren't very good at cleaning and pet training—nothing that is a moral failing on your part. You certainly didn't expect the situation to shake out this way when the pet first came to live with you.

You need to find a really potent meaning to motivate you to do something as unpleasant as facing up to a stinky pet house. It isn't fun, even if the house is yours. Maybe *especially* if the house is yours.

One of my clients, who lived solo with her dogs in an out-of-control house, found her meaning in the same place where the problem started.

She confessed to me: "I'm not hiring you for me. I'm getting my house cleaned up for my dogs. They deserve a good home. And they can't clean the house, because they're dogs, obviously." She laughed. "So, I have to do it for them. I *want* to do it for them."

No matter how stinky your house, you are not hopeless. You are not crazy. Your pet is not bad. You just need a path out of the stink. Instead of focusing on your failure, just focus on solutions.

A note before we begin: This chapter deals with the daily work of managing pet-related cleaning and care. Adjacent to this topic are the very important issues of pet health, pet safety, and pet training. I entrust those topics to the experts. Follow your veterinarian's recommendations and enlist the help of a pet behavior specialist if necessary.

Troubleshooting Pet-Related Chaos

- Unresolved pet accidents
- Litterbox issues
- Pet hair buildup
- Lingering pet odor
- Pet-related clutter
- Feeding issues
- Dog-walking fatigue

PROBLEM: UNRESOLVED PET ACCIDENTS (URINE, FECES, VOMIT)

SOLUTION: ENZYME CLEANERS

As a society, we have a strong belief that people shouldn't coexist in the same space as body waste. It's a useful social taboo, since body waste can carry disease, so it's best to keep it as far from you as possible. Plus, it's stinky.

But if you're unwell—depressed, exhausted, overwhelmed—you might find that strong belief dissipating under the strain of cleaning up your pet's messes. The bending, the scrubbing, the smell, the futility of cleaning the floor only for your beloved pet to immediately pee in the same place: All can start to feel pointless.

The tricky part about pet accidents isn't just the stains; it's the lingering smell. Pet accidents will continue to stink, even after they're gone. Luckily modern technology gives us a solution: enzyme cleaners. Enzyme cleaners, which help break down biological odors, are thankfully available wherever cleaning supplies are sold.

Sniff around your house to find any lingering accident smells. Really get in there. This process is gross but effective!

If you find an unresolved pet mess (or one you've previously cleaned up that continues to stink) on a hard surface, such as a tile or wood floor, resolving it is easy. Just spray with an enzyme cleaner, let it sit for the requisite number of minutes, wipe with a paper towel, and move on.

If the pet accident happened on fabric—such as a rug or couch—things get a little more complicated. Small throw rugs, blankets, or drapes can be thrown into the washing machine. Carpets can usually be cleaned semi-effectively with a rented steam cleaner.

But it's genuinely difficult to remove the smell of urine from deep within furniture or rugs. If you're in complete chaos, I suggest a radical solution. Just get rid of the offending item and start fresh. Put it out on the curb and forget it existed. Even if it leaves your house looking a little empty. I know that seems drastic—furniture costs money! But you can't imagine the time, money, and suffering it could cost you to completely remove pet waste smell from furniture otherwise. Sometimes, it's a relief to just cut your losses and move on.

PROBLEM: LITTERBOX ISSUES

SOLUTION: STREAMLINE YOUR LITTERBOX ROUTINE

Litterbox care is a grim job. Neglecting it, even for a day or two, can leave your house smelling like cat urine—an eye-watering aroma so pungent, it's hard to believe it could originate from your darling kitty-cat. If you don't want your house to smell like that, you have to be a diligent steward of litterbox cleaning. Here are a few tips to reduce your litterbox-related suffering.

Location, Location, Location: Keeping your litterbox in a low-traffic area can buy you a little time when it comes to dealing with tracked litter and smell. I always sacrifice a hallway closet to my cat's litterbox. I put a pet lock on the door so my cat can get in but the dog (seeking cat turds) can't.

Use Flushable Litter: Scooping the litterbox isn't really one chore, it's three: scooping, bagging up the waste, and taking it to the outside trash so your house doesn't stink. To get around that chore cascade, I switched to flushable crystal litter. You can flush the solid waste down your toilet, circulate the rest of the litter, and you're done. The entire process takes less than sixty seconds.

Increase Scoop Frequency: Do you frequently have this conversation with yourself? "Should I scoop the litter? I should, but I don't want to. But I should! But I don't want to!"

No one likes scooping litter. But the longer you let the litter sit, the worse scooping is. My unpleasant secret weapon for this problem is to scoop the litter every single day, at the same time every single day. This removes the element of choice. It also makes the task easier because scooping a mostly clean litterbox is way more pleasant than scooping a litterbox that's gone untouched for many days.

Sensory Issues: Cleaning the litterbox can be sensorially fraught for those who struggle with odors. Make your life easier by creating a sensory kit for tackling litterbox maintenance. Keep a small bin near your litterbox with sensory supplies.

Sensory Kit for Litterbox Cleaning

- A surgical mask lined with essential oils or Stink Balm, to help with odors
- A box of disposable rubber gloves, to quash contamination fears
- A cat litter scooper with a long handle
- A can of air freshener to spray when you're done

Prevent Tracked Litter: Ideally, at least 95 percent of litter should stay in the litterbox. If your cat is a litter kicker, equip the litterbox with a litter-trapping mat. If your cat kicks litter far outside the box, as my maniacal old cat used to, get a litterbox with a roof so litter can't go far. If that doesn't help, keeping a small handheld vacuum next to your litterbox can help you zap spills.

Lingering Odors: If your litterbox continues to stink even after scooping, you might need to change out your litter more often. Make sure to empty all litter from the litterbox at least once per month. Spray the litterbox with an enzyme cleaner, rinse it, then dry it. Line the bottom of the litterbox with plain, unscented baking soda before adding fresh litter. This will help keep your litterbox odor-free (or as odor-free as a substance as noxious as cat urine can be).

PROBLEM: PET HAIR BUILDUP

SOLUTION: VACUUM LIKE YOUR LIFE DEPENDS ON IT

Besides excessive pet hair being an aesthetic issue, it can be a smell issue, as well as a health issue. If your household is covered with dog hair, it's going to smell like dog hair. Pet hair can also trigger some allergies.

Excess pet hair is also a hospitality issue. When people come over, if your household is covered in pet hair, they'll leave covered in pet hair. Close friends and fellow pet lovers don't mind, but it is nice to send your guests home fur-free, if possible.

Frequent vacuuming should help keep pet hair at bay: at least once per week. If that's too tiring for you, I highly suggest investing in a robot vacuum.

When my husband and I divided up chores, I volunteered to do the vacuuming. After Tom watched me neurotically vacuuming pet hair every other day, he took pity on me and bought me a robot vacuum as a surprise gift. I told him it was the best gift he'd ever bought me.

"But I've bought you a diamond ring!" he reminded me.

"I said what I said," I confirmed. It was that life-improving. I love the diamond ring, but being able to go a week—or even *two*—without vacuuming? Divine.

FAVORITE STRATEGIES FOR PET HAIR MANAGEMENT

- Frequently brush and groom your pets. (As a bonus, if you compost, pet hair is compostable! It can also be thrown outside for wild birds to use as nesting material—as long as your pets haven't received any recent flea or tick treatments.)
- Wipe down furniture with a lint roller, pet hair scraper, or wet rubber glove. Keep these supplies near the couch in a "pet hair remediation kit" to streamline the process.
- Place designated blankets over the spots where pets frequently lounge. It's much easier to throw a blanket in the wash than it is to remove pet hair from furniture.
- Vacuum floors and furniture as often as you can stand it.

PROBLEM: LINGERING PET ODOR

SOLUTION: AIR THE HOUSE & RULE OUT MEDICAL ISSUES

If your pet smells linger beyond the resolution of pet messes and litterboxes, you might have to do a bit more detective work.

Make sure your home has adequate airflow by periodically opening the windows if your climate allows. If not, add an air purifier to the stinkiest rooms. Fabrics will absorb the smell of your pet's hair and dander, so wash your pet's bedding or blankets every week or two.

If your pet just emanates excessive odor, a visit to the vet might be in order. They can help advise you on any medical issues that might be causing the smell, and give you information about appropriate grooming for your pet's breed.

PROBLEM: PET-RELATED CLUTTER

SOLUTION: DECLUTTER THEIR STUFF JUST AS YOU DECLUTTER YOURS

Even people who are suffering greatly often enjoy doting on their pets. I've seen highly nonfunctional people set up extremely elaborate cat tree villages. It's admirable. Those cats are living the dream.

When it comes to pets, we want them to have everything good: toys, treats, beds, that one cardboard box they love to play in. It's all fun and games until the pet supplies accumulate to the level that you can't see your floor anymore.

When you have a pet, even if you're a thoughtful shopper, the supplies just build up. I once spent an hour persuading my client to get rid of three of her five cat trees so she had a fighting chance at vacuuming her floor. I myself have a collection of demolished dog toys, expired pet medication, and treats my cat was too picky to eat. Pet clutter is acquired with the best of intentions. That doesn't mean it can't be a barrier to a functional home.

It can be painful to get rid of pet items, but let's keep it in perspective. **Your pet can't declutter. It's your job to do it for them.** It's okay to get rid of things you don't have room for, even if your pet likes them, as long as they have other things they like just as much. Pet supplies can easily be regifted by posting them online for free.

After the death of a pet, decluttering their possessions can be particularly gut-wrenching. It's okay to wait until you feel totally ready to let them go—whether that's a week, a month, a year, or more. It can feel meaningful to donate those pet supplies by taking them to the local animal shelter, or giving them to someone who has a new pet.

PROBLEM: FEEDING ISSUES

SOLUTION: AUTOMATE FEEDINGS & FOOD DELIVERY

Even struggling people are usually very diligent about feeding their pets. But if you worry your forgetfulness will extend to your pet care, an automated feeder can give you (and your pet) peace of mind. Automated feeders are also helpful if you have a cat that tends to "scarf and barf," like my cat. Program the feeder to give your cat several small meals throughout the day and night rather than one or two big meals once a day. The cat is happy, and you don't have to clean up daily barf piles. It's a win for all! There are also online services, such as Chewy, that will deliver your pet's food on a recurring schedule, so you don't have to worry about forgetting to buy food. And don't forget to consult with your vet on your pet's digestive issues.

PROBLEM: DOG-WALKING FATIGUE

SOLUTION: DO WHAT YOU CAN & OUTSOURCE THE REST

When you're struggling physically, or overloaded with tasks, taking half an hour to walk your dog can seem like an insurmountable obstacle. Enlisting the help of a dog walker—whether they're a professional or a friend—can help decrease the burden and keep your dog happy.

Beware of all-or-nothing thinking. Walking your dog for five minutes is still an improvement on no exercise at all. Doing a few mini-walks, rather than one big one, can help conserve your energy while your dog gets the stimulation they need.

REMEMBER, CLEANING IS CARING

As inconvenient as pet messes can be, cleaning up after an animal is an integral part of caring for them. I spent nearly every day of ten years cleaning up dog hair from my long-haired dog Copper, who was my best friend. I mean this as a compliment to the dog, not a criticism of my other friends who got outranked by a dog.

When he died, I found myself totally unable to clean *anything* that might have his hair on it. Which, because he was so fluffy, was everything.

I couldn't vacuum, I couldn't do laundry, I couldn't change my sheets. I also couldn't throw away the half-eaten hamburger I'd made him for his last meal. Because I knew it would be the last time I ever got to clean up after him, something I had done diligently for a decade.

Remember that every time you clean up a mess for your pet, it is an act of love—making a home for your companion. It isn't glamorous, but it is meaningful.

19 In Sickness & in Health

Troubleshooting Caregiving & Illness

In the early days of our marriage, Tom and I had an elderly neighbor named Ms. Nanette. One day, we were raking leaves and saw Nanette tottering outside, looking ill-tempered, dragging a wooden ladder. She set the ladder against her house and timidly stepped onto the first rung. The ladder shook alarmingly, as did Ms. Nanette.

"*Wait*," called my husband, running to the fence. "Let me do that for you!" He wasn't sure what he was volunteering to do, but it was clear that Nanette, upward of eighty years old and in poor health, shouldn't be climbing a ladder to anywhere.

Tom spent the next hour cleaning Nanette's gutters. When he climbed down, she fixed him with a beady eye.

"Remember," she rasped. "I didn't ask you to do that. You offered."

Which was a creative alternative to *thanks*!

Nearly ten years later, I balanced on a ladder and scooped gunk out of our gutters. Tom, permanently retired from ladder climbing due to MS, watched through the window, giving me encouraging looks. It was blazingly sunny, like every day in Colorado, and the glare was giving me a headache. I finished the job and retreated into the dim house, where Tom handed me an ice water.

"I'm really sorry I can't help," he said. I thought of the last time he climbed a ladder, slipping off the bottom rung, and landing sideways on a can of blue house paint, bruising his hip badly and (less important but still problematic) sloshing a large quantity of paint all over our rented apartment's original hardwood floors.

"You are helping." I gulped my water and came up for air. "You're helping by not falling off a ladder. I'd rather clean the gutters than have to take you to the hospital."

"Remember," he rasped comically. "I didn't ask you to do that. You offered."

Nothing disrupts the delicate balance of household chores quite like an unexpected disability. For our purposes, let's define *disability* as not being able to do something due to illness, injury, psychological suffering, or cognitive difficulties. That may be short-term or forever.

Caregivers carry a vast workload of chores and nursing tasks. That responsibility can be heavy. And yet, I can't think of anything more spiritually enriching than caring for the ill. Caregiving requires sacrificing your comfort for someone else's, an idea that's become increasingly unfashionable in today's hyperindividualistic culture of self-care. It isn't easy work. Spiritually enriching things never are easy, are they?

As I learned to be a caregiver and, then in an astounding reversal of fortune, learned to be cared for myself, Ms. Nanette's words came back to me. *I didn't ask. You offered.* Not as a sullen dodge of expressing gratitude but as instructions for caring well.

When you commit yourself to caring for someone else, you become a detective of their needs. The height of good care is that the sick person doesn't have to ask—the caregiver offers. The ability to anticipate need is a skill like any other. And like all skills, you can approach it begrudgingly or with enthusiasm. Here are a few resources to help caregivers and the chronically ill adjust.

Troubleshooting Caregiving & Illness

BEING A CHRONICALLY ILL HOMEMAKER

Knowing Your Abilities

The funny thing about living with chronic illness, chronic pain, or mobility difficulties (and, honestly, you really have to reach to find something funny about it) is that sick days become completely meaningless.

When I was able-bodied, I never would have cooked or cleaned if I felt as I do now. I would have urgently arranged a week off work, school, and life in general.

But now, I feel like garbage all the time and likely will continue to for the foreseeable future. I still *can* do housework; it just costs so much more than it did before. When you operate under conditions that other people would find intolerable, it is very difficult to discern the correct level of effort to give your home.

SPECTRUM OF EFFORT

TOO LITTLE	JUST RIGHT	TOO MUCH
Assuming you can't do anything It's understandable to restrict your effort and refuse to attempt new chores or accommodations out of fear of making things worse. But this can lead you to feel helpless, overwhelmed, and guilty. *Tip: Treat any depression or anxiety associated with your disability.*	*Knowing what you can & can't do* You channel your energy into the chores that matter most to you. Your chores aren't effortless, but they don't leave you suffering for hours or days afterward. You have a sense of control over your home without getting burned out. *Tip: Outsource tasks you cannot do.*	*Ignoring your limitations* You keep disregarding your limitations and doing way too much. You end up in flare-ups for days afterward, unable to do anything. Your grit is admirable, but it's an inefficient use of your effort. *Tip: Practice radical acceptance of your capabilities.*

The trick to managing your illness while managing your home is trying to stay within that "just right" window of effort. That will take some trial and error. If your "just right" level of effort isn't enough to keep your home going, consider outsourcing some chores. Or, if you live with someone else, move on to the next step on how to divide up chores in a disability household.

CHRONICALLY ILL COUPLES

How to Divide Housework

When a member of your household becomes disabled, your preconceived notions of competence and fairness in household labor are no longer relevant. You're in new territory. None of the old maps apply.

It isn't fair to expect a disabled person to do things completely beyond their ability level. But it also isn't very respectful to assume disabled people can't contribute at all. Sometimes that's true, but usually it's not. Disabled means disabled; it doesn't mean useless.

When dividing up household chores with a chronically ill family member, communication is key. The goal is for both caregiver and caregivee to stay in their "just right" window of effort. You can try to find your way to the just-right level of effort by identifying which chores are easiest for you.

First, make a list of your household responsibilities. Then, sort them into three categories per the disabled partner's ability level.

SORT YOUR CHORES BY ABILITY LEVEL

"Yes" Chores	"Maybe" Chores	"No" Chores
Chores that you can do relatively easily, without causing a flare-up	Chores that you could do partially or with breaks Chores that you could do only with support, such as: • Reminders • A guide with steps • A helper • Assistive technology	Chores you absolutely cannot do Chores you could do but shouldn't because you would suffer for hours or days afterward
These chores can be delegated to the disabled partner.	Divide these up thoughtfully.	These chores can be delegated to the able partner.

DIVIDE CHORES BASED ON YOUR FINDINGS

Try to make your lists as even as seems fair or feasible. You might measure fairness based on "effort put in" rather than "results produced." If the lists are vastly uneven still, consider these tweaks:

- Explore the feasibility of the disabled partner taking on a few "maybe" chores.
- Outsource a few "no" chores to family, friends, or professionals if feasible.
- Reassess standards to see whether you can get by without some chores, or with chores being done less often.

GET CREATIVE

There are lots of household contributions that can be done from bed. If you are the disabled partner, consider the ways that you can contribute to the household without sacrificing your health. Here are a few examples.

- **Online Admin:** Handling bill pay and arranging appointments and maintenance
- **Online Orders:** Planning meals and ordering groceries/household supplies
- **Cheerleader:** Giving compliments and encouragement
- **Recumbent Laundry:** Sorting and folding the laundry for someone else to put away

DON'T FORGET TO CONSIDER ENERGY LEVEL

Chronically ill folks often experience decreased energy levels—an important consideration when splitting up chores. You might technically have the ability to do lots of chores, such as:

- Folding the laundry
- Walking the dog
- Cooking dinner
- Doing the dishes

But just because you can do each task individually doesn't mean you can do them all in the aggregate. If you don't carefully consider your energy level, that chore list will play out something like this in real time:

Folding the laundry—*Oh no, my back hurts really badly.*

Walking the dog—*Wow, I feel really dizzy and faint.*

Cooking dinner—*Oops, I almost passed out while chopping vegetables and now I'll be in bed for six days. Forget the dishes!*

Figuring out how much you can give your home might require a bit of trial and error. Just continue to check in with your partner and adjust your plan. And make sure to plan for bad days when your energy level fluctuates lower than normal.

PLAN FOR BAD DAYS

Even a good plan can go out the window when flare-ups put a partner completely out of commission. That's why it's important to have a Bad Day Plan—a pre-agreed-upon protocol that can be put into action when flare-ups happen.

Example: Adjusted Household Standards During a Flare-Up

- Able partner takes on all household chores and responsibilities.
- To make that easier, reduce household responsibilities by outsourcing anything possible: grocery delivery, dog walking, childcare, and takeout.
- Temporarily decrease standards to a pre-agreed-upon level. Focus on only essential tasks, such as trash and dishes.

HOW TO TAKE CARE OF A SICK PERSON

| A Beginner's Guide to Caregiving |

Caregiving is a household task. It's somewhere between cleaning, cooking, and being nice. To some, it comes naturally. To others, not so much. Remember: No one knows how to give care until they have to do it.

Here's a caregiving guide for beginners. Follow the next four steps to take care of someone who is acutely ill. Remember, everyone's different, and everyone likes to be cared for differently. Be ready to adjust your caregiving style to suit your patient based on their feedback.

1. **Assume Responsibility:** Once your loved one is sick, you're in charge. Graciously assume all responsibility for your chores, their chores, and all other household tasks, such as caregiving. Don't make the sick person ask; you offer.
2. **Make a Sick Nest:** Find a comfortable place for the sick person to sit or lie down, away from the hustle and bustle of the house.

Give them a pillow and blanket, put on a movie, and let them rest.

3. **Arrange Nourishment:** Continually bring the sick person fluids to drink—sick people need hydration! Cook or order some food for both of you. Don't make them decide what to eat—they're already tired enough. Mild foods, such as toast, rice, or soup, are usually a good bet.
4. **Obtain Supplies:** If needed, run to the store to pick up any helpful medication or supplies. If you don't know what to get, reference the following table.

SUPPLIES NEEDED FOR ILLNESS	
Nasal/Sinus	AM and PM cold or allergy medicine
	Fever-reducing medicine if necessary
	Neti pot and saline
	Nasal spray
	Nasal strips
	Moisturizing tissues
	Nasal ointment
	Hot tea and soup
Cough/Sore Throat	Cough medicine
	Fever-reducing medicine if necessary
	OTC pain medicine, such as ibuprofen or acetaminophen
	Lozenges and Chloraseptic throat spray
	Hot tea and soup
Nausea/ Vomiting	Electrolyte drinks
	Crackers and dry toast
	OTC medicine for nausea and indigestion
	Ginger tea and peppermints
Pain	OTC pain medicine, such as ibuprofen or acetaminophen
	Ice packs and heating pads
	Pain-relief salves and patches
	Epsom salts for baths

5. **Check In:** Now, simply leave them alone. Ensure, as much as you can, that they don't have to get up and do anything demanding. Check in on them every few hours to make sure they have enough fluids and snacks. Be ready to take them to the doctor if they don't improve within a day or two.
6. **Self-Care:** Remember to take care of your own needs too. If you're not hydrated, rested, and fed, you'll be a worse caregiver. If your patient is frustrating or annoying when sick (I know I am!), don't share that information with them. Complain to someone else. Your job is to be patient and reliable until they are well.

HOW TO TAKE CARE OF A CHRONICALLY ILL PERSON

| A Partner's Guide |

When an illness is permanent rather than acute, caregiving looks a little different. Most chronically ill people have flare-ups, or times when their illness is more severe or symptomatic than others. Treat flare-ups the same as acute illness with the preceding guide. Beyond flare-ups, you're playing the long game.

LEARN ABOUT THEIR CONDITION

Familiarize yourself with their condition. Remember to read trusted sources. There's a lot of weird information out there, and not all of it is helpful. Educate yourself on treatments and triggers.

HELP WITH MEDICAL APPOINTMENTS

If they agree, accompany them to doctors' appointments. Medical appointments can be nerve-racking. Be there to take notes, corroborate their description of their symptoms, and be an advocate for anything they've forgotten. For bonus points, get a treat after the appointment.

HELP WITH FOOD

Learn what they can eat and try to have easy snacks nearby. Arrange groceries and delivery meals. Don't necessarily expect them to have the energy for meal preparation.

BE AN ACCESSIBILITY SCOUT

Investigate outings ahead of time for your loved one. Is there food they can eat? Places to rest? How are the temperature, light, and noise level? Are parking, bathrooms, and walkways accessible? Having this information ahead of time can help prevent disasters.

BE MINDFUL OF SUGGESTIONS

It's normal to want to help by giving suggestions on what the sick person could do to improve their health. But remember that the chronically ill have typically exhaustively researched their conditions and options, and can feel hopeless after trying lots of things with no discernable difference. Avoid suggesting something obvious—such as yoga or hydration—that they may have tried before.

REMEMBER CHRONIC ILLNESS IS CHRONIC

Chronic means that they will not recover. Be patient and don't expect them to suddenly be healed, just because their illness is wearing on you. Process your own feelings about illness and mortality.

HELP, I'M TERRIBLE AT TAKING CARE OF SICK PEOPLE

Troubleshooting Emotional Barriers for Caregivers

Now that you have a step-by-step guide for caregiving, let's get into the complications.

As a society we're generally aligned on the belief that sick or disabled people should be taken care of. And that if one of your family members gets sick, it's your responsibility to care for them with patience and compassion.

But theory is one thing, and practice is another. Caregiving is all tied up with your early childhood experiences of illness. It brings up all this junk you'd rather not think about, such as death, vulnerability, and abandonment.

When someone you love gets sick, those feelings can rise up to surprise and inconvenience you. And as the housework piles up, the sick person calls for more assistance, and you start to buckle under the weight of responsibility, those feelings can make you act in a way completely out of line with your values. Let's explore a few genres of challenged caregivers and some advice for how they can better cope.

THE HARSH CAREGIVER

| As a Caregiver, You Feel Irritated, Impatient, or Baffled |

You just want the sick person to get well—immediately! You see illness as an obstacle to be powered through. Possibly, you come from a family that would never (or could never) lie in bed and take a day off work, no matter how sick. As a sick child, you got brisk treatment and were encouraged to toughen up ASAP.

Now, as an adult, you hate being coddled when sick. It feels icky and frustrating as if people think you're not good for anything just because you have the sniffles! You're likely to chug some DayQuil and pretend that the flu is "just allergies."

Your flaw is that you assume everyone else feels the same way. This can lead you to be harsh or judgmental toward sick people who—shockingly—want to sleep off an illness and—even more shockingly—expect to be brought chicken soup?! By you?!

Advice for Those Who Can Relate

Interrogate Your Beliefs: Reflect on the experiences that made you feel that it was lazy or selfish to indulge being sick. Was that a fair assumption at the time? Do those facts still fit your current situation?

Find Compassion: Give yourself, and others, a break. Not everyone has your admirable work ethic and strength of character. You had experiences that made you toughen up fast. Others didn't. That might be an upsetting reality. But it also isn't their fault (or yours).

Take Breaks: When you feel frustrated with a sick loved one, take a break before your feelings boil over. Vent your feelings to someone else (not the sick person).

Be Efficient: Remember, resting while sick is efficient. The more people rest, the faster they get well. Your caring actions will help expedite the healing process.

Try It Out: The next time you're sick, do a risky experiment: rest. Let someone take care of you, just a little bit! By understanding what you need when you're sick, you'll build your awareness of how to care for others.

THE INEXPERIENCED CAREGIVER

As a Caregiver, You Feel Clueless, Incompetent, or Quietly Envious

In an amazing stroke of luck, none of your loved ones ever got seriously ill. And if they did, there was always a responsible adult or seasoned professional around to handle the work of caregiving. When it came to caregiving responsibilities, you were pretty much off the hook!

That's all well and good until someone you love finally falls ill, and you're out of your depth.

You just don't know what to do with sick people. You have too little experience. You have no role models to call on for advice. You only know how to receive care, not give it, which leaves you feeling confused and incompetent in a caregiver role. You find that sick people often seem frustrated with you because you don't know how to anticipate their needs. That makes you feel upset and frustrated, too, which doesn't help matters at all.

You might even find yourself unconsciously finding ways to avoid the crushing responsibility by usurping the role of Sick Person. *Oh, you're sick? Oh no, I think I'm coming down with something too! Cough, cough, sniff, sniff.* It's okay—I'm not judging you. But you can't get away with that move forever!

Advice for Those Who Can Relate

Identify the Problem: Admit to yourself, and to your closest loved ones, that you're no good at taking care of sick people—yet. Admitting the problem out loud can help break the tension and move you toward finding solutions.

Use Yourself for Data: Reflect on what kind of caregiving you enjoy when you're sick. Make note of all the small things that help you feel better. This will help you build awareness of helpful caregiving tasks.

Interview Your Loved Ones: Next, ask your loved ones how they like to be cared for. Do they want space, or enjoy company? What do they like to eat? What helps them feel better?

Create a Manual: Compile this information—a personalized how-to guide for caregiving—in a list you can access easily later. When illness strikes, pull out your list and proceed. Not clueless anymore!

THE FREAKED-OUT CAREGIVER

When People Get Sick, You Feel Anxious, Smothered, or Terrified of Failure

The truth is, sick people unsettle you. Especially if it's a person you know well.

Seeing someone you love and admire incapacitated totally freaks you out. You're scared. Of what? Of plenty! Illness, aging, and death, for starters. Even more privately, you're terrified of being in charge because what if you screw it all up?!

Your fear can lead you to do all sorts of wacky things. Denying that the person is actually sick, for one. Avoiding any closeness with them is a classic move as well. You might come up with perfectly reasonable explanations for your behavior: They don't *really* need you, they're not *really* that sick, and after all, what if their illness is contagious?!

But deep down, you know that you feel smothered by their neediness, as if it will swallow you whole if you get too close.

Advice for Those Who Can Relate

Start Processing: Being near illness is bringing up a lot for you. Those feelings need to be sorted through. Slowly, patiently, face your own feelings about illness, aging, and death. That's not easy, so don't hesitate to enlist the help of a therapist or spiritual adviser well versed in those subjects.

Explore Your Fear of Engulfment: These caregivers often have a strong fear of being drawn into and smothered by a difficult situation. You might fear that if you start caring for someone, you'll lose all your independence and sense of identity. Reflect on experiences that made you feel that closeness was threatening. Do those beliefs still fit your current reality?

Build Your Confidence: When you have the opportunity, try out taking care of a sick person, in small doses, ideally with a backup caregiver to take over if you start to feel overwhelmed. If you get anxious, retreat to your own space until you regain your balance.

THE INTERNALIZED HEALTHISM CAREGIVER

When People Get Sick, You Feel Judgmental, Suspicious, or Superior

Healthism is a form of discrimination against disabled people. Healthism is the belief that illness is totally preventable through individual behavior. So, if someone gets sick, it's their fault for not trying harder to be healthy.

Healthism is everywhere. We absorb these beliefs from all around: from family, from ads, from our coworkers in the breakroom at lunch. Healthism makes you take an attitude of suspicion and judgment toward the sick and disabled rather than one of compassion.

It's not that you don't care about your sick loved ones. It's just that when they get sick, you feel so frustrated with them for not taking better care of themselves. You're so absolutely certain what they need to do to be well. *Why won't they just listen?*

Even if you're right—and you might be—frustration and self-righteousness are rarely a good starting place for being a good caregiver. You're like a harsh coach, running the sick person through a gauntlet of health-improving behaviors with little care for their emotional needs. When they start to resist your advice, you only get more suspicious that they're not trying hard enough to get well. This is exhausting to both you and the sick person.

Advice for Those Who Can Relate

Rethink Illness: Healthy behaviors are wonderful and worthwhile. And they do give you a better chance of avoiding illness. That doesn't mean that nutrition, exercise, and supplements can totally prevent illness. The scary truth is, illness can happen to anyone at any time.

Find Compassion: Imagine yourself in their position. Being sick can make you feel very vulnerable, even helpless. Blame or judgment will only make those feelings worse.

Practice Acceptance: Seeing someone you love ill can be scary. It's tempting to try to fix the situation by undertaking an aggressive effort to get them out of bed and make them well again. This is an admirable mission, but remember: Personal effort can't fix everything. Sometimes, illness must simply be accepted.

THE OVERLOADED CAREGIVER

When People Get Sick, You Feel Desperate, Overwhelmed & Resentful

You are already at capacity on household responsibilities. So, when someone in your family gets sick, it pushes you over the edge into chaos. You're always taking care of the needs of those around you. But when you get sick, your family can't function without you. You have no chance to rest. And so you end up feeling jealous and resentful when you're in a caregiver role.

Mothers often find themselves in this position when their partners and grown children aren't very capable caregivers. Long-term caregivers can also experience what's called caregiver fatigue or caregiver burnout, when the demands of caregiving completely overwhelm their abilities. This can leave you feeling helpless, scared, and angry—not just at the person you care for, but at the world in general.

Advice for Those Who Can Relate

Recognize the Problem: Admit, to yourself and others, that you are overwhelmed and exhausted. Assert your need for rest and care.

Let Your Loved Ones Process: Admitting that you're overwhelmed might be a shock to your loved ones, especially if they're used to you subverting your own needs. Remember, it's not necessarily true that they don't care about your needs. It's that you've been performing so well, they're not aware that you have any needs. Give them a moment to adjust to the new awareness that you are a regular human being.

Enlist Backup: You might be perfectly correct that things can't run effectively without you. That doesn't mean you don't still need a break. Enlist backup caregivers to fill in. Or begin training your loved ones on how to temporarily assume your responsibilities. Even better, ask a friend with more capacity than you to help arrange backup!

Give Your Support System a Chance: If you've been performing spectacularly well, it's going to take your loved ones some time to get up to your level. This can be really frustrating to watch. But try to be patient as they clumsily learn to take over cleaning, cooking, and caregiving responsibilities. They will never learn if they don't have the chance to try.

THE JOY OF CAREGIVING COMPETENCE

Caring well for someone, and helping ease their illness, can be incredibly rewarding. The more successes you have, the more satisfying you will find it. Practice, improve, and enjoy the confidence that competence brings.

20 Training the Next Generation

Troubleshooting Home Care with Children

THERE ARE A THOUSAND IMPEDIMENTS TO KEEPING A CLEAN HOUSE, BUT you will never meet an impediment more potent than living with children. **Children are guaranteed to throw even the most orderly domestic life into chaos. Parents of young children survive on little sleep, meager meals, and manage to pull off twice the domestic work as a single adult. All while trying to raise little humans up to be good people!**

Having a functional household with children means engaging children in the running of the household. That's hard, because kids are really bad at chores. It's not their fault—they just got here! It's their first day on the job!

My great-aunt Dorothy, a lifelong educator, used to say, "You have to have toddler help if you want teenage help."

"Ha!" her daughter told me once. "She never did tolerate toddler help."

That's because toddler help isn't actually help. They're not helping you. You are helping them, under the guise of them helping you. You are helping them learn what they are capable of. And in my experience, kids are capable of a lot.

For a while, I was a social worker in a Montessori school. If you aren't familiar with the Montessori Method, teaching practical life skills is part of the curriculum. On my first day, I saw toddlers carrying big pitchers of water across a room to wash dishes. If you've never seen a toddler carry a pitcher of water across a room, I will tell you that the urge to snatch it out of their hands is almost overpowering. Every second is horror movie–level suspense, just waiting for them to drop the pitcher and flood the floor.

But the kids never did drop the water. Ever. They did an extremely competent job. Watching the kids wash and sweep, with apparent enjoyment, completely changed my notions of what children are capable of. So, why is it still so hard to teach kids how to clean? It's because they're just like us.

A Few Cleaning Truths About Kids (& Adults)

- Like you, kids are busy! It's hard to find the time to squeeze in life skills lessons around school, homework, playdates, and activities.
- Kids struggle to choose nonpreferred tasks over preferred tasks. Before you get frustrated with a kid for not stopping playing to clean up, remember how hard it is to stop scrolling to do the dishes.
- Kids don't like to attempt stuff they're bad at. They feel embarrassed when they detect they're doing a bad job, and would often rather not try than do a job badly.
- Kids enjoy feeling competent, appreciated, and that their workload is fair. But a child's perception of what is fair may be very different from yours.
- Young kids don't distinguish cleaning from play. They hate cleaning because they see we hate cleaning.

HOW TO TEACH A KID TO CLEAN

Choose Your Method

You can clean faster, better, and more easily than a child. So, why would you outsource a job to someone who's so obviously bad at it?

Teaching a child to clean is an investment in the future. It won't pay off now. It will pay off in the years to come.

It isn't very hard to teach a child to clean, but it does take patience. *Lots* of patience. Patience is your most powerful tool. You must be more patient than the child you're teaching. So, take a deep breath before you begin.

METHOD #1: CLEANING LESSONS

Teach Your Child a New Cleaning Skill with Direct Instruction

Choose the Right Moment: When you have ten to fifteen minutes of free time and your child is unoccupied, tell them you want to teach them a skill. Don't teach "cleaning" as a general concept. Choose one cleaning task at a time, such as sweeping.

Teach Step-by-Step: If the task involves multiple steps, show them how to do each step of the process. Then, repeat the same process (even if the cleaning task is already technically done) with the child. Young children may need help positioning their hands.

If you notice the child is doing the task wrong, don't say, "That's wrong!"

Say, "Let me give you a tip to make it a little easier." Then, demonstrate the correct technique. Continue until the child does it correctly.

Let Them Try It Alone: Tell the child, "Okay, you've got the hang of it! Now try it on your own. I'll be here to help just in case." Watch them do the task independently, praising anything you see they do right, and giving tips, not criticisms, if they do it wrong.

Repeat and Repeat Again: Expect to repeat this process several times over the course of a few weeks before the child can do the task independently. It's best if you can give these lessons without more than a week or two going by in between, so children have a chance to build their skills. If your child isn't catching on after a few lessons, they may just not be developmentally ready for that chore yet. Give them an easier version of the task that they can do competently and independently.

METHOD #2: MODELING GOOD CLEANING BEHAVIOR

| Show Your Child That Cleaning Is a Natural Part of Life |

One of the most natural ways to teach children to clean is by modeling positive cleaning behaviors. Young children are like little sponges for their environments. They soak up beliefs about cleaning from adults.

So, if adults stomp around, huff, and complain about cleaning, if they always look frustrated or annoyed when it's time to clean, children will learn that cleaning is unpleasant. Why would they want to try something that's unpleasant?

On the other hand, modeling cleaning as a positive, normal part of life helps children naturalize cleaning into their daily routines. When you are cleaning something, narrate what you are doing and why. Try to keep things neutral and functional. This method doesn't teach skills very well, but it helps kids develop a good attitude about cleaning.

MODELING CLEANING ATTITUDES

Too Negative *Expressing Hatred of Chores*	Just Right *Focusing on Function*	Too Critical *Moralizing about Chores*
I hate doing the dishes! Why is this my job? I've been working all day. Can't someone else deal with this?	I'm going to wash the dishes, so we have clean cups to drink from tomorrow. Plus, it's easier to cook dinner if the sink is clear.	This kitchen is disgusting! I can't believe you let it sit all day. I didn't know my family was so gross!

METHOD #3: ANNUAL CHORE ROLLOUT

| Give Your Child a Specific Responsibility Appropriate for Their Age |

At the beginning of every school year, have a family meeting to announce the chore that your child will be responsible for that year. Give the occasion a little fanfare! Your child gets to "graduate" to a new household responsibility. The idea is to assign a chore that's suited to each child's interests and developmental level. Here's a guide.

DEVELOPMENTALLY APPROPRIATE CHORES

Each of these tasks will need to be patiently taught until a child can do them independently.

Toddlers (ages 2 to 4)

- Picking up toys and returning them to a designated location, with supervision to help them stay focused
- "Cleaning"—wiping spills, tables, or chairs with a sponge or wet cloth
- Throwing away trash
- Bringing dirty dishes and cups to the sink
- Helping you load laundry into the washer

Lower Elementary (ages 5 to 7)

- Sorting toys or school supplies into designated cubbies
- Bringing dirty dishes to the sink and rinsing them (with the help of a stool to stand on)
- Learning to wipe down an entire table
- Sweeping with a small broom or a mini-vacuum
- Sorting their laundry by type (shirts, socks, etc.) and putting away into cubbies, with supervision to stay focused

Upper Elementary (ages 8 to 11)

- Spraying surfaces with nontoxic cleaner and wiping
- Folding and putting away laundry, with reminders (you will need to help them set up their laundry storage system first)
- Begin learning to tidy up Doom Piles by cleaning out their desk or backpack
- Making the bed
- Dusting with an old sock over their hand

- Learning to sweep, vacuum, or mop one room at a time, with help
- Learning to wash dishes or load the dishwasher
- Making sandwiches, toast, or cereal independently

Middle School (ages 12 to 14)

- Organizing school papers
- Resetting a table or desk after working on a project independently
- Feeding and walking pets
- Watering houseplants
- Loading the dishwasher independently (with reminders)
- Learning basic cooking, such as grilled cheese and scrambled eggs
- Vacuuming and sweeping independently
- Cleaning the bathroom sink, toilet, or tub

High School (ages 14 to 18)

- Defining their own functional cleaning standards
- Learning to prepare simple meals (rice, pasta, baked potato, soup, and more)
- Learning to do administrative tasks, such as school registration, with an adult
- Independently cleaning an entire room (bathroom, kitchen, or bedroom)
- Doing own laundry independently without reminders
- Learning to make grocery lists and go grocery shopping

CONTROVERSIAL TEACHING METHODS

Proceed with Caution

Far be it from me to tell parents what to do in the privacy of their own homes. It's hard out there! Child-rearing can be very intense and confusing, and parents are assailed on all sides by advice. Please consider this my modest contribution as a professional who has seen these well-intentioned teaching methods go sideways a time or two.

REWARDS FOR CHORES

| Giving Children an Allowance of Money or Treats for Completing Chores |

This is a popular method, which I will endorse with a few caveats.

If household work is a child's first exposure to labor, it's reasonable to give them a reward (e.g., allowance, treats, or special activities) to help teach them about the value of work. **The tricky part is that children won't be compensated for doing daily household tasks as adults. And so teaching them to do chores to get rewards is, in some ways, poor preparation for the realities of adulthood.**

If you want to use this method, I suggest paying kids for doing out-of-the-ordinary chores, not everyday tasks. Sweeping the driveway, washing the windows, deep-cleaning the tub, scrubbing the floors: If you're going to pay a child for a task, try to make it a task that you would conceivably pay someone else to do if the child didn't do it. Make sure to intersperse daily tasks, such as dishes and laundry, as just "part of life," not necessarily tasks that will be rewarded, unless children take on an outsize amount of responsibility by cleaning up after others, not just themselves.

USING CHORES AS PUNISHMENT

| Assigning Housework as a Form of Discipline |

Remember Martha and the Admiral from Chapter 5? If a parent was physically disciplined as a child, then assigning chores to their own children as a form of punishment feels very progressive. It's like community service but contained in the home! Unfortunately, there are a few ways this method can go awry.

It's a poor learning environment. If you assign chores as a punishment, it's likely that in that moment, you're frustrated with your child. And they're likely frustrated with you too. Because you're both frustrated, you are both ill-equipped for teaching and learning. This leaves kids feeling anxious and incompetent while attempting the assigned chore, and you feeling frustrated and overwhelmed when the child does the chore badly. Plus, it puts you into a power struggle with the child if they do a bad job.

This method can also teach children to associate chores with punishment. So when they grow up, they have a negative emotional association with chores. That doesn't happen to every kid, and it can be subtle. But functional adults are produced by teaching children that chores are a natural part of life, not a punishment when something goes wrong.

If you're going to use chores as discipline, make sure the consequence is logical. Don't make your kid mop the floor because they were mean to their sister. That doesn't make any sense. Instead, assign chores as discipline if the child's behavior was destructive to the home environment. If they broke something or made a big mess, having the child repair their mistake (with support if the repair is beyond their skill level) is a good preparation for the responsibilities of adulthood.

NOT TEACHING YOUR CHILDREN CHORES

Saving Children from Responsibility as a Form of Affection

I've seen parents who feel guilty about their parenting—for not being patient enough or kind enough, for not being able to spend as much time as they'd like with their child, or for not being able to provide the lifestyle they hope for—take responsibility away from their child as a form of affection. These parents often mistakenly believe that children will naturally learn how to do chores on their own, given enough time. They want them to have complete freedom from responsibility in childhood.

The problem with this method, though very sweet, is that it produces very loved but very incompetent young adults, like Alex from Chapter 5. This is not a gift. Domestically incompetent young adults are ill-equipped to navigate roommate disputes and cohabitation. They feel embarrassed about their lack of skill. They often need to rely on a peer or partner to teach them how to do chores, which puts that person in a pseudo-parent role and creates an unequal relationship dynamic.

That's why it's a loving act to give your child a bit of responsibility at home. Of course, it's still kind to give children a break when they're overloaded with schoolwork or having a bad day. Just make sure they have adequate opportunity to learn, so that, by the time they leave home, they can perform home care tasks independently.

COMPLETELY OUTSOURCING DOMESTIC WORK

| Giving Children No Opportunity to Learn About Home Care |

I'm happy for families that are lucky enough to be able to outsource domestic work. After all, I have many times benefited from being hired! The downside is that children raised in homes where all domestic work is taken care of never have an opportunity to learn—like Zoe in Chapter 5.

As young adults, they usually aren't financially secure enough on their own to hire a domestic helper. And so they end up grappling with their lack of skill for their first decade of adulthood.

If you're lucky enough to outsource home care, refrain from communicating to children that you outsource cleaning because it isn't worth your time. These beliefs do not support new adults, who will certainly need to clean and aren't served by feeling too good for the work.

Instead, communicate that professional cleaners are worth paying because they do a great job. Make sure children know that there is no functional living without cleaning. And make sure your child still has opportunities to learn domestic skills.

TROUBLESHOOTING THE TEACHING PROCESS

| Dealing with Barriers to Learning |

BARRIER #1: YOUR CHILD IS AN UNWILLING STUDENT

It's maddening to hear that your child hates cleaning because there's no chance that they hate it more than you already do.

In this case, it's important to try to create some positive experiences of cleaning. Try to prevent problems before they start. Don't tear your child away from their favorite hobby to give them a (definitely boring) cleaning lesson. Don't do it when they're hungry or tired. If they say they don't want to learn, ask why. It may be that they (like you) can identify a sensory barrier to the task that you can fix. If they don't have a good reason, and there is no other obvious barrier, it's okay to insist that they learn.

BARRIER #2: YOUR CHILD IMMEDIATELY FORGETS WHAT THEY'VE BEEN TAUGHT

Remember, they're children! Just like you, they sometimes need support to remember complex processes and new habits. Don't expect that they will be able to do a task independently after learning one time.

If they seem to forget steps, print out a list of the steps and post it next to where the chore is done. If the child can't read, add pictures or icons to illustrate the steps.

BARRIER #3: YOUR CHILD LACKS CONFIDENCE

Children, like adults, are prone to crises of confidence. That's especially true when learning a new skill, which they need correction and guidance to learn. If they're especially sensitive to failure, cleaning lessons can easily lead to meltdowns of "I can't do it! It's too hard! I'm so bad at this!"

This can, admittedly, also be a delaying tactic for savvy children, who get wise to the fact that outbursts like these tend to result in being comforted, not taught. (We won't judge the kids for their clever ways. They're still learning to be people!)

In this instance, you have to walk a fine line: Keep the mood light but the message firm. You have to communicate two seemingly contradictory messages:

Cleaning is no big deal, and failing at cleaning doesn't matter.

But also, *it's actually really crucial that you learn to do this, and I will be teaching you whether you like it or not.*

That isn't easy. Respond to cries of "I can't! It's too hard!" with validation.

It is hard. It's hard because it's new.

I was so bad at this when I first tried it. That's okay.

It just takes practice. It will be easy soon.

But don't let up teaching the lesson. Continue teaching, calmly, with a sense of humor. If your child becomes truly overwhelmed and dysregulated, let them take a break, and resume the lesson later in a lower-pressure situation. Make sure to aggressively and relentlessly praise everything they do right during the process with whatever method makes sense to you: hugs, high fives, or words of encouragement.

YET

One of my favorite mentors was a kindergarten teacher. She had a tattoo on her wrist that read "yet."

As in: *My students can't read—yet. They can't control their bodies—yet. They can't play nicely with others—yet.*

They can't clean—yet!

Remember that you were once a child too, who couldn't clean—yet.

You, too, were assailed by the forces of adult expectation. Remember how unfair it felt to be obligated to clean. Remember how unfair it sometimes *still feels* now, as an adult. Not to mention decluttering, organizing, doing your taxes, and all those other unwelcome responsibilities of life.

But these are skills that everyone learns to master, however clumsily, slowly, and unwillingly. And it's a privilege to learn, because those who never learn suffer for it. Competence is a gift. Parents that never received that gift can still give it to their children.

A Tidying Benediction

ORGANIZATION ISN'T A ONETIME ACT. IT'S A PROCESS. IT'S A PRACTICE.

Like all other healthy habits—exercise, nutrition, fiscal responsibility—there will be times of waxing and waning. Times when you're on top of everything, and times when everything is on top of you. May all your chaos come into order, again and again.

When it comes to home care, grieve what your body and brain cannot do. Embrace and enrich what they can. Barriers aren't your fault, but they are yours to take care of. May you treat your homemaking quirks with patience, persistence, and curiosity.

Having a home—no matter how messy, temporary, or complicated—is a blessing. It's your little corner of the world to take care of. Taking care of it is what makes it yours. Treat it seriously. Treat it lovingly.

May your home be a place of restoration rather than a place of obligation.

Acknowledgments

THE BIGGEST THANK-YOU TO MY MOM, CONNIE, FOR TEACHING ME EVERYthing I know about making a home. Thank you to my dad, Matt, for confirming that there is, indeed, a correct way to load the dishwasher: our way. Thank you to my husband, Tom, for many valuable lessons about love, and for always sending me off to write with the same phrase his mentor used to make him finish his dissertation, half encouragement, half order: "Keep going!"

Thank you to Jeff at Curious Minds for finding me and believing that I could write a book. Thank you to the team at Balance for giving me a chance to write it. Thank you to all my clients for letting me into their homes to rummage through their clutter. Thank you to Switchback Coffee Roasters for the corner booth in the back, where I trapped myself for many long hours to write this book, which I couldn't write at home because I got too distracted by chores.

Bibliography

Anderson, Bridget. *Doing the Dirty Work?: The Global Politics of Domestic Labour.* New York: Zed Books, 2000.

Bauer, Gerrit. "Gender Roles, Comparative Advantages and the Life Course: The Division of Domestic Labor in Same-Sex and Different-Sex Couples." *European Journal of Populism* 32, no. 1 (January 27, 2013): 99–128. https://doi.org/10.1007/s10680-015-9363-z. PMID: 30976211; PMCID: PMC6223479.

Davis, KC. *How to Keep House While Drowning: A Gentle Approach to Cleaning and Organizing.* New York: Simon Element, 2022.

Folbre, Nancy. *For Love and Money: The Distinctive Features of Care Work.* YouTube, December 6, 2011. Accessed May 22, 2024. www.youtube.com/watch?v=91N5HtMbVHY.

Holmes, Dave. "Are We Not Men?" *Esquire*, October 9, 2023. Accessed May 22, 2024. www.esquire.com/lifestyle/a45236217/be-a-man-dave-holmes/.

Lark, Regina F. *Psychic Debris, Crowded Closets.* Createspace Independent Publishing Platform, September 24, 2017.

New Economic Thinking. *The Economics of Care.* YouTube, February 23, 2016. Accessed May 20, 2024. www.youtube.com/watch?v=vZEJV3kBQH0.

Poo, Ai-jen, and Ariane Conrad. *The Age of Dignity.* New York: New Press, 2009.

Rodsky, Eve. *Fair Play: A Game-Changing Solution for When You Have Too Much to Do (and More Life to Live).* New York: Putnam, 2021.

Seeley, Evelyn. "Our Feudal Housewives." *The Nation*, May 28, 1938.

Wight, Vanessa R., Suzanne M. Bianchi, and Bijou R. Hunt. "Explaining Racial/Ethnic Variation in Partnered Women's and Men's Housework." *Journal of Family Issues* 34, no. 3 (April 27, 2012): 394–427. https://doi.org/10.1177/0192513x12437705.

Index

About the Author

Amanda Stuckey Dodson is a clinical social worker, professional organizer, and artist from East Texas. Amanda trained as a psychodynamic therapist, with a specialization in eating disorders and trauma recovery.

In 2021, Amanda created her company, Nesting Your Life, to fill an underserved niche: functional organizing for people with mental illness, developmental disorders, or chronic physical conditions. She is a sought-after life skills coach, helping chronically disorganized clients across the world create order in their lives.

Amanda lives with her husband on the Front Range in Colorado, where she runs a youth art program. She holds an MSW from Simmons College in Boston and a BSW from the University of Texas at Austin.

RAISING READERS

Books Build Bright Futures

Thank you for reading this book and for being a reader of books in general. We are so grateful to share being part of a community of readers with you, and we hope you will join us in passing our love of books on to the next generation of readers.

Did you know that reading for enjoyment is the single biggest predictor of a child's future happiness and success?

More than family circumstances, parents' educational background, or income, reading impacts a child's future academic performance, emotional well-being, communication skills, economic security, ambition, and happiness.

Studies show that kids reading for enjoyment in the US is in rapid decline:

- In 2012, 53% of 9-year-olds read almost every day. Just 10 years later, in 2022, the number had fallen to 39%.
- In 2012, 27% of 13-year-olds read for fun daily. By 2023, that number was just 14%.

Together, we can commit to **Raising Readers** and change this trend. How?

- Read to children in your life daily.
- Model reading as a fun activity.
- Reduce screen time.
- Start a family, school, or community book club.
- Visit bookstores and libraries regularly.
- Listen to audiobooks.
- Read the book before you see the movie.
- Encourage your child to read aloud to a pet or stuffed animal.
- Give books as gifts.
- Donate books to families and communities in need.

BOB1217

Books build bright futures, and **Raising Readers** is our shared responsibility.

For more information, visit **JoinRaisingReaders.com**

Sources: National Endowment for the Arts, National Assessment of Educational Progress, WorldBookDay.org, Nielsen BookData's 2023 "Understanding the Children's Book Consumer"